THE COMPLETE CAR
OWNER'S MANUAL

By
Jerrold Clifford

BONANZA BOOKS • NEW YORK '76

Copyright © MCMLXXVI by Jerrold R. Clifford
Library of Congress Catalog Card Number: 75-10569
All rights reserved.
This edition is published by Bonanza Books
a division of Crown Publishers, Inc.
by arrangement with Drake Publishers Inc.

a b c d e f g h

Manufactured in the United States of America

CONTENTS

To ROSA VERONIKA

INTRODUCTION

Every day, people buy and drive cars. Advertisements indicate the virtues of various makes and models, while beautiful girls and handsome men in magazine layouts or television commercials try to seduce us into buying the latest automobiles. Yet, most people know little or nothing about how these cars work, what maintenance is required for continued smooth performance, or even the correct way to keep them looking attractive. While most people are concerned with the cost of a new car, few stop and consider that the regular maintenance, repair, and operating costs can amount to several times the original purchase price over the service life of the car. By knowing what services are required and how to perform them, these costs can be reduced significantly and the maximum service life of the car can be obtained. Knowing where to get replacement parts and how to install them can save the car owner a considerable amount of money.

This book explains how a car works and how to keep it operating, what to do in emergencies, how to diagnose and cure many common problems, and how to maintain the car inside and out. Hints for saving gasoline are included, and a special chapter explains how to save money on auto insurance and still protect yourself.

The author wishes to thank Martin Clifford for his invaluable assistance and encouragement, and acknowledges with thanks information supplied by Ford Motor Company, Quaker State Oil Refining Corporation, and Filter Dynamics International, Inc. (Lee products).

Jerrold Clifford
Stamford, Conn.

CHAPTER 1

GETTING STARTED

There is no such thing as a perfect car. The perfect car would give years of faithful service, require no repairs, maintenance, use only a modicum of fuel, be self-cleaning, always perform faultlessly no matter how badly treated, and last of all (and certainly not least), have an extremely low purchase price. Unfortunately, automobiles do require maintenance, an occasional cleaning and, hopefully, only occasionally, repairs, which are unavoidably expensive. And, since they are expensive, you will want to protect your investment and extend its useful life.

You can do many common repairs and most of the maintenance yourself, and save considerable money at the same time. It doesn't matter that you are all thumbs, or that you are not mechanically inclined. Many of the procedures do not require a great deal of manual dexterity; indeed, they can often be accomplished by nothing more complicated than the turning of a nut or screw. You don't need expensive and specialized equipment either. Most of these procedures require the simple tools found in most homes and apartments:

1. Various slot-bladed screwdrivers.
2. A regular Phillips blade screwdriver.
3. Adjustable pliers (preferably with insulated handles).
4. A set of key wrenches.
5. A set of regular wrenches.

It is also a good idea to have a heavy gauge, well-insulated screwdriver, as well as an inexpensive ratchet wrench set. These tools can be found in most hardware stores, and wherever do-it-yourself supplies are sold. However, if you need any of these items, many reputable discount department stores sell quality tools at generally lower prices than hardware and tool stores. A number of these discount stores also have automotive sections which, in addition to specialty items, sell many replacement parts such as filters, light bulbs and lamps, wiper blades and arms, ignition wires and other components.

The repairs, maintenance procedures, and tips in this book are presented in an easy to follow step-by-step manner. A list of all required tools and parts precedes each procedure. Thus, you do not have to be an automobile mechanic to execute them; you do not even have to have any experience with cars. Remember, garages have mark-ups on parts, and more importantly (and expensively) must charge for labor in order to compensate for rent, telephones and other overhead costs. And, since they may have many cars to repair in a day, they may not give your car the attention it should have, or adjust it as accurately as possible. This costs money—your money. If your car is not performing properly, its life may be shortened.

Every car will, most likely, need occasional repairs, requiring specialized tools and experience in using them. In addition, every car should have periodic safety checks. Although these repairs and safety checks should be performed by qualified personnel, you needn't be an expert to do many of the basics yourself. You will be driving a safer vehicle, and saving money at the same time. And, by catching potential problems early, you can prevent them from becoming serious and expensive, thereby shortening the service life of your car.

CHAPTER 2

AUTOMOTIVE ENGINES, FUEL
AND OIL SYSTEMS

We all know that uncontrolled fire is destructive. It can destroy homes and forests, kill animals and people. But, under controlled conditions it is extremely useful. We use fire to cook food, heat our buildings, and even, in a fireplace on a snowy winter's night to create a romantic mood. Similarly, explosions can be destructive. But, like fire, if controlled, they can be made to perform useful functions.

Basically, an automobile engine is nothing more than a device for controlling the explosions that occur when gasoline and oxygen are combined and ignited. Left uncontrolled, the destructive power of one gallon of gasoline is roughly equivalent to that of 14 sticks of dynamite. But, when used as fuel in an automobile engine, that same gallon of gasoline enables us to travel many miles. Once you know what an automobile engine is, it is easier to understand how it works.

The basic parts of an automobile engine.

Figures 2-1 through 2-5 illustrate these components.

The block

This is the part of an engine most people visualize first, when they think of an engine. It generally has four, six, or eight holes, called cylinders in which a corresponding number of cylindrically shaped objects, called pistons, slide. Since we are dealing with combustion, the block gets quite hot—hot enough to damage the engine. Since an internal combustion engine has many moving parts, lubrication is necessary for smooth

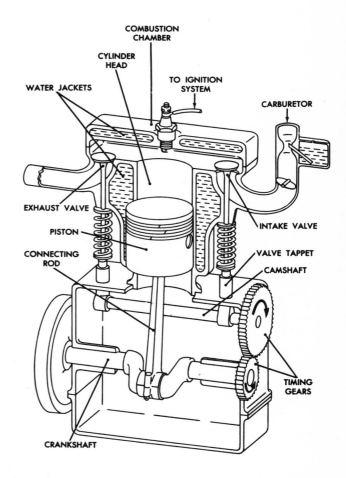

Fig. 2-1—A cutaway view of a single-cylinder, 4-stroke cycle, internal combustion, gasoline engine. 4-, 6-, or 8-cylinder engines work in a similar manner, but have more parts.

operation, and to increase engine life. Thus, the block contains tubular passageways, in which coolant and lubricating oil circulate. It is topped by the cylinder head containing bearing saddles, the purpose of which is to hold the crankshaft and allow it to turn.

Cylinder head

Attached to the top of the block, the cylinder head forms the cover for the combustion chamber. It contains two valves which control the flow of gases into and out of the combustion chamber. The cylinder head also contains passageways in which coolant and lubricating oil circulate.

Crankshaft

The crankshaft (see fig. 2-2) is a rotating shaft with appendages. As it revolves, it changes the up and down motion of the piston into a rotary one. It is connected to the clutch and transmission which drive the vehicle.

Pistons (see fig. 2-3 and 2-4)

The pistons move up and down within the cylinders, pumping gases in and out of the cylinder. The force exerted on them by the expansion gases, (as a result of the controlled explosions mentioned earlier) causes them to move. This motion is transmitted to the crankshaft via connecting rods, forcing it to turn.

Piston rings

Each piston has a set of rings which seal the space between the piston, and the cylinder walls. There are three types of rings: compression, scraper, and oil control. Compression rings prevent flame and blow-by from the combustion chamber from burning the oil film (used to reduce engine wear) from the cylinder walls. Scraper rings, similar to compression rings, assist the compression ring in the task of preventing flame,

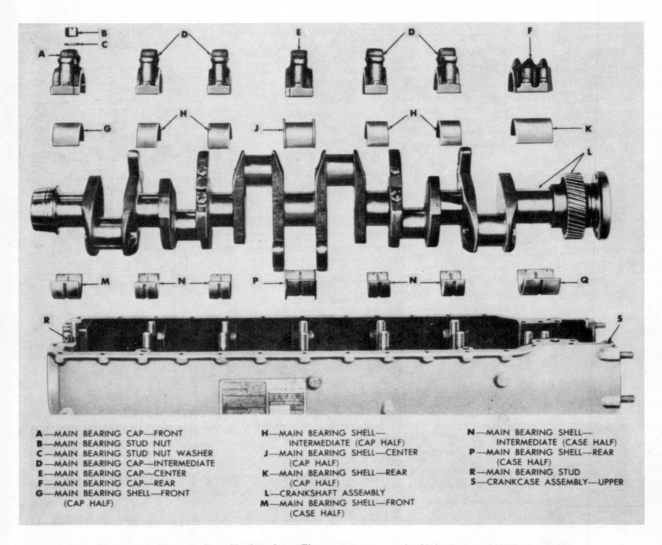

A—MAIN BEARING CAP—FRONT
B—MAIN BEARING STUD NUT
C—MAIN BEARING STUD NUT WASHER
D—MAIN BEARING CAP—INTERMEDIATE
E—MAIN BEARING CAP—CENTER
F—MAIN BEARING CAP—REAR
G—MAIN BEARING SHELL—FRONT
(CAP HALF)
H—MAIN BEARING SHELL—
INTERMEDIATE (CAP HALF)
J—MAIN BEARING SHELL—CENTER
(CAP HALF)
K—MAIN BEARING SHELL—REAR
(CAP HALF)
L—CRANKSHAFT ASSEMBLY
M—MAIN BEARING SHELL—FRONT
(CASE HALF)
N—MAIN BEARING SHELL—
INTERMEDIATE (CASE HALF)
P—MAIN BEARING SHELL—REAR
(CASE HALF)
R—MAIN BEARING STUD
S—CRANKCASE ASSEMBLY—UPPER

Fig. 2-2—A crankshaft and its bearings. The component marked L is the crankshaft assembly.

and combustion gases from escaping from the combustion chamber. But this is not their only function. They are called scraper rings because they scrape oil on the downward stroke of the piston, ensuring that less of it reaches the combustion area. Thus, they also assist the oil control rings whose purpose is to stop oil from getting into the combustion area.

Connecting rods (see fig. 2-3)

Connecting rods provide the linkage between each piston and the crankshaft.

Valves

Just as windows permit air to enter and leave a room, the valves act as a sort of window, allowing an air-fuel mixture to enter the combustion chamber and burned gases to leave. To control air flow, windows must be opened and closed. Similarly, to do their job, valves must also be opened and closed. Toward this end, a mechanism consisting of the camshaft, push rods, and rocker arms is used. There are two valves for each cylinder: one is the intake valve, and the other is the exhaust valve. Driven by the crankshaft, the camshaft is a shaft containing egg-shaped discs, or cams. As the camshaft turns, the cams open and close the valves.

Flywheel

The flywheel (see fig. 2-5) is a heavy rotating plate attached to the rear end of the crankshaft. Since each piston moves up and down four times within its cylinder, and only one of these strokes delivers power, energy is needed to move the pistons during the other three strokes. Some of the power supplied during the power stroke is used to rotate this plate. This rotational energy, in turn, is used to move the pistons during the three phases when they are not delivering power.

How do these basic parts work together? The internal combustion engine is a four phase engine; each upward and downward motion of the piston is called a stroke (see fig. 2-6). At the start of the first, or intake stroke, the piston is in the upper part of the cylinder; the intake valve is open, allowing a mixture of gasoline, and air to enter the combustion area, and the exhaust valve is closed, preventing any of this mixture from escaping. As the flywheel and crankshaft turn, the connecting rod and piston are pulled downward causing more of the mixture to be sucked into the combustion chamber. As the crankshaft continues turning, the rod and piston

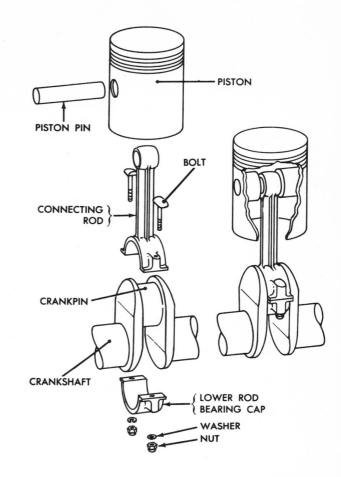

Fig. 2-3—The piston, connecting rod, and piston pin fit together.

are pushed upward. The intake valve closes. With both valves now closed, the fuel and air mixture have nowhere to go, and are compressed at the top of the cylinder, as the piston continues its upward journey. For this reason, this motion is called the compression stroke. When the piston is at the top of its compression stroke, an electric spark is sent into the cylinder via a spark plug. The spark ignites the mixture. When this happens, the mixture burns rapidly, and expanding gases are created, which force the piston downward. As the piston moves, the connecting rod moves with it, pushing hard on the crankshaft causing the flywheel to move faster. The engine is said to be delivering power; hence, this phase is called the power stroke.

When the piston is at the bottom of the power stroke, the crankshaft, now under engine power, pushes the piston upward. The intake valve is still in the closed position, but the exhaust valve now opens. As it continues its upward journey, the piston pushes the gases through the exhaust valve opening. The entire four stroke process is repeated until the driver stops the engine.

The automobile internal combustion engine has many moving parts. If any of these parts are damaged or broken, the engine will not work properly and expensive repairs may result. As an engine is used, each part begins to wear. And when this happens, little can be done to reverse the process. However, it is never to late to start maintaining your car. The rate of wearing can be slowed, and the service life of the engine can be increased.

WANKEL ROTARY ENGINES

Another type of gasoline engine which has become popular recently is the *Wankel rotary engine*, named for Felix Wankel, who developed it in 1954. It is best known for its use in small cars, such as the Mazda. This type of engine has about 40% fewer parts than the conventional internal combustion engine, takes up less space, and is lighter than a conventional piston engine with comparable horsepower.

Energy from combustion is converted directly to rotary motion (see fig. 2-6A) in the Wankel engine. Rather than having pistons which move up and down within the cylinders, the Wankel engine uses one or more curved triangular rotors, which rotate in enclosed housings. However, like the conventional piston engine, the Wankel rotary engine has four cycles—intake, compression, ignition, and exhaust. The rotor housing contains two spark plugs. To assure maximum combustion, the fuel-air mixture enters through an *intake port*, and burned gases exit through an *exhaust port*. The rotor is connected to the drive shaft via an *eccentric shaft*. As the rotor turns through one complete revolution, all four cycles occur, and the drive shaft turns. Fig. 2-6B demonstrates how these cycles occur as the rotor turns. For convenience of reference, the letters A, B, and C are shown at the "corners" (apexes) of the triangular rotor.

The first part of the diagram shows that ignition has occurred between apexes A and B. The

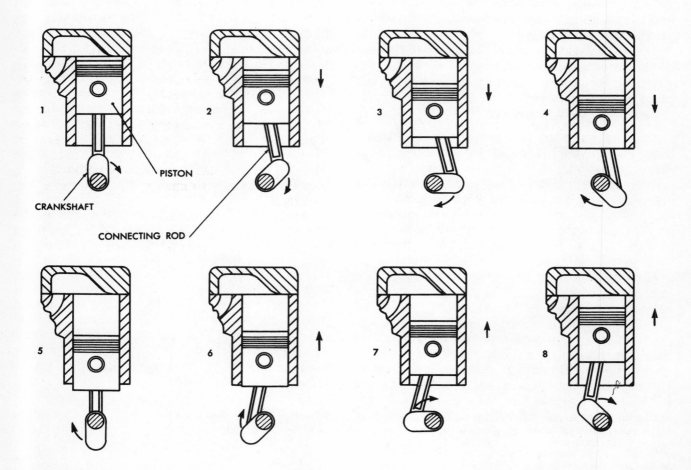

Fig. 2-4—The relationship of the piston, connecting rod, and crank on the crankshaft as the crankshaft turns one revolution.

air-fuel mixture, which is compressed between the rotor and the wall of the housing, is ignited. Exhaust is taking place between apexes B and C; the burned gases are forced through the exhaust port. While all this is occurring, intake of fresh fuel-air mixture takes place between apexes A and C.

The second diagram shows that combustion is producing power between apexes A and B; rotary movement in a clockwise direction occurs. This movement is transmitted via an eccentric shaft to the drive shaft. The exhaust phase continues to occur between B and C, while between apexes A and C, the intake of fresh fuel-air mixture is almost completed.

As the rotor advances to the position shown in diagram 3, intake of the mixture occurs between B and C, while compression occurs between A and C. Between apex A and apex B, power continues to be produced from the burning mixture. As the rotor continues to turn, the exhaust phase between B and C is completed.

Finally, the rotor moves to the position shown in diagram 4. The intake phase continues between B and C, compression of the mixture continues between A and C, while the power phase is completed between A and B.

To prevent gases from escaping, and because of the rotor's shape, special seals had to be developed. Metal and aluminum-carbon seals have been tried as apex seals, and spring loaded seals are generally used on the faces of the rotor.

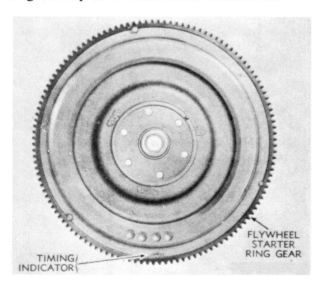

Fig. 2-5—A flywheel. Its purpose is to reduce fluctuations in engine speed, and so its size varies with the number of cylinders and the construction of the engine—the more cylinders an engine has, the more overlapping of power impulses; thus, the flywheel can be relatively smaller. The rim has a gear that meshes with the starter driving gear when the engine is started.

In order for this engine to work as efficiently as possible, the rotor has to be synchronized with the ignition. To do this, an *internal gear* is placed in a hole which is bored in the center of the rotor. This gear meshes with a smaller one that is attached at the center of the rotor housing. As the rotor turns, it causes an eccentric shaft to rotate, which turns the drive shaft. The eccentric shaft turns three times for each rotation of the rotor.

The cooling system for most vehicles equipped with the Wankel rotary engine is the same as that used on cars with conventional internal combustion engines. However, the rotor can only be cooled by the lubricating oil, since it is enclosed in the rotor housing.

The carburetor, lubrication, and electrical systems are similar to those found on vehicles with piston engines.

You have just read how air and fuel are mixed, and then ignited. The device that does this mixing is called the *carburetor* (see fig. 2-7). If the air passing into the carburetor is dirty, some of this dirt may stay in the carburetor, and keep it from performing properly. To prevent this, most cars have an air filter (see fig. 2-8) which is usually a disposable cylinder that traps dust and dirt particles. As the car is driven, these filters become clogged, and prevent sufficient air from mixing with the fuel to allow clean combustion. This means your engine will not operate efficiently; the car uses more fuel which, in turn, means higher operating costs. Thus, the disposable air filter should be changed regularly. Most manufacturers recommend that this be done at least every 6,000—10,000 miles. Of course, if the area you drive in has very dusty or polluted air, it may be necessary to change the filter more frequently.

There are two other services provided by the air filter: arresting flames which result when an engine backfires, and muffling the hissing sound when air enters the carburetor.

How to Replace the Disposable Air Filter

Tools required

None

Where to find the air filter

The air filter is located above the engine block. It is placed in a large container (usually cylindrical in shape or cylindrical with a flat tube in front) which is generally painted black or blue.

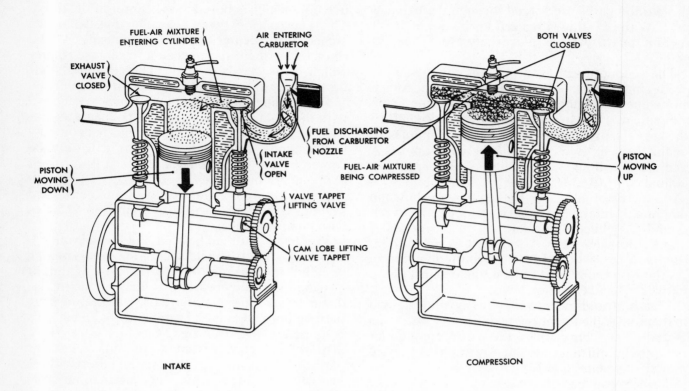

FUEL-AIR MIXTURE
ENTERING CYLINDER

AIR ENTERING
CARBURETOR

EXHAUST
VALVE
CLOSED

FUEL DISCHARGING
FROM CARBURETOR
NOZZLE

INTAKE
VALVE
OPEN

PISTON
MOVING
DOWN

VALVE TAPPET
LIFTING VALVE

CAM LOBE LIFTING
VALVE TAPPET

INTAKE

BOTH VALVES
CLOSED

PISTON
MOVING
UP

FUEL-AIR MIXTURE
BEING COMPRESSED

COMPRESSION

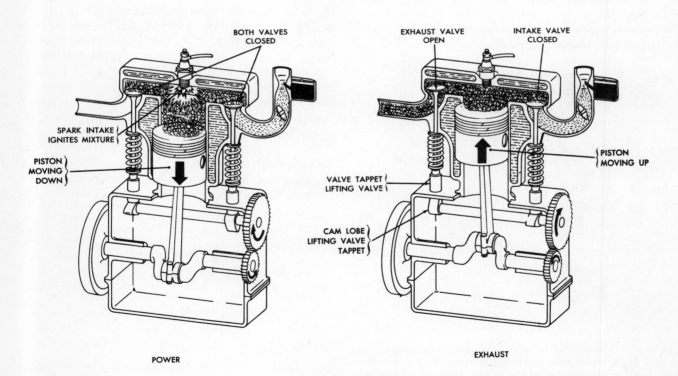

BOTH VALVES
CLOSED

SPARK INTAKE
IGNITES MIXTURE

PISTON
MOVING
DOWN

POWER

EXHAUST VALVE
OPEN

INTAKE VALVE
CLOSED

PISTON
MOVING UP

VALVE TAPPET
LIFTING VALVE

CAM LOBE
LIFTING VALVE
TAPPET

EXHAUST

Fig. 2-6—The four strokes of a 4-stroke cycle gasoline engine. The relationship of the valves, and the piston are clearly seen as the engine passes through the intake, compression, power, and exhaust strokes.

Fig. 2-6A—A rotary engine.

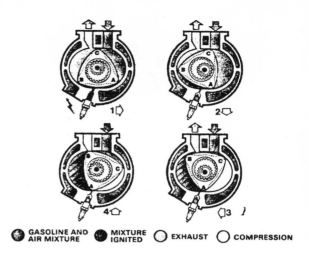

● GASOLINE AND AIR MIXTURE ● MIXTURE IGNITED ○ EXHAUST ○ COMPRESSION

Fig. 2-6B—The four basic positions of the rotor in the combustion chamber of a rotary engine.

Procedure

1. Loosen and remove the wing nut, in the center of the top of the air cleaner assembly.
2. Some cars have a removable plate at the top of the air cleaner. If yours is of this type, lift off this plate. Other cars have an air cleaner, which can be separated into two parts. If yours has this form, lift off the upper portion.
3. Remove the cylindrical air filter, by simply lifting it upward. Replace it with a new filter, by putting the new filter in the bottom portion of the air cleaner assembly.
4. Using a clean rag, wipe the air cleaner assembly.
5. Replace the upper portion of the assembly or the plate.
6. Replace and tighten the wing nut.

The air cleaner on many late model GM cars (such as the Vega and Monza 2+2 with a 4-cylinder engine, and a one or two barrel carburetor) consists of a one piece welded unit. Under normal driving conditions, this unit should not require servicing for 50,000 miles. When this interval is reached, (or sooner if the air in the area where you drive is dusty, sandy, or very polluted) replace the air cleaner by detaching it from the air horn and silencer. Examine the gasket that fits on the air horn; if it is damaged or cracked, replace it with the colored adhesive surface facing the carburetor. Attach the replacement unit.

The purpose of the carburetor is to mix the fuel and air, and prepare this mixture for ignition. You can view it as an atomizer with a

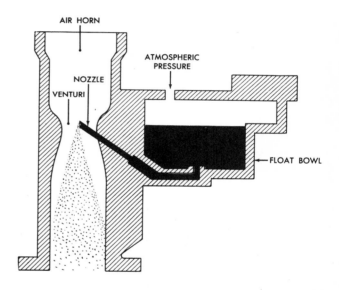

Fig. 2-7—A simplified carburetor consisting of an air horn, float bowl, and nozzle. The venturi is an hour glass shaped constriction which creates a partial vacuum at the outle of the nozzle, permitting the greater (atmospheric) pressure on the surface of the gasoline in the float bowl to force the gasoline through the nozzle. The gasoline sprays very finely in the passing air to form the fuel-air mixture.

thermostatically controlled device, (the butterfly valve) which controls the passage of exhaust gases. For good gas mileage, and proper engine performance, it is important that the carburetor be as clean as possible. This is ensured by the air filter. However, due to some of the chemical compounds in gasoline, and tiny particles of dirt, which can pass through the air filter, the carburetor can become dirty. A badly dirty carburetor should be overhauled and cleaned, a job requiring time, patience, care, and practice. But, it is a simple matter to prevent this condition from occurring; all that is required is the ability to use a spray can.

How to clean the carburetor

Tools required:

None

Materials needed:

1 spray can of choke cleaner, or carburetor cleaner.
1 clean rag.

Where to find carburetor: The carburetor is located above the engine block. It is surrounded by the air cleaner assembly, which houses the air filter.

Procedure:

1. Loosen and remove the wingnut in the center of the top of the air cleaner. The front of the air cleaner of your car may also be clamped or clipped to a support; if so, loosen this clamp or clip.
2. Gently lift the entire air cleaner assembly. If your car is a late model, the air cleaner may have several hoses leading from it; try not to pull on them when lifting the air cleaner.
3. When the air cleaner assembly is lifted, the carburetor will be exposed. Move the air cleaner assembly so that it does not obstruct the carburetor.

4. Spray the entire exterior area of the carburetor.
5. Using a clean rag, gently wipe any access liquid and dirt from the carburetor. Do not allow the dirty fluid to drip into the carburetor.
6. To one side of the carburetor, there is a rod leading into a moveable assembly which usually has a spring. Spray this assembly, and wipe away any excess fluid.
7. Wait a few minutes, and replace the air cleaner assembly.

Remember, a clean carburetor will not only increase gas mileage, it will also help make it last longer, and thus save you money. The carburetor should be cleaned regularly, at intervals of 2000-4000 miles.

Does your car buck or shake, or sometimes have a temporary loss of power? This condition can be frustrating and dangerous, and might lead you to believe you need expensive repairs, or perhaps, even a new car. While the problem may, indeed, be serious, it may be nothing more than a dirty or clogged fuel filter.

As mentioned before, the carburetor can become dirty due to unclean air, and impurities or chemical compounds in the fuel. Just as the air filter serves to clean the air before it enters the carburetor, the fuel filter is designed to "clean" the fuel. Some cars have a cartridge type fuel filter in the vicinity of the carburetor, while others have an in-line filter.

Where to Find the In-line Gas Filter

The in-line gas filter is a small cylindrically shaped object which, as its name implies, is

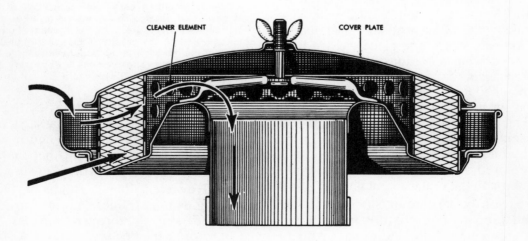

CLEANER ELEMENT   COVER PLATE

Fig. 2-8—The flow of air through an air filter.

located in the fuel line. It can be found by tracing the fuel line forward from the carburetor. Some of these filters are transparent, making it easy to inspect for dirt or clogging. The liquid seen inside the filter should appear clear, and have a uniform color throughout. If the liquid does not satisfy these conditions, or if the in-line gas filter in your car has a metallic case, (and so can't be examined) and hasn't been changed in 6000 miles, the filter should be replaced.

How to Replace the In-line Gas Filter

Caution. Gasoline vapor mixed with air is flammable. (Remember, it supplies the power for your car.) While changing the filter, DO NOT smoke, light matches, or use any items that might cause sparks in the vicinity of the engine. Some fuel will probably spill during this procedure; so allow sufficient time, following the replacement procedure, before smoking in the general vicinity of the car.

To avoid the possibility of a fire, which could result from gasoline spilling on hot engine parts, perform this procedure when the engine is cold.

Tools required

Clamp pliers, or if not available, regular pliers

Procedure

(To prevent gasoline from accidentally splashing into your eyes, wear safety glasses.)

1. Using pliers, compress both ends of the clamp closest to the carburetor and slide it toward the gas filter. (Be careful not to let your hand get pinched by the clamp in case the pliers slip.)
2. Again using pliers, compress the ends of the other clamp, and move it toward the gas filter.
3. Work the small hoses on both sides of the gas filter loose from the fuel line, being careful not to twist, kink, or break the fuel line.
4. Replacement gasoline filters usually come with new rubber hoses, and sometimes with new clamps. If the hoses are separate from the filter, slide the replacement hoses onto the ends of the filter, so the entire assembly resembles the one just removed. If it is necessary to use the old hoses, remove them from the old filter, and examine them for cracks or other damage. If they are not damaged, slide them onto the ends of the new filter.
5. Install gasoline filter in only one direction;

thus, each new filter has a direction marked on it, usually in the form of an arrow. This arrow should point towards the carburetor.
6. Compress the ends of a clamp and move it so that it is next to the gas filter, on the side of the filter towards the carburetor.
7. Join the side of the filter towards the carburetor to the fuel line using the rubber hose.
8. Compressing the clamp, move it towards the carburetor, until it is over the portion of the hose over the fuel line.
9. Compress the ends of the other clamp, and move it next to the filter, on the side away from the carburetor.
10. Work the hose over the fuel line.
11. Compress the ends of the clamp, and move it over the portion of the hose that is over the fuel line.
12. Examine the finished job to make sure there are no gasoline leaks. If there are leaks, readjust the hoses, and clamps until there are no leaks.

Many General Motors cars have a fuel filter which is really not in the middle of the fuel line, but located between the end of the fuel line and carburetor. This type of filter is different from the type just described, and requires a different replacement procedure.

Where to Find the On-the-carburetor Gas Filter

This type of gasoline filter is located at the end of the fuel line, where the fuel line joins the carburetor.

Tools Required
Wrench

Procedure

Caution. The same caution described in the section on "In-line Gas filters" is applicable here.

1. At the end of the fuel line is a nut, called the inlet fuel filter nut. Using the wrench, disconnect fuel line connection at this nut.
2. Remove nut from the carburetor.
3. Between nut and carburetor is a gasket, the filter, and a spring. Remove filter and spring.
4. Install the spring and new filter element in the carburetor, making sure the hole in the filter is towards the nut.
5. Install a new gasket on the inlet fitting nut.
6. Install the nut in the carburetor, tightening it securely.

7. Now install the fuel line, tightening the connector.

8. Examine the connection, to make sure there are no leaks.

Power companies and public officials stress the need for conservation of energy. With rising gasoline prices, poor gas mileage is a luxury few can afford. Poor fuel economy may even force you to trade in your car. But, before you consider this course of action, there are several things that can be done to increase fuel economy.

First of all, examine your air filter, and (if it is the see-through type) gasoline filter. Replace them, if necessary, using the procedures already described. While the air filter is removed, clean the carburetor, using the previously described procedure. Cleaning and gapping the spark plugs, (described elsewhere in this book) will also help.

But, in the final analysis, the largest factor affecting gas mileage can be found just behind the steering wheel—the driver. How you drive determines how much fuel is used, and hence, the gas mileage you get with any car.

Tips on Saving Gasoline

1. Avoid sudden starts and stops. When you change your speed suddenly, you use more gasoline as opposed to doing it gradually and smoothly.

2. If possible, try to keep your speed constant. When you accelerate unnecessarily, extra fuel is injected into the fuel system—fuel which is wasted.

3. Keep your speed down. For example, reducing your highway speed from 70 miles per hour to 50 miles per hour can give you up to a 25% improvement in fuel economy. This is largely due to the wind resistance. Wind resistance increases as your car's speed increases; thus, more energy (more fuel) is required to move the car at higher speeds.

4. If your car has air conditioning, use it only when absolutely necessary, since it requires power (supplied by the fuel) to run the compressor of the air conditioner. In fact, using the air conditioner reduces gas mileage by about 10%.

5. Don't let your engine idle unnecessarily. In cold weather, let your engine idle for about 30 seconds before driving the car; idling for longer intervals does not help it, and, in addition, wastes fuel.

6. Avoid very short trips. Since combustion is not as efficient in a cold engine as in one that has reached its designed operating temperature, a one mile trip, for example, can decrease fuel economy by as much as 70%.

By this time, if you've checked your gasoline and air filters, and followed the driving tips mentioned above, you've probably noticed a signifi-

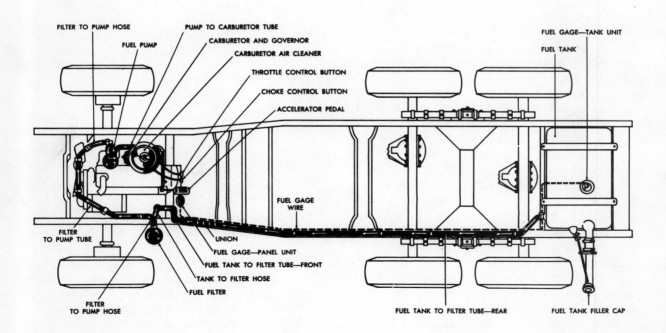

Fig. 2-9—An automotive fuel system.

cant improvement in your gas mileage. However, poor performance may still be plaguing you.

It is important for gasoline entering the carburetor to be "clean." However, clean or dirty, gasoline must get to the carburetor to allow the car to operate at all; this is the job of the *fuel pump*. (see fig. 2-10).

Located on the side of the engine, the fuel pump may either be driven mechanically from the camshaft, or driven electrically. If there is a leak in the fuel pump, gasoline may get into the crankcase (the reservoir for the oil), necessitating an oil change. If you have difficulty maintaining a constant highway speed, a faulty fuel pump may be the problem.

How to Test Your Fuel Pump Without Using Any Tools

If your car has a standard shift, or an automatic transmission, and your owner's manual indicates that the car may be driven in low gear at highway speeds, there is a quick and easy way to test the condition of the fuel pump. Place the shift lever in second gear, and operate the car at highway speeds. If the fuel pump is performing properly, the car will reach speeds of over 50 miles per hour, and the vehicle should be able to maintain these speeds. If the fuel pump is defective, the car will reach a high speed, but soon after, the speed will decrease rapidly. Should the fuel pump need replacement, it is best that you don't do it yourself. Although it is not a difficult procedure, a certain degree of experience with engines is required.

Another factor concerning the fuel system, which affects performance and economy, is the fuel line itself. The fuel line is a tube which serves as a passageway, allowing fuel to get from the gas tank to the carburetor. Sometimes these lines are damaged, or the connections become loose. Certain periodic checks should be made to ensure that the fuel flow is not being restricted, or that fuel is not leaking. Remember, leaking fuel never gets to the combustion chamber so gas mileage will suffer.

How to Inspect Fuel Lines

Tools required
None

Caution. Do not smoke or use matches while inspecting fuel lines. Gasoline, flame, and sparks are a dangerous combination.

Procedure

1. Start at the carburetor. Using just your fingers, examine the fittings (connectors) at the end of the fuel line, where it meets the carburetor. The nuts should be tight. If they are loose, tighten them with a wrench. Be careful not to damage the fuel line.
2. Examine the fuel line; it should be dry and free from kinks. If wet spots or kinks are present, point them out to your mechanic—part or all of your fuel line may need replacing.
3. If your car has an in-line gas filter, make sure there are no leaks in the area of this filter. Examine the short hoses on both sides of the filter, to make sure that they are not cut or damaged. Replace them if damaged. Inspect the clamps to make sure they are fitting tightly. If loose, replace them; if they are not fitting properly, re-position them and inspect for leaks. If leaks are still present, repeat this procedure.
4. Using your fingers, make sure the connections to the fuel pump are tight. If loose, carefully tighten them, avoiding twisting, or damaging the fuel lines.
5. Trace the fuel lines toward the gas tank as far as possible. If any leaks are found, point them out to your mechanic; part or all of the fuel line may need replacement.

Although it is not part of the fuel line, also examine your gas tank for leaks. While you can examine the gas tank by crawling under the car, this is a dangerous practice, and should be avoided. Instead, examine it the next time the car is raised

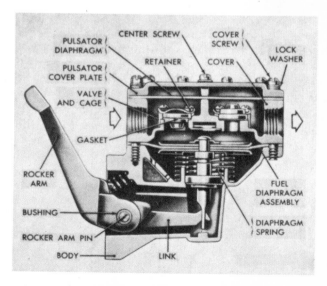

Fig. 2-10—A sectional view of a fuel pump.

on a lift. Sometimes pin-holes in the tank allow gasoline to form drops. Gas tanks are often in an exposed position; and are scraped and bruised while entering poorly designed driveways. Sometimes they are damaged by pebbles or rocks found on highways. Small leaks can be repaired by home remedies. However, these usually do not last long and other trouble spots often develop. Indicate these areas to your mechanic; he can drain and remove the tank, and see that a repair is made, or else replace it, if necessary.

Despite the care, inspection procedures, and preventive maintainence techniques afforded the fuel system, difficulties and performance problems may still occur. Here is a description of many of the commonly encountered problems affecting the fuel system, and what you can do to cure the problem.

Troubleshooting the Fuel System

Problem—the car stalls in cold weather

Possible Cause—frozen fuel. When the gas tank isn't full, there will be air in the tank. The moisture in this air can condense, forming drops of water. In cold weather, these water drops may freeze and obstruct the fuel line. When this occurs, engine does not get a sufficient supply of fuel; hence, the engine stalls. One indication that this may be the problem, is the presence of frost on the inside of the gas cap.

Solution—Your gas tank has a fixed volume. The more gasoline in the tank, the less moisture-laden air. Thus, in cold weather, it is best to keep the tank as full as possible. A good preventive measure is to pour a can of gas line anti-freeze into the gas tank once a month during cold weather, following the directions on the can. If the gas line is blocked due to icing, try to get the car to a warm area (such as a heated garage) for several hours. Here, prevention is the best solution, since gas line anti-freeze will not melt ice, but will prevent its formation.

Problem—A pause or flat spot when accelerating.

Possible Cause—The fuel mixture may be too lean. Remember, for your car to deliver its best performance, the proper amount of fuel must mix with the right amount of air in the carburetor. If either ingredient is missing, or present, but in the wrong quantity, efficient combustion will not take place.

Solution—The problem may be in the carburetor itself. To check this, remove the air cleaner assembly (see procedure for changing the air filter). Have someone depress the gas pedal several times. A stream of gasoline should flow into the carburetor. If this stream is not present, or if it is present, but is thin or weak, moves sideways, or just dribbles out; then the carburetor needs to be overhauled. Sometimes a lean condition causes backfiring.

It is also possible for this condition to be caused by an obstructed fuel line, or a weak fuel pump (see "How to Test the Fuel Pump Without Using Any Tools"). Your mechanic can determine if there is an obstruction in the fuel line. Regular inspections of the fuel line and the see-through gasoline filter (if there is one), or regular replacement of the in-line metallic case gasoline filter (as previously described), will help prevent this situation from occurring.

Problem—No power on heavy acceleration, or at high speed.
Possible Cause—Carburetor throttle valve may not be going wide open. Check this by pushing accelerator pedal to the floor.
Solution—If the carburetor throttle valve does not open properly, your mechanic can easily adjust the throttle linkage to obtain a wide open throttle on the carburetor.
Possible Cause—Dirty or plugged fuel filter.
Solution—Replace the filter or filter element, using the procedures described earlier.
Possible Cause—The carburetor needs cleaning, adjustment, or overhaul.
Solution—Have your mechanic check the carburetor, and clean, adjust, or replace it if necessary.
Problem—Engine is difficult to start when hot.
Possible Casue—A sticking choke valve.
Solution—Clean choke valve and linkage (see How to Clean the Carburetor). If it still sticks, some parts may have to be replaced; your mechanic can easily do this.
Possible Cause—No fuel in the carburetoɪ.
Solution—Check the fuel pump (see How To Test Your Fuel Pump Without Using Any Tools). It may be defective. If it is, have it replaced.
Problem—The engine runs unevenly or surges.
Possible Cause—Fuel flow is restricted.
Solution—Check all hoses, and fuel lines for bends, kinks, or possible leaks. If any unplanned bends are present, straighten the line. If this isn't possible, have the kinked or bent section replaced. It is advisable to have leaking sections replaced.
Possible Cause—A plugged or dirty fuel filter.

Solution—Replace the fuel filter (see the sections on how to replace the gas filter).

Possible Cause—Dirt or water may be present in the fuel system.

Solution—Have your mechanic check for this condition, and, if it is the problem, the fuel tank and lines should be cleaned, and, the carburetor should also be removed and cleaned.

Possible Cause—Vacuum leakage.

Solution—First make sure that all hoses are properly connected, with no air leaks. If they are installed properly, check their condition, replacing any that are defective.

If any of these problems still occur after you have followed the listed procedures, the problem may be defective carburetor parts. If the carburetor was not checked, see that this is done.

THE OIL SYSTEM

The modern automotive internal combustion engine has many moving parts, and the distances between these parts is often very small. Thus, without preventive action, operation of the engine would soon cause these parts to wear, necessitating their repair or replacement. The preventive action to reduce this wear is the lubrication of these vital parts. The oil system exists for this very purpose. Proper lubrication is essential for long engine life, and proper vehicle performance.

To provide for proper lubrication of engine parts, specially formulated oils are circulated under pressure. The oil reduces friction, and extends the life of engine parts. When combustion occurs within the engine, deposits are also formed. Modern automobile engine oils are designed to "trap" these deposits, and hold onto them. When the oil is allowed to drain from the engine, these deposits go with it. Special additives found in quality oil are designed to clean the engine, trap dirt, and coat and protect moving parts. In addition, circulating oil helps cool the engine, by carrying away the heat which results from the friction of moving parts. And, along with lubricating and reducing friction, cleaning the engine, and aiding in the cooling process, there is a fourth function oil provides—it forms a thin film on the cylinder walls, helping the piston rings make a good seal against the cylinder walls.

So that the oil can effectively perform its four functions, it must circulate properly within the engine. Bolted to the under part of the engine block is a pan, the oil pan (see fig. 2-11). At the bottom part of the pan is a reservoir for the oil, the sump, which is equipped with a drain plug for changing the oil. The function of the oil pump is to circulate the oil.. Driven by gears from the camshaft and crankshaft, the oil pump is usually located in the sump. And finally, to keep the oil as clean as possible, an oil filter is used. The oil filter is in an accessible spot on the outside of the engine, as it should be changed regularly.

In fact, since oil is so important to the operation of the engine, an oil pressure gauge or warning light tells the driver when the oil system is malfunctioning. Most cars have a warning light on the instrument panel, which goes on when you start the car—this is not an indication of trouble, but merely tells the driver that the bulb is working properly. If the bulb does not light when the car is started, check to see if it is burned out. If it is functional, have your mechanic check to see that the warning system is operating properly; there may be a loose connection.

You may notice that the oil warning light sometimes flickers when the engine is idling, or when you make a sudden stop. This is normal. However, if the light comes on and stays on above idle speed, stop the engine as soon as it is safe to do so, and check the oil level. If you continue to run the engine, you may end up with a large repair bill.

HOW TO CHECK THE OIL LEVEL

On the side of the engine is a stick which generally has a curved handle. This is the dipstick, which leads down through a tube into the sump. Its purpose is to indicate when oil must be added to the engine. (Note: Do not confuse the oil dipstick with the transmission fluid dipstick which is usually found near the rear of the engine block on cars with automatic transmissions. The transmission fluid is usually red, while oil is generally clear or brown.)

To check the oil, make sure the engine is off. An idling engine will not give an accurate reading. Wait a minute or two, then remove the dipstick by pulling if from the holding tube. Wipe it with a clean rag, and re-insert it in the tube. Remove the dipstick and note the oil level. It should be between the "add" and "full" marks, or the "safe area" marks. If the oil level is low, add one or more quarts until the reading is between the lines. (Caution: Do not overfill.)

To do its job effectively, oil must flow freely over a wide temperature range. It is a physical fact that oil has a certain resistance to flow; this resistance is called *viscosity*. The basic rule for oil is the higher its viscosity, the thicker the oil. Your owner's manual should indicate the proper oil for your car. Look for the SAE grade (Society of Automotive Engineers). Generally, lighter grade oils are recommended for cold weather usage (a grade of SAE 10, for instance), and a heavier grade for use during the warmer months (a grade such as SAE 30). It is often convenient to use an all year oil, a multigraded oil, such as SAE 10W-40.

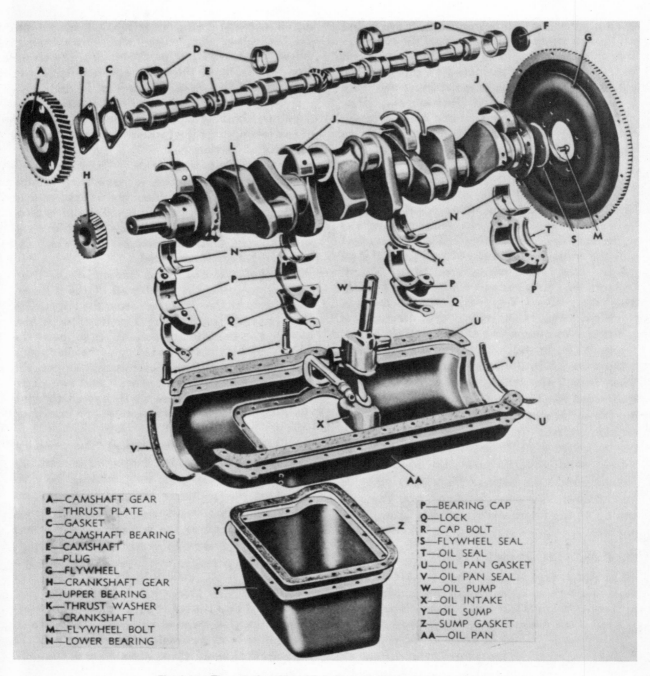

A—CAMSHAFT GEAR
B—THRUST PLATE
C—GASKET
D—CAMSHAFT BEARING
E—CAMSHAFT
F—PLUG
G—FLYWHEEL
H—CRANKSHAFT GEAR
J—UPPER BEARING
K—THRUST WASHER
L—CRANKSHAFT
M—FLYWHEEL BOLT
N—LOWER BEARING

P—BEARING CAP
Q—LOCK
R—CAP BOLT
S—FLYWHEEL SEAL
T—OIL SEAL
U—OIL PAN GASKET
V—OIL PAN SEAL
W—OIL PUMP
X—OIL INTAKE
Y—OIL SUMP
Z—SUMP GASKET
AA—OIL PAN

Fig. 2-11—The relationship of the oil pan to the lower engine parts.

THE IMPORTANCE OF CLEAN OIL

Oil serves a vital role in the protection of your engine. But while it is doing its job, it is literally taking a beating. The oil is attacked by friction, assaulted by heat and chemical changes, and contaminated by water, soot, acids, and impurities. To help protect the oil, and your engine, higher quality oils have additives that help prevent rapid deterioration. Eventually, however, even the best oil loses its protective abilities. Therefore, change the oil at regular intervals, as suggested in your owner's manual. Older cars generally require changes at least every 2,000 miles, while newer cars have recommendations of from 4,000-6,000 miles. If your car is used under severe conditions, frequent changes are recommended. However, no matter what mileage interval is recommended, change the oil at least every three months.

It is not well known, but an engine tends to burn dirty oil more readily than clean oil. This is because deposits are contained in the oil, along with a small amount of gasoline introduced after prolonged use of the choke on the carburetor. Thus, deposits in dirty oil cause the oil to be burned more easily than if the oil were clean.

How to Change the Oil

Tools required

Wrench, pan or other container to collect dirty oil

Procedure

Note: Let the engine warm up to its normal operating temperature, and then shut it off for about 10 minutes before performing this procedure. This ensures that harmful particles will be suspended, or "trapped" in the warm oil, and so, will be eliminated when the oil is drained. If the oil is changed while the engine is cold, these particles may remain at the bottom of the crankcase and be mixed with the fresh oil. It is important to eliminate any such particles, since the abrasive wear which they cause on the moving parts of the engine can reduce the life of the engine considerably.

1. On the bottom side of the engine is a large bolt, which is found in a threaded opening in the bottom of the oil pan. Place the container for catching the dirty oil beneath this bolt, and slightly toward the back of the car.
2. Using the wrench, loosen the bolt slowly and remove it. The old oil will then drain from the engine.
3. If you are going to change your oil filter (see "How to Change the Oil Filter", below), do so now.
4. Replace the drain bolt, tightening it firmly but do not overtighten it.
5. On top of the engine (where it is generally painted), there is an oil filler cap (if you are in doubt as to its exact location on your car, check the owner's manual). Remove the cap, by either lifting it (on most older cars) or twisting and lifting (on many newer cars).
6. Pour fresh oil through the opening which is now visible, being careful not to spill any on the engine. (Should some spill, wipe it up with paper towels or a rag, but be careful to prevent any dirt in the area from setting into the engine.) Check your owner's manual for the capacity of the crankcase, so you can add the proper amount of oil; if the manual is not convenient, simply add oil one quart at a time, checking the oil level with the dipstick (as described above) until the oil level is between the marks. Be sure *not* to overfill the crankcase.
7. Start the car. The oil light may come on, but it should go off after a moment or so.
8. Stop the engine, and examine the engine to make sure there are no leaks.

CLOGGED OIL FILTERS MEAN TROUBLE

There are many types of particles that get into the oil of an operating engine. These particles act as abrasives and, if allowed to remain in the oil, could destroy the precision fit of engine parts. Thus, some means of removing these particles is necessary; this is the job of the oil filter. By trapping abrasive particles, the oil filter not only protects the engine from abrasion, but also helps the engine remain clean. Any particles that get trapped by the oil filter can not be deposited in the engine.

Engines are generally designed to ensure that oil will circulate, even if the filter is clogged. But remember, oil that is not properly filtered will contain harmful substances which can damage the engine, or cause it to wear prematurely. Therefore, to guarantee proper filtration, it is important to replace the oil filter regularly. Your car owner's manual should indicate the proper replacement interval for your vehicle. Many car manufacturers recommend that the oil filter be replaced every second oil change. Often, a manufacturer of oil filters will list a replacement interval (in miles) on the filter package. Use this information as a rough indicator only, since filters need replacement when they are too plugged with carbon, dirt, or deposits to perform efficiently.

The proper replacement interval can not be determined by mileage alone; there are other factors, for example, the condition of the oil and that of the engine. As an example, engines with poor rings generally have operating conditions which promote oil deterioration. Such engines may require more frequent oil filter changes than new ones.

Modern oil filters are generally of a screw-on type, having a center opening in their base. They are usually ribbed, making it easier to install by hand.

How to Replace an Oil Filter

Where to Find the Replaceable Oil Filter

Oil filters are designed to screw on to an opening on the bottom or side of the engine. They are usually easy to recognize, since they are generally painted a bright color, and have a ribbed end.

Tools required

Oil filter wrench (available at most auto parts stores and most automobile supplies departments of discount department stores), container for catching dirty oil and a rag.

Procedure

1. Place the collection pan beneath the filter, to catch any dirty oil that spills when the filter is removed.
2. Using the filter wrench, turn the filter counter-clockwise.
3. When the filter is loosened, the filter wrench is no longer necessary. Remove the filter by turning it by hand, being careful to prevent any warm, dirty oil from spilling. (Oil filters generally hold about ¾ quart of oil.)
4. Using a rag, clean the space on the engine around the filter.
5. There is a rubber ring around the threaded opening. Coat this ring with a small amount of clean oil.
6. Screw on the new oil filter until it is finger tight. Do not overtighten, but attach the filter tightly enough so there are no oil leaks.

How to Replace an Oil Filter

Change oil filter only if the oil is also changed. (See "How to Change the Oil".)

OIL ADDITIVES MAY HURT

Most automobile parts stores sell a variety of products designed to be added to the oil. Manufacturers state that they are designed to reduce friction and engine wear, quiet engine parts, increase compression and gas mileage, and reduce oil burning. While some of these products may satisfy all of their claims, some experts feel that the use of such products—when a quality motor oil of the proper viscosity (SAE number) containing specially formulated additives, has been added—might actually be harmful to the engine. At any rate, if the car is performing properly and a quality motor oil is used containing special additives, additional additives are an unnecessary expense.

HOW TO REDUCE OIL BURNING

Every car with an internal combustion engine will occasionally have "smoke" coming from its exhaust pipe. Often, the major ingredient of this smoke is water vapor, and is most noticeable when the engine is first started on a cold or rainy day. A small amount of smoke may also be visible when a car accelerates very rapidly and suddenly. These conditions are normal, and not necessarily an indication that a problem exists. Occasionally, a darker color smoke then is usual for your car may be seen when the engine is cold. This probably means that the choke or carburetor needs an adjustment, which your mechanic can easily do for you. However, if the smoking continues, even after the engine has reached normal operating temperatures, or is blue or very dark in color, this is an indication that excessive oil is being burned and that expensive engine work may have to be done. If this is the case, chemical additives (as mentioned in the previous section) may temporarily alleviate the situation. Only the necessary repairs will solve the problem.

It is normal for cars to consume oil as they age, and so regular checks of the oil level using the dipstick (as mentioned earlier) is recommended. The oil level should be between the indicated marks. If the level is low, add more oil.

If the car needs oil too often (say, more frequently then every 1,000 miles), the car may have an oil leak, or be burning oil. If an examination of the engine reveals no oil leaks, then burning oil is most likely the problem. However, if you have been performing the regular examinations of your car, then you most likely have found the problem early enough to minimize it and prevent expensive repairs.

An engine is more likely to burn dirty oil than clean oil, and an engine which has poor rings is operating under conditions which may promote oil deterioration; thus changing the oil, and the oil filter at more frequent intervals should help. Driving the car at high speeds for long periods, or driving a vehicle which is carrying unnecessary weight puts additional strains on the engine. This is particularly true if the engine is small. Reduc-ing your speed (but staying above the safe minimum speed), helps to ease the strain on the engine. An additional benefit is the increase in gas mileage that should accompany the reduction in speed. Removing unnecessary weight, such as extra tires in the trunk (but always carry a good spare!), also helps take the load off the engine and should also lead to reduced oil consumption along with the added benefit of increased fuel economy. Finally, avoid unnecessary sudden changes in speed. This will help to reduce oil consumption, save gasoline, and lead to a more comfortable ride for you and your passengers.

CHAPTER 3

THE IGNITION SYSTEM

No matter how well the fuel system performs, unless the fuel mixture is ignited, no combustion will occur, and the vehicle will not operate. Toward this end, an electric spark is used, and it is the job of the ignition system to supply a sufficiently strong spark at just the right time to cause efficient combustion, and allow the engine to deliver its maximum power.

The ignition system can be divided into two parts—the *primary circuit* and the *secondary circuit* (see fig. 3-1).

THE PRIMARY IGNITION CIRCUIT

The primary ignition circuit is a low voltage circuit. When you turn the key to the proper position, a switch, called the *ignition switch*, will be in the "on" position. Current flows from the battery through an electrical part called a *resistor*, which "restricts" the voltage and current. The current passes through the resistor, and arrives at another electrical device called the *ignition coil*.

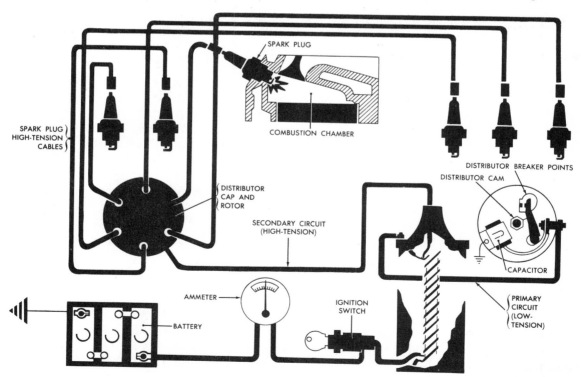

SPARK PLUG

SPARK PLUG HIGH-TENSION CABLES

COMBUSTION CHAMBER

DISTRIBUTOR BREAKER POINTS

DISTRIBUTOR CAM

DISTRIBUTOR CAP AND ROTOR

SECONDARY CIRCUIT (HIGH-TENSION)

CAPACITOR

AMMETER

BATTERY

IGNITION SWITCH

PRIMARY CIRCUIT (LOW-TENSION)

Fig. 3-1—A wiring diagram showing the circuits of an ignition system. The primary and secondary circuits are shown, as is the relationship of the spark plugs to the combustion chambers.

The ignition coil (see fig. 3-2) contains two loops of wire; a *primary winding* and a *secondary winding*. Although these windings do not touch, when current starts flowing through one winding, current, it will also start flowing through the other one. The ignition coil is designed so that when a low voltage is placed across the primary winding, a high voltage is produced across the secondary winding. It is this high voltage that produces a strong spark in the combustion chamber. However, for this to occur the current in the ignition coil must be interrupted, and restored continually. This is the purpose of the *breaker points*.

The breaker points are located in the *distributor*, a partly electrical, partly mechanical device, which has a shaft through its center (see figs. 3-3 and 3-4). This shaft is driven from the camshaft; as the distributor shaft turns, a cam is used to open and close the breaker points. This, in turn, opens and closes the circuit. Thus, the breaker points may be viewed as a sort of switch. When the points are open, the secondary winding may produce more than 20,000 volts. To make certain that current does not jump across the points as they open, another electrical component called the condenser is used.

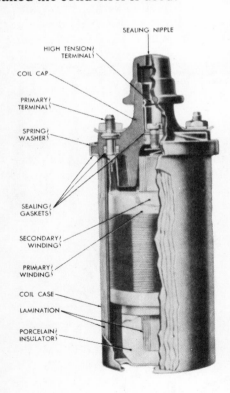

Fig. 3-2—A sectional view of an ignition coil.

SEALING NIPPLE
HIGH TENSION TERMINAL
COIL CAP
PRIMARY TERMINAL
SPRING WASHER
SEALING GASKETS
SECONDARY WINDING
PRIMARY WINDING
COIL CASE
LAMINATION
PORCELAIN INSULATOR

Finally, a connection is made from the breaker points to "ground", completing the circuit back to the battery. (Ground refers to the practice of connecting one side of electrical parts to the car body or frame; thus, the vehicle itself serves as a sort of wire, or series of wires joining electrical components attached to it.)

Current in the primary circuit flows from the battery, through the resistor, and the primary winding of the ignition coil, through the closed breaker points and—via a ground connection—back to the battery. (When the points are open, current passes to ground via the condenser.)

THE SECONDARY IGNITION CIRCUIT

It is the secondary ignition circuit that is responsible for supplying a spark of sufficient strength to cause efficient combustion; it is a high voltage circuit. Current flows from the secondary winding of the ignition coil, and via a wire, to the center of the distributor cap. Here, contact is made with a *rotor*, located atop the distributor shaft which, as its name implies, rotates within the distributor cap.

Arranged around the inside of the distributor cap are metal terminals. There is one terminal for each cylinder in the engine. There are separate wires connected to each of these terminals in the distributor cap. Each wire joins a terminal and a *spark plug* (see fig. 3-5).

Each spark plug is an electrical device that is screwed into the engine. Each has two electrical terminals separated by a small gap, and these are called the *central electrode*, and the *side electrode*. The side electrode is grounded to the engine.

As the rotor in the distributor turns, it makes contact with one of the terminals in the distributor cap. Current passes through the cap, and one of the connecting wires to the central electrode of one of the spark plugs, and jumps the gap separating the two electrodes. This is the spark which ignites the fuel mixture in the combustion chamber.

While this is occurring, the rotor continues to turn and make successive contact with each of the terminals in the distributor cap.

Sparks are produced in the different spark plugs. If these sparks occur at the proper time, the result will be a properly performing engine.

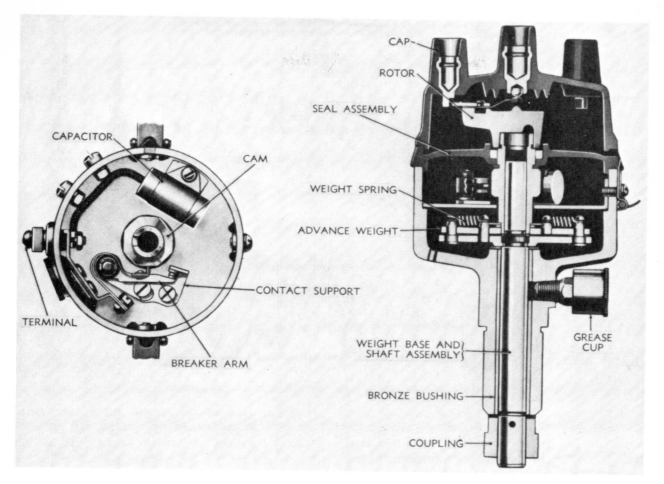

Fig. 3-3—Top and side sectional views of a distributor. The distributor cap is not shown in these views, but does appear in Figure 3-4. The capacitor shown in these figures is still referred to by the older term condenser.

Many late model cars do not have points. Instead they use an electronic ignition system which has a magnetic switching device. These ignition systems use transistors to increase their efficiency.

A FAULTY IGNITION SYSTEM CAN MAKE YOU WANT TO CHANGE CARS

The ignition system consists of mechanical as well as electrical components. If any of these parts fail to perform, or perform at the wrong time, the engine will not operate at full capacity. Starting problems, loss of power, and shaking are a few of the problems a faulty or improperly adjusted ignition system can cause. The smaller the engine, the more noticeable these problems are

likely to be. Problems created by a faulty ignition system might even make you decide to change cars. Before you take this drastic step, remember that the ignition system is not as complicated as it looks. Simple inspection and maintenance procedures can help alleviate, and prevent ignition problems.

HOW TO INSPECT THE IGNITION SYSTEM

A thorough analysis using electronic equipment is often used to locate ignition problems. However, a simple visual check can often locate problem areas before they cause trouble. Using a flashlight, check to see if any ignition parts are damaged; the distributor cap sometimes cracks, insulation covers at the spark plugs sometimes

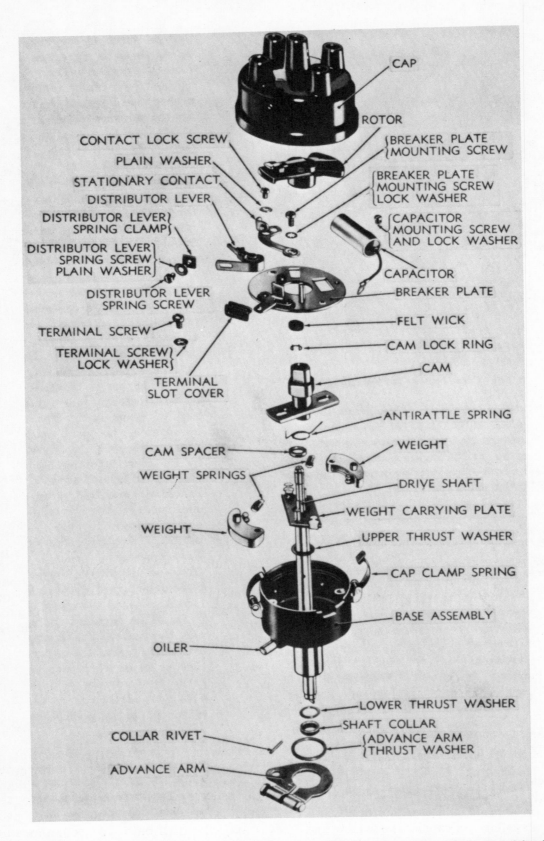

CAP

ROTOR

CONTACT LOCK SCREW

PLAIN WASHER

STATIONARY CONTACT

DISTRIBUTOR LEVER

DISTRIBUTOR LEVER} SPRING CLAMPS

DISTRIBUTOR LEVER} SPRING SCREW PLAIN WASHER

DISTRIBUTOR LEVER SPRING SCREW

TERMINAL SCREW

TERMINAL SCREW} LOCK WASHERS

TERMINAL SLOT COVER

BREAKER PLATE MOUNTING SCREW

BREAKER PLATE MOUNTING SCREW LOCK WASHER

CAPACITOR MOUNTING SCREW AND LOCK WASHER

CAPACITOR

BREAKER PLATE

FELT WICK

CAM LOCK RING

CAM

ANTIRATTLE SPRING

CAM SPACER

WEIGHT SPRINGS

WEIGHT

WEIGHT

DRIVE SHAFT

WEIGHT CARRYING PLATE

UPPER THRUST WASHER

CAP CLAMP SPRING

BASE ASSEMBLY

OILER

LOWER THRUST WASHER

SHAFT COLLAR

COLLAR RIVET

ADVANCE ARM THRUST WASHER

ADVANCE ARM

Fig. 3-4—A disassembled view of the distributor. The distributor cap can be seen in this view. The provision for four wires around the outside of the cap indicates that this distributor is designed for a 4-cylinder engine.

30   The Complete Car Owner's Manual

develop wear spots, or don't fit snugly over the spark plug connections, and ignition wires can develop cracks or other faults in the insulation. If any component is found to have a fault, replace it.

If no damages are readily apparent, place the vehicle in a dark area, such as a darkened (but well-ventilated) garage. Open the hood and start the vehicle. Being careful to stay clear of the rotating fan (which can cause serious injury when the engine is on), examine the ignition system for sparks, or light flashes. If any are apparent, or a damaged or faulty component is present change it.

The ignition wires on modern cars are generally not solid; rather, they are made of conductive particles that are compressed to form a continuous electrical conductor. As these wires age, heat from the engine, and other factors cause them to lose their electrical "efficiency". When this point is reached, they are in capable of supplying the proper voltage (current mix for a strong spark), and engine performance will suffer. To prevent this from occurring, change the ignition wires in accordance with the recommendations in the owner's manual. If this information is not available, you should change the ignition wires every second tune-up.

How to Change the Ignition Wires

Tools required

None

Procedure

Note: Let the engine cool first. A cool engine is easier to work with, and the possibility of accidental burns is eliminated.

1. Start with any wire. Gently but firmly, pull the wire from its connection inside the distributor cap. (Pull the wire from the end, not the middle, to avoid a strain on any connections.)
2. Holding the wire near its other end, gently, but firmly, pull that end from its connection.
3. Ignition wire replacement sets generally come with various lengths of wires. Match the removed wire with the appropriate replacement wire.
4. Slide each end of the replacement wire onto its terminals.
5. Repeat steps 1-4 for each of the other ignition wires. It is important that each wire join the proper terminals. Therefore, change the wires one at a time, to avoid the possibility of an accidental mismatch.

SPARK PLUGS

The spark plugs are, in a sense, "where it all happens." Unless a spark occurs, the fuel mixture will not be ignited, and the engine will not operate. The center of a spark plug is made of copper, and is surrounded by porcelain, which does not conduct electricity. One end of a spark plug consists entirely of metal, and is designed to screw into the engine. The other end has the two electrodes mentioned earlier. If the ignition system is functioning properly, a strong spark (at the right time) will travel between the electrodes. If there is a problem within the engine it can often be spotted by examining the spark plugs.

SPARK PLUGS CAN INDICATE ENGINE PERFORMANCE

New spark plugs have electrodes which are square faced, and when installed, the distance separating the electrodes (called the *gap*) is adjusted to the proper setting for your car. As the car is driven, the electrodes tend to wear in a curved or circular fashion. When this curvature becomes too severe, the engine will "miss" on acceleration, and the car will not have the power you may be expecting. Thus, to prevent this from happening, spark plugs should be replaced at every tune-up, or approximately every 10,000 miles.

If the spark plugs are fairly clean, or perhaps slightly grey in color, and the spark plug electrodes are wearing in a rounded fashion, this is an indication of proper engine operation. Sometimes, however, the spark plugs may be wet. If so, smell the plug. If the wetness is due to raw gasoline, then the engine may be overchoked, a situation that can arise from a faulty carburetor. Have your mechanic check the carburetor.

If the spark plug is dry, but burned, then either a spark plug with the wrong heat range was installed, or the engine is running too hot due to a lean mixture. Having the mixture checked could prevent an expensive repair bill. Your mechanic can easily do this, perhaps using a meter to examine the exhaust gases.

Spark plugs that have oil on them, or dark deposits, may indicate faulty rings. Have your mechanic check for this condition, particularly if the car is using an excessive amount of oil. Unfortunately, ring work is generally expensive.

As the vehicle is driven, the spark plugs will show signs of wear. The electrodes tend to wear in a curved manner, but depostis from lead compounds in the fuel may also accumulate on the plugs. Although spark plugs can be reconditioned, generally the plugs are replaced. However, use of low lead, or no lead fuels will reduce these deposits, and spark plug life can be extended. You should use these fuels only on cars which are designed to run on them; otherwise the result can be expensive engine damage.

Spark plugs play an important part in the efficient operation of vehicles with internal combustion engines. Toward this end, they are generally designed to withstand considerable (electrical) punishment. If you have an 8-cylinder car, and its engine operates at about 4000 rpm (revolutions per minute), the spark plugs must supply approximately 300 strong sparks *each second*. It is not surprising, then, that spark plugs do wear, even in an engine that is operating as efficiently as possible.

REMOVING AND CHANGING SPARK PLUGS

Since spark plugs can indicate the operating condition of an engine, and are designed to be replaced at regular intervals, there is a very simple procedure for the removal of spark plugs. However, despite the simplicity of the technique, two difficulties are sometimes encountered:

1. Because of design, particularly on some of the larger engines, or the presence of added-on features such as power steering, brake units or air conditioning equipment, and other items, the spark plugs may not be readily accessible. Usually, special tools are available to aid in the removal and replacement of these spark plugs. If your car has spark plugs which cannot be reached easily and you don't want to buy special tools, have your mechanic change the plugs. Since some garages have high mark-ups on parts, you may have to use the spark plugs supplied by them, or else pay an additional installation charge. However, some mechanics are willing to install parts supplied by the customer, charging only for labor. Thus, you can still save money on this type of maintenance, even if you do not do the job yourself.

2. Sometimes spark plugs may have been installed too tightly. Although this is usually not the case, it may be difficult to remove the spark plugs using tools which are not long enough.

How to Remove Spark Plugs

Where to Find the Spark Plugs

The spark plugs are screwed into the engine, one spark plug for each cylinder. Each plug has an ignition wire leading from it to the distributor.

Tools required

Spark plug wrench or ratchet wrench with a spark plug socket.

Procedure

Note: The engine should not be operating while this procedure is performed. To avoid accidental burns, it is advisable to follow these steps when the engine is cool.

1. Start with any spark plug. Holding the ignition wire by the end joining the plug, pull the ignition wire off the plug.
2. Insert the spark plug socket into the block, until it completely engages the nut shaped portion of the spark plug. Be careful not to hold the tool at an angle, or the plug may break.
3. Rotate the wrench in a counter-clockwise direction. The spark plug should unscrew from the engine.

When performing any procedure involving the removal of ignition wires, care should be taken to ensure that the proper wire is matched to the correct plug. Therefore, it is a good idea to completely finish with one spark plug (removal, examination, re-adjustment or replacement, and re-installation) before working on the next one. To remove the other plugs, follow steps 1-3 above.

EXAMINING THE SPARK PLUGS

Many auto repair and diagnostic centers have various checks, both electronic and mechanical, to determine the malfunctioning of engine parts. However, much of this information can be determined from a thorough examination of the spark plugs. If the electrodes are rounded, and the spark plug is dry and fairly clean, this is an indication that the cylinder from which the plug was taken has good operating conditions within it; however, rounded electrodes indicate that the plug has served for over 10,000 miles and should be replaced.

The heat range, under which the spark plug was operating, can be checked by examining the removed plug for color and for the amount and type of deposits. The deposits should be at a minimum; the insulator around the center electrode may be a light gray color, and the electrodes should not be burned. Burning of the electrodes indicates the plug was operating in too high a heat range, probably due either to the installation of the wrong plug, or an improper air-fuel mixture. A soft carbon coating is an indication that the air-fuel mixture is too rich. If the insulator is a light gray, but the shell is coated with either carbon or soot, this tells you the low-speed adjustment is too rich.

A serious problem is indicated if there are hard flakes of carbon present, and the insulator is wet. The engine is pumpimg oil. In severe conditions, the plug may not fire, causing the engine to operate roughly, resulting in a loss of power.

Check to see there are no deposits between the center insulator and the shell. Sometimes such deposits form an unwanted electrical path (called a *short circuit*); such a plug will not operate properly. These deposits do not necessarily mean a problem with the engine, since they are usually the result of additives in the fuel.

SPARK PLUGS CAN BE CLEANED

When a spark plug has been removed, and found to be in good condition, its service life can be extended by cleaning it and re-adjusting the gap between the electrodes. Most auto repair services do not supply this service. They prefer simply to replace the spark plugs. Remember, they get a mark-up on parts, and can still charge for labor. Also, badly dirtied spark plugs might require special reconditioning; the time required for this processing, coupled with the high cost of labor, and the relatively low price of new spark plugs, makes it economically unfeasible to do this procedure. However, for the low cost of a spark plug file, gapping tool, and a small amount of solvent, you can do the job and extend the service life of the plugs.

How to Clean Spark Plugs

Note: Do not perform this procedure on burned plugs, plugs with cracked or damaged insulators, or plugs with severely rounded electrodes. These plugs should be replaced.

Tools required

Spark plug file, gapping tool, solvent, stiff brush

Procedure

1. Clean the plug or plugs with solvent, using the stiff brush to remove any deposits. Be

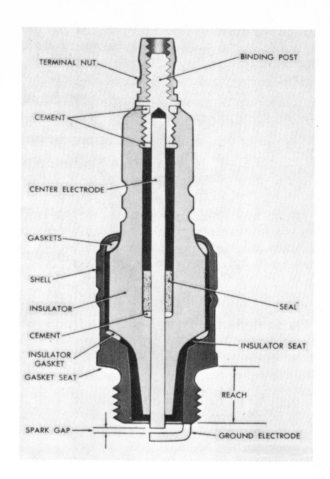

Fig. 3-5—A sectional view of a spark plug.

sure to remove any deposits that might be present beneath the side electrode.
2. Allow the plug to dry thoroughly.
3. It is very important that the electrodes are flat, otherwise the spark plug will not fire at full efficiency. Using the file, make sure that the surfaces of the electrodes are flat.
4. Be sure to brush away any filings that might be present.
5. Follow the simple procedure for gapping spark plugs.
6. Examine the plug to make sure there are no loose filings, or dirt that can come loose, and get into the cylinder.

Once the spark plug has been removed, examined and a determination has been made to either clean the plug to extend its service life or to replace it, the next step is to make sure the distance between the electrodes is correct. This is extremely important if the engine is to operate efficiently. The procedure for adjusting this distance to specified values is known as *gapping* the spark plugs, and should be performed on cleaned, reconditioned, or new plugs.

How to Gap Spark Plugs

Tools required

Spark plug gauge (also called spark plug tool)

Note: To avoid errors in setting the gap, a round wire gauge tool should be used.

Procedure

1. Check your owner's manual to determine the proper setting for your car. If not available, use the table in the back of this text.
2. Check the gap, using the wire on the gauge which corresponds to the correct setting for your car. If you use a blade type of gauge be sure to hold the blade level, or else you will get an improper indication. The wire or blade should just be able to fit between the electrodes.
3. If an adjustment is necessary, use the adjusting part of the tool to bend the *side* electrode; attempting to bend the center electrode will crack the insulator, and ruin the plug. Do not bend the electrode sideways, or the spark plug may not operate efficiently.
4. Check the gap again, as indicated in step 2, until the gauge just clears the electrodes. If necessary, repeat step 3.

Once the spark plugs have been cleaned and gapped, or new plugs have been gapped, the next step is to install these plugs in the engine.

How to Install Spark Plugs

Tools required

Spark plug wrench or ratchet wrench with spark plug socket, clean rag.

Procedure

1. If you have not already done so, gap the plugs using the previously described procedure.
2. Using a rag, wipe the gasket surfaces, (the "holes", where the spark plug is to fit. If possible, use a new gasket where one is used, since this gasket affects the operating characteristics of the plug; if a new gasket is not available, clean the gasket, as best you can, before using it.
3. If your car is designed to use spark plug gaskets, screw the spark plug into the engine until it is finger-tight.
4. On some engines, some Chrysler cars, for example, the spark plugs are installed in tubes, and no gasket is used. If your engine is of this type:

a) Make sure the tube has no cracks; if it does, replace it.
b) Place the plug in the socket of the tool, and hold the socket so that it is upright.
c) Slide the tube over the plug.
d) Thread the plug into the engine, holding the tube and the plug together.
5. Using the wrench, tighten the plug. The plug should be seated firmly, but be careful not to overtighten it. Overtightening may result in changing the gap, or squeezing the gasket (if present) out of shape.
6. Holding the end of the ignition wire, slide it onto the spark plug, making sure a good connection is made.

DETERMINING THE BEST SPARK PLUG FOR YOUR CAR

All spark plugs are not the same. Although the specific function they perform within the internal combustion engine is the same, and they have somewhat similar shapes, different spark plugs can have quite different operating characteristics. Although spark plugs can differ as to size, construction, and efficiency, a major difference between plugs is the temperature range at which they are designed to operate.

Some plugs are known as *hot plugs*, because they are designed to run at a higher temperature than the ones normally found in a specific engine. New engines are generally designed to operate with *cold plugs*, that is with spark plugs of a specific "normal" heat range. However, as an engine gets older, oil and carbon deposits begin to appear on the plugs. A badly worn engine may result in an excessive amount of oil and carbon formation on the plugs, and in severe cases ignition misses may occur. Under these conditions it is adviseable to replace the usual cold plug with a hotter one, as hotter plugs are supposed to burn off these accumulations more efficiently than the normal cold plugs.

Car manufacturers generally recommend the particular plugs that are to be used in their engines. These recommendations are in the form of a spark plug brand code number or name. An auto parts store can tell you which plug is recommended for your car, and can suggest a hot plug replacement.

THE BATTERY-ELECTRICITY UPON DEMAND

When you are at home, and you operate an electrical appliance such as a radio, television, or even just a lamp, rarely are you concerned with whether the device supplying the power is in good condition; you probably don't even know where it is located or what it looks like. What concerns you is whether or not the device works. Most of us only consider the source of the electricity when the power fails, or the electric bill is to be paid.

When you operate a car, however, you must concern yourself with the electrical system, even if it is only during periodic maintenance intervals.

Although some people do live in motor vehicles, there is a basic difference between a motor vehicle, and most homes or apartments: homes and apartments are stationary, vehicles are mobile. Because they are mobile, vehicles can not be attached to remote generators via fixed lines, the way homes and apartments are; the source of electrical power must be mobile too. And, although the power supplied to the home or apartment might be disrupted, the residence can still be used. However, if the electrical source in a

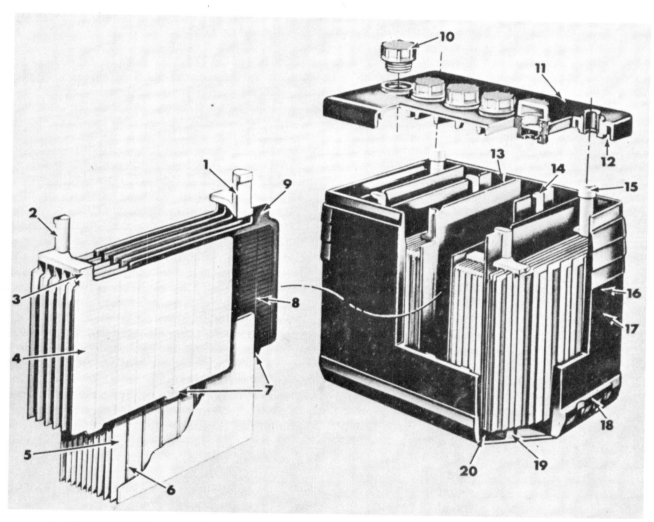

1. POSITIVE CELL TERMINAL AND STRAP
2. NEGATIVE CELL TERMINAL AND STRAP
3. NEGATIVE TERMINAL LUG
4. NEGATIVE PLATE (GRID AND SPONGE LEAD)
5. SEPARATOR
6. SEPARATOR RIB
7. PLATE FEET
8. POSITIVE PLATE (GRID & LEAD DIOXIDE)
9. POSITIVE TERMINAL LUG
10. VENT PLUG
11. ONE-PIECE COVER
12. EPOXY RESIN SEALING LIP
13. CELL PARTITION
14. OVER-PARTITION CONNECTOR
15. TERMINAL POST
16. CONTAINER
17. AMPERE-HOUR RATING
18. MOUNTING LEDGE
19. ELEMENT REST
20. SEDIMENT SPACE

Fig. 3-6—The components of an automotive storage battery.

vehicle is incapable of functioning, the vehicle may not be used to go anywhere, except perhaps, downhill.

The mobile source of electricity used in cars is called the *automotive storage battery*, or simply the *battery* (see fig. 3-6). Every car manufacturer establishes its own requirements for the batteries used in different makes and models. Although these batteries may look somewhat the same, their physical size, construction, and operating characteristics are generally different.

HOW AN AUTOMATIC STORAGE BATTERY WORKS

The battery is nothing more than a sturdily constructed box, divided into different compartments called *cells*. Within each cell are plates, which have a grid-like structure. Compounds such as lead or lead peroxide are pressed into these grids. Those plates that consist of grids filled with lead peroxide are connected to a terminal on the battery case called the *positive (or plus) terminal*, usually denoted POS or +. The other plates that are filled with metallic lead are connected to another terminal on the battery case, called the *negative (or minus) terminal*, usually denoted NEG or -. Finally, a solution of sulfuric acid and water, called *electrolyte*, is added until plates are covered.

When this battery is installed in a car, and an electrical circuit is completed, as, for example, when the ignition key is turned to the start position, a chemical reaction occurs within the battery. The result of this chemical reaction is electricity (see fig. 3-7).

Because of its construction, this type of battery is sometimes referred to as a lead-acid storage battery. Recently, battery manufacturers have made available to the consumer batteries that are lighter, sturdier, and more powerful than those previously produced. Some of these are completely sealed and require practically no maintenance. The service lives of some batteries have been extended over what they were previously, and some manufacturers are guaranteeing their product for as long as the purchaser owns the vehicle into which it is installed. Batteries which have this guarantee usually cost more, but if you intend to keep your car for many years, it may be a worthwhile investment.

ACCESSORIES RELY ON THE BATTERY

Modern vehicles (cars and trucks) require relatively large amounts of electrical current. On most cars, the alternator or generator can supply the demand for electricity, so conservation of electrical energy is not normally necessary as long as the engine is operating. However, using accessories with the engine off can strain a battery severely.

For example, if the high beam headlights are left on with the engine off, there is a 12 to 18 ampere (a unit of electrical current) drain. This can reduce a fully charged 40 ampere-hour rated battery by as much as 50%, if they are left on for about 40 minutes. Fig. 3-8 shows the current drain on a 12-volt system when various common accessories are in the on position.

Battery Tips For Your Protection

1. Do not use electrical accessories more than is absolutely necessary when the engine is not running. Doing so can put a severe strain on the battery, and could lead to starting difficulties.
2. If accessories must be used with the engine off, turn the ignition key to the ACCESSORY position. When the key is placed in this position, power will be supplied to the accessories, but the ignition curcuit is shut off. This reduces the strain on the battery, and protects the distributor points from damage.
3. Keep your car in tune, particularly in cold weather. At 70°F or above, a start can drain ½% of the useful charge of a 40 ampere-hour rated battery. Starting the same car in cold weather can drain 3% to 5% of the useful charge of the same battery. Keeping the car in tune can reduce cranking time, and thus lessen the strain on the battery.
4. Use the proper weight (viscosity) oil (see "The Oil System"). Oil that is too viscous can act almost like molasses on a cold morning. It makes it more difficult for the engine to crank, and can overwork the battery.

BATTERY CARE CAN ELIMINATE PROBLEMS

Proper battery care is vital to the dependable operation of your car. A car with a weak or dirty battery may not start (especially on cold or wet days), and accessories such as headlights, windshield wipers, heaters and air conditioners will not operate properly.

TAKING CARE OF THE BATTERY

Batteries are generally located on a flat surface

FULLY CHARGED BATTERY

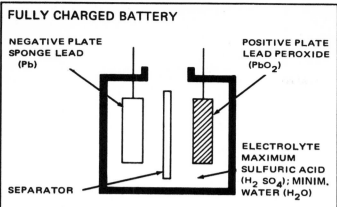

NEGATIVE PLATE SPONGE LEAD (Pb)

POSITIVE PLATE LEAD PEROXIDE (PbO_2)

ELECTROLYTE MAXIMUM SULFURIC ACID (H_2SO_4); MINIM. WATER (H_2O)

SEPARATOR

In a charged battery, active material of the negative plate is sponge lead (Pb); active material of the positive plate is lead peroxide (PbO_2); the electrolyte contains sulfuric acid (H_2SO_4) and a minimum of water.

BATTERY DISCHARGING

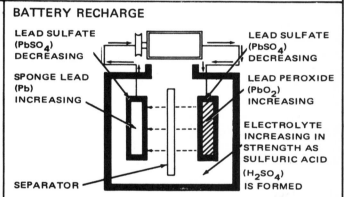

LEAD SULFATE ($PbSO_4$) ACCUMULATING

SPONGE LEAD (Pb) DECREASING

SEPARATOR

LEAD SULFATE ($PbSO_4$) ACCUMULATING

LEAD PEROXIDE (PbO_2) DECREASING

ELECTROLYTE BECOMING DILUTED AS SULFURIC ACID IS CONSUMED AND WATER IS PRODUCED

When the battery discharges, the electrolyte reacts with both the positive and negative plates . . . oxygen from the lead peroxide in the positive plates combines with hydrogen from the sulfuric acid to form water . . . lead from the lead peroxide combines with the sulfate from the sulfuric acid to form lead sulfate . . . hydrogen from the sulfuric acid combines with oxygen from the lead peroxide to form more water . . . lead from the sponge lead in the negative plates combines with the sulfate from the sulfuric acid to form lead sulfate . . . and electric current flows.

DISCHARGED BATTERY

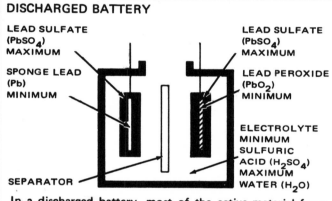

LEAD SULFATE ($PbSO_4$) MAXIMUM

SPONGE LEAD (Pb) MINIMUM

SEPARATOR

LEAD SULFATE ($PbSO_4$) MAXIMUM

LEAD PEROXIDE (PbO_2) MINIMUM

ELECTROLYTE MINIMUM SULFURIC ACID (H_2SO_4) MAXIMUM WATER (H_2O)

In a discharged battery, most of the active material from negative and positive plates has been converted to lead sulfate ($PbSO_4$), and the electrolyte is greatly diluted with water (H_2O).

BATTERY RECHARGE

LEAD SULFATE ($PbSO_4$) DECREASING

SPONGE LEAD (Pb) INCREASING

SEPARATOR

LEAD SULFATE ($PbSO_4$) DECREASING

LEAD PEROXIDE (PbO_2) INCREASING

ELECTROLYTE INCREASING IN STRENGTH AS SULFURIC ACID (H_2SO_4) IS FORMED

When the alternator recharges your battery, the chemical reaction between plates and electrolyte is reversed . . . lead sulfate from positive and negative plates reacts with the electrolyte to form sulfuric acid . . . removal of sulfate from the negative plates restores sponge lead as the active material . . . oxygen from the water recombines with the lead in the positive plates to form lead peroxide . . . and the strength of the battery is restored.

Fig. 3-7—How an automotive storage battery works.

attached to the side or front of the engine compartment. A holding clamp is used to prevent the battery from sliding or bouncing. As a car ages, this clamp corrodes, and the battery may not be firmly attached to the vehicle. Examine the battery hold-down clamp occasionally, and if it is broken or corroded, replace it.

While you are checking the battery hold-down clamp, examine the battery case. It should be free of cracks; if any are present replace the battery. Moisture, grease, or dirt on the battery case, and around the terminals, can lead to a slow

leakage of electricity, even though the vehicle may not be in use. Thus, the case should be as free of dirt and grease as possible; occasionally wiping the case with a rag will help to keep it in good condition. If the battery case is badly soiled, you can clean it using a cloth dipped in a mild solution of baking soda and water (2 ounces of soda to 1 quart water). Be careful to avoid getting this solution into the battery itself, and splashing it on the car's finish. Carefully rinse the case with cold water.

One very important area of battery main-

ACCESSORY	CURRENT USED (amperes)
Air conditioner	10 – 14
Heater	6 – 7
Ignition system	2 – 3
Parking lights	4 – 8
Low beam headlights	8 – 14
High beam headlights	12 – 18
Radio	0.4 – 2
Windshield wiper	2 – 3

Fig. 3-8—Current drain on a 12 volt electrical system when various appliances are used. The numbers shown represent units of electrical current called amperes. The amounts shown vary with the car model and the accessories used.

tenance, often overlooked by experienced mechanics, is the care of the battery terminals. One of the results of the chemical reactions taking place within the battery is the formation of deposits on the terminals (particularly the negative terminal). Unless these deposits are removed occasionally, they will build up, forming a resistance to the flow of electricity from the battery. This can prevent the battery from delivering all the power for which it was designed, and could lead to problems in starting, difficulties with the lights, and other electrical devices.

How to Clean Battery Terminals

Tools required

Terminal cleaning tool (usually very inexpensive and available wherever auto parts are sold), or a stiff brush with a wooden or plastic handle. Wrench.

Procedure

1. Using the wrench, loosen the nut on the clamp, holding the battery cable to the positive terminal.

Caution: When working with the positive terminal, do not let the wrench (or any metal object) touch the terminal, clamp or nut, and any object attached to the car frame (or the frame itself) at the same time. To do so can cause a serious accident.

2. Lift or slide the cable from the terminal.
3. If the terminal cleaning tool is used, work with the end of the tool which has a circular wire brush. Place the brush over the terminal, and press down while rotating the tool in a circular motion. To remove the tool from the terminal, lift up and rotate tool in the opposite direction. Note: Some batteries

have terminals on the side of the case instead of on top; for this type of terminal, use a sideways motion instead of up and down movements.

3a. If you use a stiff brush, move the brush across the entire exposed surface of the terminal. To avoid damaging the terminal, do not press too firmly.

4. Using the straight brush end of the terminal cleaning tool or the stiff brush, clean the clamp on the end of the battery cable.

5. Place the clamp over the battery terminal, and using the wrench, tighten the nut on the clamp until a good, tight contact is made. To avoid damaging the terminal, do not overtighten.

6. Repeat the previous steps for the other terminal. When removing the cable from the negative terminal, avoid letting it come in contact with the positive terminal.

If you have followed these procedures for battery care, there is only one remaining step to make sure the battery can deliver maximum power. For the battery to work properly, the level of the electrolyte (the fluid level inside the battery) must be correct. Some batteries are of the sealed variety, and there is no way to change the level of the electrolyte. However, most batteries still in use today are the refillable kind. As the battery is used, some of the water in the electrolyte evaporates, and should be replaced.

How to Add Water to a Battery

Tools required

None

Note: Ordinary tap water sometimes has a large mineral content. These "impurities" can accumulate inside the battery, and eventually damage it. Thus, if distilled water is available, it should be used instead.

1. Depending on the battery, unscrew or lift the caps on top of the battery.
2. Check the fluid level in each cell of the battery. In each case, the level should be even with an indicator mark. This mark is usually the point where there is a split in the ring portion of the case. Do not add water to any cell which is at or above this level.
3. Slowly and carefully add water to any cell which has a fluid level below this mark. Stop when the level is even with the mark. *Do not overfill.* Be careful to avoid splashing any battery liquid on any metal surfaces or the finish of the car, as the acid will attack metal

or paint. Should any battery solution get on the car, wash it off with large amounts of cold water. More importantly, should any get on your skin or in the eyes, wash the affected area with lots of cold water, and see a physician.

TESTING THE BATTERY

As a battery is used it "gets used up." More accurately, the battery is *discharging*. When a battery supplies power (that is, when it is discharging), the sulfuric acid in the electrolyte combines chemically with the plates. The remaining solution then has more water. Since the acid is heavier than water, the remaining solution becomes lighter than before. If a device existed which could determine how "light" the solution is, we could tell how much electrical energy the battery is capable of delivering.

Fortunately there is such a device, and it is called a *hydrometer* (see fig. 3-9). A hydrometer is a very simple gauge; it is nothing more than a weighted float within a glass cylinder, sort of a thermometer with a float inside it. When the hydrometer is filled with liquid, the depth to which the float sinks indicates the weight of the liquid when compared with water. A scale is usually printed on the side of the cylinder, so that the condition of the battery can be determined.

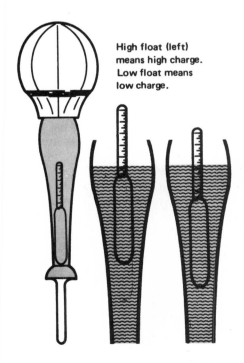

High float (left) means high charge. Low float means low charge.

Fig. 3-9—A professional type of hydrometer with a close-up of high charge and low charge readings.

You may have noticed that batteries strong enough to start a car in warm weather may fail to do so when the temperature drops. This is understandable. When a battery discharges, the battery solution contains proportionately more water than previously. As the temperature drops, the electrolyte may begin to freeze, and the chemical reactions needed for the production of electricity will not take place as readily. In severe cases, the electrolyte will freeze, and cause the battery case to crack.

THE IMPORTANCE OF THE PROPER BATTERY FLUID LEVEL

The level of electrolyte in the battery not only is a factor in the delivery of the maximum power, of which your battery is capable, it is also a factor in determining its useful life. If the water level is too low, the "acid strength" (that is, the concentration of acid) becomes too high. This can damage the battery.

As a battery is used, it becomes discharged. With the demands made upon it by the electrical system, and the accessories in a modern automobile, the battery would soon become "dead," that is, incapable of satisfying the demands made upon it. The situation can be reversed, however. The battery can be charged. This can be done by passing a current through the battery in the direction opposite to that of discharge. This is the purpose of the *generator* or *alternator* and the electrical circuit used for this is called the charging circuit.

Most modern cars come with an electrical device called an alternator, while older cars have generators. Both perform the same job—providing an electrical power source. A generator will generally supply power only at higher engine speeds, while an alternator supplies electrical needs at all engine speeds. Both the alternator and the generator are operated by means of a "loop," called the *fanbelt*, which slips over a pulley on the crankshaft. Thus, the alternator or generator operates only when the engine does. Neither device can be used to supply the electrical energy needed to start the engine.

Helping the generator or alternator supply the electrical needs of the car is the job of the *voltage regulator* (see fig. 3-10). The voltage regulator is like a sensing device that can detect the amount of power the battery can provide and which, as its name implies, controls or regulates the alternator or generator.

CHARGING-REPLENISHING THE BATTERY

If your battery is in good shape, and the charging system in your car is functioning properly, the battery will be replenished (recharged) as you drive. However, as a battery ages, it may not hold a charge as well as it used to; that is, the battery may no longer be capable of supplying all of your car's electrical needs without recharging. Sometimes, even a good battery will get weak, if the car is not operated for extended periods. In either case, as long as the battery is not damaged, charging the battery with an external battery charger will probably help.

BOOSTER CABLES CAN HELP IN EMERGENCIES

Occasionally, something can go wrong with a battery, despite careful attention to maintenance. When this happens, the battery may not be able to supply sufficient power to start your car. If an external battery charger is not available, having a pair of booster cables in the car could save you from the cost of an expensive road call. Booster cables allow you to use the battery in another car to start your own vehicle.

How to Booster start a Car

Note: If the weather is very cold, remove the vent caps from the battery, and check to see if the electrolyte is frozen. If it is, do not booster start the car; to do so may damage the battery beyond repair.

Tools required

A pair of booster cables.

Note: This is an emergency procedure, and is not part of a regular maintenance program. It is necessary to have the brief use of another vehicle with a good battery, having the same voltage rating as your own. If you are in doubt, voltage ratings are usually printed somewhere on the battery.

Procedure

1. Position the "good" vehicle so that its battery is close enough to your car, for the booster cables to join the batteries.

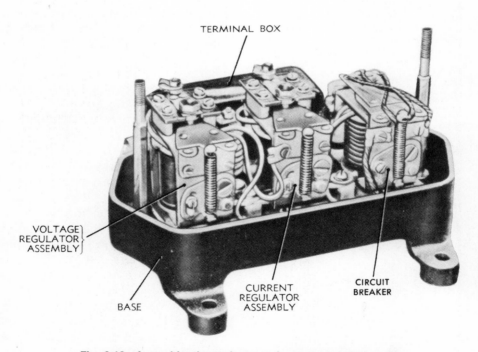

TERMINAL BOX

VOLTAGE REGULATOR ASSEMBLY

CURRENT REGULATOR ASSEMBLY

CIRCUIT BREAKER

BASE

Fig. 3-10—A combination voltage and current regulator with the cover removed. The voltage regulator protects the battery, but if the battery is badly discharged or if a heavy electrical load were to be connected, the generator or alternator might try to satisfy the current demand and be damaged; thus the current regulator is often needed in addition. A circuit breaker is also present for protection.

2. Turn all accessory switches, and the ignition key to the OFF position.
3. Place the car in neutral with the park brake set, or in park with the brake set.
4. Remove the vent caps from both batteries.
5. On the "bad" battery, follow the regular battery cables. One of these will lead to the starter switch, or solenoid. Note whether the terminal from which this cable leads is marked positive (POS or +), or negative (NEG or −). Connect one end of the jumper cable to the terminal on the booster battery, which is marked the same way (see fig. 3-11).
6. Connect the other end of the same jumper to the terminal on the weak battery marked in the same way. Thus, both positive terminals will be connected, or both negative terminals will be connected. NEVER CONNECT A POSITIVE TERMINAL TO A NEGATIVE TERMINAL; this can result in damage to the alternator, or a possible explosion.
7. Connect one end of the second jumper cable to the other terminal of the "good" battery.
8. Connect the other end of the second cable to "ground," that is, to any metal part of the frame of the car you wish to start. *Do not* connect this end to the negative terminal itself; although this is often done, it can actually cause the battery to explode.
9. Have someone race the engine, of the "good" car *momentarily* (racing more than brief periods may cause damage), while you start your car. If the battery is the cause of your starting problems, your car should start.
10. Starting with the cable connected to the frame, disconnect the booster cables one at a time. Again, do not let the metal parts of the cables touch each other, or allow the one joining the positive terminals to touch any metal object. Always disconnect the ends of the cables connected to the "bad" car before the ends connected to the "good" car.
11. Allow the engine to run for a while. If the charging circuit is functioning properly, it will help charge the battery. If the car has a generator instead of an alternator, it may be necessary to race the engine *briefly* (as mentioned above, racing an engine can cause damage) or to drive the car at highway speeds, in order to charge the battery.
12. Replace the vent caps on both batteries.

As soon as you get the chance, determine the

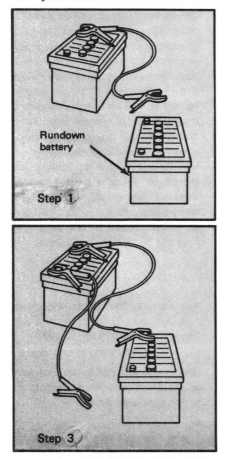

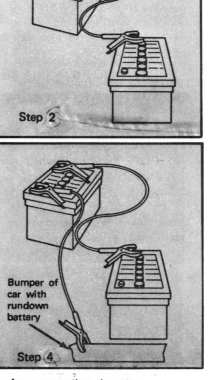

Fig. 3-11—The proper sequence for connecting booster (jumper) cables.

cause of the battery failure, and correct the situation. It could happen again.

BATTERY CABLES DELIVER ELECTRICAL POWER

The finest battery in the world will not start your car, without some way of delivering power to where it is needed. This is the job of the battery cables. Although these cables are not mechanical in nature, and have no moving parts, they have been known to cause starting problems, and even to cause stalling engines in moving cars. While they are very simple to inspect and maintain, most people (and many mechanics) seem to neglect doing this.

How to Inspect Battery Cables

Tools required

None for inspection.
Wrench if tightening is necessary.
Battery cleaning tool, or stiff brush if cleaning is necessary.

Procedure

1. Examine the insulation on the cables. If it is cracked or frayed, the cables should be replaced.
2. Wipe the cables with a rag. This will remove any grease, oil, or dirt that may have gotten on them.
3. Make sure the connections on the ends of the cables, away from the battery, are tight. If either connection is loose, tighten it with a wrench, but *do not* let the wrench touch any metal parts, or the frame at the same time the wrench touches the connection if the cable is connected to the positive (POS or +) terminal.
4. Check to see that the battery terminals are clean. If they are not, clean them. (See How to Clean the Battery Terminals.)
5. Tug at the cables where they are connected to the battery. Gently try to twist them. If either cable moves, tighten it using a wrench. When tightening the connection, be sure the wrench *does not* touch the negative and positive terminals at the same time, or that the wrench *does not* touch the positive terminal or cable clamp at the same time it touches any other metal object or car frame.

If your inspection reveals that the battery cables have worn or frayed insulation, or are bad-

ly corroded, buy new cables. They are not expensive, and can be replaced in a few minutes.

How to Replace Battery Cables

Tools required

Wrench.

Procedure

Caution: Do not let the wrench touch the positive terminal (or the cable clamp on the positive terminal), and any metal object (or the car frame or negative terminal) at the same time. To do so can be dangerous.

1. Using the wrench, loosen the nut holding the cable clamp to the positive (POS or +) terminal of the battery.
2. Slip the cable off the positive terminal.
3. Using the wrench, loosen the connection at the other end of this cable. Remove the cable.
4. Place one end of the new cable at the connection point away from the battery. Tighten the connection using the wrench.
5. Place the other end of the new cable over the positive terminal. Tighten the nut using the wrench.
6. Using the wrench, loosen the end of the other cable that is away from the battery, and then slip the cable from this connection.
7. Use the wrench, loosen the nut holding the cable to the negative (NEG or −) terminal, and slip the cable from the terminal.
8. Place the end of the cable, without the terminal clamp, at the connection point away from the battery, and use the wrench to tighten the connection.
9. Place the battery terminal clamp over the terminal, and tighten the nut using the wrench.
10. Check to see each connection is tight.

Following the inspection, maintenance, and replacement procedures will help ensure that your car will start when you want it to, and that the engine and electrical accessories will operate smoothly. In addition, a properly adjusted ignition system will help your fuel economy, and aid in extending the service life of the engine.

Occasionally, however, problems involving the ignition system may still develop. Here is a description of the more common difficulties involving the ignition system, and the procedures to be followed to correct the difficulties.

Troubleshooting the Ignition System

Problem—No response at all when key is turned.

Possible Cause— A loose battery cable connection, or defective battery. Remember, the battery supplies the electrical power needed to start the engine. To get the power to where it is needed, the battery cables must make good contact with the battery terminals. To check for a bad connection, hold a screwdriver by the handle (*not* the blade), and insert the blade between the battery post and the cable clamp. Have someone turn the key to try to start the car, while you do this to both battery connections. If the engine starts to turn over, it is an indication that one or both of the connections is bad.

Solution—Clean the battery terminal posts (see ''How to Clean the Battery Terminals'').

Problem—The motor briefly rotates, but then rapidly slows down.

Possible Cause—The battery is discharged. A quick test to doublecheck whether this is actually the problem is to turn on the headlights, and attempt to start the engine. If the lights go out, the problem is the battery.

Solution—Use an external charger to charge the battery, or booster start the car following the procedure described for this. Check the condition of the battery (see ''Testing the Battery''), to see if it is still serviceable, and locate the cause of the trouble. Have your mechanic check the charging circuit for problems. Until the cause of the problem is determined and corrected, this type of difficulty is likely to occur again.

Problem—The car is difficult to start, or the starting motor turns over strongly, but the engine won't start.

Possible Cause—The ignition system is not furnishing sufficiently strong electric sparks, or the engine is either not getting a sufficient fuel supply or is getting too much fuel at once.

Solution—Wait several minutes, then attempt to start the engine while holding the gas pedal all the way to the floor (do not pump the pedal). If this does not work, and your car *does not* have a high energy ignition system, try the following test:

Remove one spark plug wire. Holding it by the insulation, hold it about ½ inch from the engine block. Have someone crank the engine. The presence of a good, regularly occuring spark is an indication that the primary circuit, and the ignition coil are working properly. If there is no spark, or if there is a spark but it appears weak or irregular, it is an indication of trouble in the primary circuit, or perhaps in the ignition coil itself.

Note: Sometimes difficult starting may occur during, or after a heavy rain or snow storm. Often, this is simply due to ignition wires getting wet, or moisture in the distributor. Wait until the storm stops, and then allow sufficient time for the wires to dry. Then attempt to start the car. Following this procedure can save you the expense of a road service call.

CHAPTER 4

COOLING SYSTEMS

To anyone who has ever examined the engine on a car after it has been operating for any length of time, or driven on a crowded parkway on a summer's day, and observed cars on the shoulder of the road with their hoods open—one thing is quite obvious: engines get hot. In fact, temperatures reached in the combustion chambers are in the area of 2000°F! The melting point of the iron used in the engine is not much higher than this, and so some means of protecting the engine against overheating must be used. This is the function of the cooling system.

If something is too hot, there are two methods which may be used to cool it; blow on it, or pour water on it. These two methods are commonly used to cool automotive engines. Since engines are designed to run at specific operating temperatures, there has to be a way to prevent this cooling from occurring prematurely. The components of the engine which allow the engine to reach its proper operating temperature, and then maintain this level, form the *cooling system*.

HOW A WATER COOLED SYSTEM WORKS

When cool water comes in contact with a hot object, the hot object tends to become cooler, and the water heats up. In some cases, the water may even turn to steam. This is the basic principle behind the water cooled cooling system (see fig. 4-1). The engine block and cylinder head are built with passages through which water can circulate. These are called the *water jacket*. If the water were allowed to remain within the water jacket for too long, it would turn to steam. To prevent this, the water is kept moving by a *water pump*, driven from the crankshaft, located at the front of the engine. Mounted in front of the water pump is a *fan*, which is turned by means of a pulley system. At the front of the crankshaft is a pulley over which is a flexible rubberized belt, called the *fan belt*. Attached to the frame in front of the fan is a reservoir to hold water, known as the *radiator*. Since the radiator is not actually part of the engine, some means must be provided for the water to get from the radiator to the engine and back again; rubber hoses are used for this task.

When the engine is operating, the water pump pushes water through the water jacket. Heat from the combustion chambers passes through the hollow walls of the water jacket to the water. The water circulates through the cylinder head, and one of the rubber hoses, (the upper one) into a tank at the top of the radiator.

The idea is for "cool" water to circulate and absorb the excess engine heat. The water in the radiator is now hot; thus the radiator must cool the water. The radiator is designed to do this by permitting water to flow from the tank at its top, through a series of thin metal tubes called the *radiator core*, to another tank at the bottom of the radiator. The metal tubes have fins, and air spaces between them. The heat from the water passes through the walls of the tubes in the core, and is transmitted to the fins. Air passing over the fins, cools them in turn, and this is where the fan plays an important role. Rather than just blowing air over the radiator, the fan actually helps to

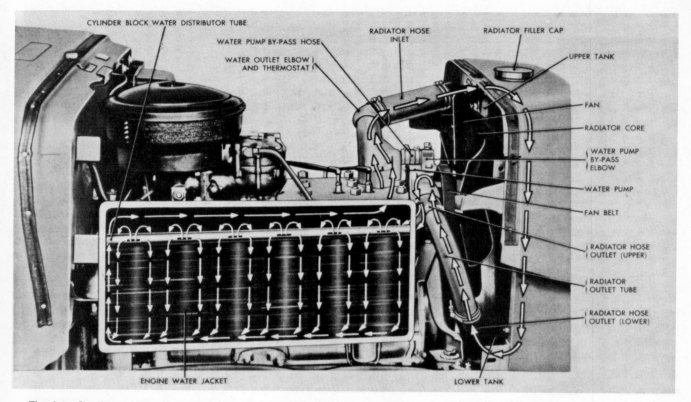

CYLINDER BLOCK WATER DISTRIBUTOR TUBE

WATER PUMP BY-PASS HOSE

WATER OUTLET ELBOW AND THERMOSTAT

RADIATOR HOSE INLET

RADIATOR FILLER CAP

UPPER TANK

FAN

RADIATOR CORE

WATER PUMP BY-PASS ELBOW

WATER PUMP

FAN BELT

RADIATOR HOSE OUTLET (UPPER)

RADIATOR OUTLET TUBE

RADIATOR HOSE OUTLET (LOWER)

ENGINE WATER JACKET

LOWER TANK

Fig. 4-1—Cooling system circulation for one type of engine. The basic principle is the same for all circulating collant cooling systems.

draw air through the radiator, speeding the air current.

Since the heat has been removed from the water as the liquid passes through the core, the water is once again cool by the time it reaches the lower tank. The water circulates from the lower tank through the lower hose, and back again to the water pump, which sends it through the water jacket again and the cooling process is repeated until the engine is stopped.

The engine is designed to operate within a specific heat range. If the proper operating temperatures are not reached, the engine will operate inefficiently. A device called a *thermostat* is used to control the water temperature. It regulates the flow of water to the radiator, preventing it from passing through the radiator when the engine is cold.

While your cooling system is helping the engine to "maintain its cool," it can also help you to maintain your "warmth." The heater in most cars is constructed like a smaller version of the radiator. Heated fluid in the cooling system passes through this heater, and a fan drives heated air into the passenger compartment. This hot air can also be blown onto the windshield to

help keep it clear of mist, snow, or ice; this is what happens when you operate the *defroster*.

COOLANT IS MORE THAN WATER

Up until now the liquid in the cooling system has been referred to as water. Indeed, water is an excellent cooling agent, and at one time was the liquid used in the cooling system, (it is still used in areas with moderate temperatures). However, there are some disadvantages in using water. In very cold weather, water may freeze. Since water expands when frozen, pressures can occur which can actually bend metal, or crack the engine block. Water can also boil, causing the engine to overheat, which may cause rust and corrosion. To overcome these difficulties, a mixture of *antifreeze*, and water is generally used.

Although it is called antifreeze, the solution serves three main functions:

1. As its name implies, it helps keep the radiator fluid from freezing.

2. It helps to raise the boiling point of the liquid, and keep it from boiling away.
3. Most good brands contain rust inhibitors, chemicals which help prevent rust formation and corrosion.

Many car manufacturers recommend that the cooling system contain a 50% antifreeze mixture—that is, half water and half antifreeze. However, more antifreeze should be used, if the car is to be used in very cold areas. Under normal conditions, the mixture in the cooling system is good for about two years.

THE COOLANT RECOVERY SYSTEM

As an engine with a water-cooled cooling system is operated, two conditions occur. The coolant becomes warm, and pressures build within the system. If there are any openings within the system (as was the case until fairly recently), a loss of coolant through overflow or evaporation can result. Openings within the system can also allow air to enter it; the combination of sufficient quantities of air and water, along with iron in the engine, can result in the formation of rust. Rust affects the efficiency of the cooling system, and if severe enough, can practically stop the cooling process.

To reduce these problems, the concept of *coolant recovery systems* was introduced. A small plastic reservoir is placed near the radiator to catch any overflow, and the standard pressure cap on the radiator is replaced with one of a different design. Should the addition of small amounts of coolant be necessary, it can be done through a cap on the plastic reservoir. The radiator cap itself is removed only when the antifreeze is changed, or if repairs are necessary.

THE SECOND METHOD—AIR COOLING

Most engines in passenger service are the water-cooled type. However, some engines in smaller cars are air cooled. These engines are usually made of metals selected for their heat conducting properties, such as aluminum, and are built with fins. The undesired heat within the engine is transmitted to these fins. A fan which is driven by the engine, directs cooler air past *baffle plates* and through the fins, cooling them. A thermostat is used to control the baffle plate openings, and maintain the desired operating temperature.

Air cooled engines are generally simpler in design than water cooled ones. They tend to warm up very quickly, and reach their designed operating heat range faster than some water cooled engines. And, because they do not have circulating water systems, there is no need to add antifreeze to prevent freeze-ups in cold weather. Air cooled engines tend to be noisier than those that are water cooled.

OVERHEATING CAN BE FRUSTRATING

The most common problem of cooling systems is overheating. It can immobilize you in traffic, damage the engine, lead to road service calls, and might even cause you to consider disposing of your car. While even the best maintained cooling systems might allow an engine to overheat under certain circumstances, in general this should not be the case. There are a few simple things that can be done to minimize the chances of this situation happening.

How to Prevent Overheating

To a certain extent, even a water cooled engine relies on air cooling. Air is continually flowing over the outside surface of the engine, helping to cool it. In fact, this process can be responsible for as much as 30 percent of the total cooling which occurs. Deposits of dirt, oil, or grease on the engine reduce the air cooling, and puts a greater load on the cooling system.

To prevent this from occurring, it is only necessary to wipe the engine occasionally with a rag. To prevent accidental burns, it should be done when the engine is cold. If this has not been done for quite a while, it may be difficult to remove some of the deposits that have accumulated. If this is the case, the engine may have to be steam-cleaned to remove them.

With the engine *off*, examine the fan belt. It should not be cracked or frayed. Press in the center of the fan belt. There should be approximately ½ inch of play. If there is more than that, the fan may not be doing its job efficiently, and the engine may not be cooled properly. *Caution*: Never put your hands near the fan belt, or the fan while the engine is on. To do so can result in a very serious injury. Do not wear ties, loose objects or jewelry, when working near this area while the engine is operating; they could get caught and cause injury.

Even if the engine is clean, and all the components of the cooling system are performing properly, a car may still overheat if there is not enough *coolant* (either water alone or a mixture of water and antifreeze) in the system. It is very easy to check the fluid level, and you should do this regularly. A good time might be while executing other inspection procedures outlined earlier.

How to Check the Coolant Level

Tools required

None

Procedure

1. Determine if your car is equipped with a closed (coolant recovery) system. This information can be found in the owner's manual. If the manual is not available, look at the radiator cap. Cars with coolant recovery systems generally are marked with a tag or label near or on the radiator, or the radiator cap may be stamped "Do Not Open." If you have this type of system, there will also be a plastic container near the radiator, joined to it by a small hose. Most older cars do not have this type of system, unless it was added after the purchase of the car.
2. If you have a coolant recovery system, allow the engine to reach its normal operating temperature. Look at the fluid level in the plastic container; it should be between the indicator marks. If the level is between the marks, no coolant need be added, and this procedure is finished. If the level is too low, follow the procedure, "How to Add Coolant."
3. If your car has a standard radiator system, it is necessary to remove the radiator cap to check the coolant level, and to add coolant if necessary. Preferably, this should be done when the engine is cold.
3a. If your radiator cap has a button in the center, press it for a moment to "release" the pressure (that is, to allow the pressure inside the cooling system to become equal to the pressure outside it). A lever may also be used for this purpose and if it is present simply lift it to equalize the pressure.
3b. Turn the radiator cap *slowly* in a counter-clockwise direction. If the cap does not have a pressure release device (such as the button or lever mentioned above), there will probably be a catch, beyond which it may be difficult to turn the cap further. Pause for a moment to allow the equalization of pressure, then press down on the cap, and continue to turn it until it is removed.

Caution: Never bend directly over the radiator cap. If the pressure has not been equalized properly, coolant may shoot out suddenly, and cause an injury.

4. Observe the coolant level in the radiator; it should be between indicator marks (if they are present), or else about 1½ inches below the top of the radiator. If it is, replace the cap and this procedure is finished; if not, see "How to Add Coolant."

REPLENISHING THE COOLANT

Despite the fact that your car may have a closed cooling system, most cars with circulating water systems occasionally require the addition of coolant. This does not necessarily indicate a problem with the cooling system (unless frequent additions are necessary), but is a result of the normal heat exchange process that is continually occurring when the engine is operated. It is easy to add coolant, takes little time, and should be done whenever the coolant level is low (See "How to Check the Coolant Level").

How to Add Coolant

Tools required

None

Procedure

1. Determine if the car has a coolant recovery system. The method for doing this is described in step 1 of "How to Check the Coolant Level."
2. If you have a coolant recovery system, and have just checked the coolant level, the engine should already be at its normal operating temperature; if not, run the engine for a few moments until it is.
2a. Open the cap at the top of the plastic coolant recovery reservoir, and add antifreeze, water, or a mixture of them until the level is between the indicator marks. Replace the cap and this procedure is finished. Note that

the level will not be indicated properly, unless the engine has reached its normal operating temperature.

3. If your car has a standard cooling system, let the engine cool before adding coolant—it is safer this way, and if a large amount of coolant is needed, it avoids the possibility of damage resulting from the introduction of a cold liquid into a hot engine. If it has not been done previously, remove the radiator cap as described in steps 3—3b of ''How to Check the Coolant Level.''

4. Slowly add antifreeze, water, or a mixture of these until the level of liquid is between the indicator marks or, if no marks are present, until the level is about 1½ inches below the top of the radiator.

5. Replace the radiator cap.

How to Prevent Freezing

A second problem often encountered with the cooling system is freezing. Since the addition of antifreeze lowers the temperature at which the solution in the cooling system will freeze, it is important to always use antifreeze in those areas where the temperature can fall below the freezing point of water (32°F)—*even if this does not occur very often.* Freezing water (ice) can severely damage an engine, and even crack the engine block. To avoid this, engines usually come equipped with *freeze plugs*, discs on the surface of the block, which are designed to pop out if the mixture in the cooling system freezes. Since these freeze plugs occasionally corrode, have your mechanic check them once in a while, and replace them if necessary. However, do not rely on them to prevent damage to the engine. Instead, they should be considered as an emergency back-up. By always having a good solution of antifreeze in the cooling system, you avoid the need to rely on them.

TESTING COOLANT STRENGTH

Having the proper amount of coolant in the cooling system is not a guarantee that the engine will not overheat or freeze. As the mixture is used, or water is added occasionally, its strength is reduced, thereby, weakening its protective abilities. Thus, to determine its effectiveness, it should be tested occasionally.

A quick and easy way of doing this involves the use of an *hydrometer,* described in the section,

TESTING THE BATTERY. There are two types of hydrometers used to check coolant ability. The first, and more accurate one, has a scale on its side to indicate the temperature range through which the mixture will provide protection. The second hydrometer is usually smaller, and has colored beads inside its glass cylinder.

How to Use the Hydrometer to Test the Coolant

Tools required

Hydrometer

Procedure

1. Determine if your car has a coolant recovery system. (See step 1 of ''How to Check the Coolant Level''.)

2. If your car has a coolant recovery system:

2a. Open the cap on the plastic reservoir.

2b. Insert the tapered end of the hydrometer into the reservoir, squeeze the rubber ball for a few seconds, then release it. This will cause some of the fluid to enter the hydrometer.

2c. If you are using a standard form of the hydrometer, read the scale; if the reading is not within the desired range, see the procedure for draining and replacing the coolant. Otherwise, with the tapered end of the hydrometer over the opening in the reservoir, squeeze the rubber ball until all of the fluid is returned to the container. Replace the cap and you are finished with this procedure.

2d. If the type of hydrometer which has floating balls is used, the number of balls which rise is an indication of the strength of the coolant. They indicate whether or not the mixture is capable of supplying an average amount of protection. (Consult manufacturer's directions to determine the actual number that should be floating for proper protection.) If the mixture is good, place the tapered end over the opening in the reservoir, squeeze the rubber ball until the liquid is returned to the reservoir, and replace the cap to complete the procedure. Otherwise, consult the procedure for draining and replacing coolant.

3. If you have a standard cooling system:

3a. If the engine has been running for a while, let it cool for a while. Remove the radiator cap as described in steps 3-3b of ''How to Check the Coolant Level.''

3b. Insert the tapered end of the hydrometer into the radiator, squeeze the rubber ball for a

Cooling System Capacity (Quarts)	QUARTS OF QUALITY ANTIFREEZE								
	3	4	5	6	7	8	9	10	11
6:	−34								
7:	−17								
8:	−7	−34							
9:	0	−21							
10:	4	−12	−34						
11:	8	−6	−23						
12:	10	0	−15	−34					
13:		3	−9	−25					
14:		6	−5	−17	−34				
15:		8	0	−12	−26				
16:		10	2	−7	−19	−34			
17:			5	−4	−14	−27			
18:			7	0	−10	−21	−34		
19:			9	2	−7	−16	−28		
20:			10	4	−3	−12	−22	−34	
21:				6	0	−9	−17	−28	
22:				8	2	−6	−14	−23	−34

Fig. 4-2—Protection offered by the addition of antifreeze. To use this chart, locate the cooling system capacity of your car in the left-most column (consult the owner's manual for this number); move to the right along the row until the desired protection temperature (in °F) is reached. Move up the column and read the number above the solid line. This is the number of quarts of antifreeze to be added to obtain this protection. The rightmost number in each row below the line represents the protection afforded by a mixture containing 50% antifreeze.

few seconds, and release it. This will cause some of the fluid to enter the hydrometer.

3c. If you are using the standard form of the hydrometer, read the scale; if the reading is not within the desired range, consult the procedure for draining and replacing coolant. Otherwise, with the tapered end of the hydrometer over the opening in the radiator, squeeze the rubber ball until all of the fluid is returned to the radiator. Replace the radiator cap, and the procedure is completed.

3d. When the type of hydrometer which has floating balls is used, the number of balls that rise indicates the strength of the mixture—whether or not the mixture is capable of supplying an average amount of protection. (The manufacturer's directions should be consulted, to determine the actual number indicating sufficient protection.) If the mixture is good, place the tapered end of the hydrometer over the opening in the radiator, and squeeze the rubber ball until all the mixture has returned to the radiator. Replace the radiator cap to complete this procedure. Otherwise, see the technique for draining and replacing coolant.

The antifreeze mixture plays an important role in protecting the engine from heat, cold, and rust. As the engine is used, however, it can lose some of its protective properties. Manufacturers generally recommend that coolant be replaced every two years; it should also be replaced if it is no longer capable of providing the necessary protection (see "How to Use Hydrometer to Test the Coolant"). This involves a two part process—draining the coolant from the cooling system, and the addition of fresh mixture.

The easiest way to drain the cooling system is to use the *drain cock* on the radiator. This is nothing more than a small faucet-like device on the bottom of the radiator. The following procedure describes how to do this.

How to Drain the Cooling System

Tools required

None

Procedure

1. Let the engine run until it has reached its normal operating temperature.
2. Shut the engine off (to avoid any injury that might occur from accidental contact with the moving fan or fan belt).
3. Turn the drain cock counter-clockwise, to permit fluid to drain.
4. Start the engine, and let it run for about 3 minutes.
5. Stop the engine, and allow all the antifreeze mixture to drain.
6. When all the liquid is drained from the system, tighten the drain cock by turning it clockwise; it should be closed firmly, but do not overtighten it.

Once the old mixture has been drained from the system, the fresh solution can be added. Car manufacturers generally recommend the proper amount of antifreeze to be added, and some antifreeze suppliers provide a chart on their packages. Usually, a mixture consisting of half antifreezen and half water is sufficient. If more protection is desired, simply use more antifreeze and less water. Fig. 4-2 indicated the range of protection afforded by the addition of different amounts of quality antifreeze.

How to Add Fresh Coolant

Tools required

None

Procedure

1. It is necessary to remove the radiator cap, to check if your car has a coolant recovery system (see step 1 of "How to Check the Coolant Level"). If the cap has a button, push it for a moment, or if the cap has a lever, lift it up. Turn the cap slowly counterclockwise (on cooling systems with a coolant recovery design, it may be necessary to press firmly on the cap while doing this). If the cap is difficult to turn, pause for a few seconds, then press down, and continue turning.
2. *Slowly* add antifreeze and water to the radiator, until the level is about 2 inches below the top of the radiator. If you have a coolant recovery system, replace radiator cap.
3. Start the engine, and allow it to reach its normal operating temperature.
4. Turn heater and defroster to their maximum on positions.
5. Wait 1 minute.
6. On cooling systems with recovery features:
6a. Observe the fluid level in the recovery reservoir.
6b. If the level is below the indicator marks, open the reservoir cap and slowly add more coolant, until the level is between the marks.
6c. Let the engine run a few more minutes, and repeat steps 6a and 6b. Be careful not to let the fluid level rise above the full indicator marks. When the coolant level remains between the marks, replace the reservoir cap and you are finished with this procedure.
7. On standard cooling systems, add mixture slowly, and a little at a time until the mixture level remains at about 1½ inches below the top of the radiator. Replace the radiator cap.

The addition of the proper quantity of a high quality antifreeze coolant assures the desired level of protection. But in order for the coolant to do its job, it must stay in the circulatory system. If there is a leak anywhere in this system, loss of coolant (and thus protection against heat and rust) will result. Often, minor adjustments of clamps or hoses can prevent coolant loss, or keep a small leak from becoming serious.

INSPECTION—THE SECOND STEP IN PROTECTION

It takes only a few minutes to inspect the cooling system for potential problems; yet this is generally not done by car owners. The assumption commonly made is that since coolant has been added, and since the temperature gauge or warning light on the dashboard is not indicating an overheating condition, the cooling system is in good condition. Unfortunately, this is not always the case. Minor problems have a way of revealing themselves at the most inopportune times: in heavy traffic, or miles from the nearest service station. Then, minor problems become major headaches.

A major source of cooling system problems is the rubber hoses that allow coolant to circulate to and from the radiator and heater. Heat from the engine and air can cause the hoses to dry out with time, and the normal motion of the engine, and contraction can cause these hoses to leak or break. Sometimes, the clamps holding the hoses become loose or break, allowing a loss of coolant. Since the hoses and clamps can create problems, they should be examined when inspecting the entire cooling system.

How to Inspect Cooling System Hoses and Clamps

Tools required

Screwdriver, rag.

Procedure

1. Start at the hose at the top of the radiator. Check to see that hose is dry. If it is, go to step 2.
1a. Examine hose for cracks. If any are present, the hose must be replaced (see "How to Replace Cooling System Hoses").
1b. Examine the ends of the hose. Sometimes the ends split or cut. If so, the hose should be replaced, using the procedure mentioned in 1a.
1c. See if water is coming from the area around the clamps, at the ends of the hose. If it is, try tightening the clamp; this is done by turning the screw clockwise with the screwdriver.
2. Check to see that there are no bulges in the hose. A bulge often means the hose is about to break, and should be replaced, using the

procedure mentioned in 1a.

3. See if the hose appears brittle. This often happens as the hose gets older. Brittle hoses can cause trouble, and should be replaced as indicated in "How to Replace Cooling System Hoses."

4. Examine the clamps at both ends of the hose. They should be tight and holding firmly. If secure, go to step 5.

4a. Try tightening the clamp by turning the screw in a clockwise direction. If this works, go to step 5. If not, the clamp should be replaced, as described in "How to Replace Hose Clamps."

5. Examine the lower radiator hose, and heater hoses; if both are dry, repeat steps 2 through 4. If clamps are tight and holding firmly, no further action is necessary. If a clamp can not be tightened, it is an easy and inexpensive procedure to replace the clamp. However, you should have a little extra antifreeze handy, since some coolant may be lost when the old clamp is removed.

How to Replace Hose Clamps

Tools required

Screwdriver

Procedure

1. To prevent accidental burns, wait until the engine is cool.
2. If your car has a pressure release radiator cap, push the button, or lift the lever.
3. Using the screwdriver, turn the clamp screw counterclockwise, and remove it; if the screw is not engaging the clamp, force the screw from the clamp.
4. Remove the old clamp, straightening it if necessary.
5. Examine the area of the hose where the clamp had been positioned. If there are any cuts or damage, reposition the hose or replace it (see "How to Replace Cooling System Hoses").
6. Slip the new clamp into position, and tighten it by using the screwdriver to turn the screw in a clockwise direction. The clamp should be tight and holding firmly, but be careful not to overtighten it.
7. Make sure the pressure release mechanism (if any) on the radiator cap is in the proper position, and then start the car. Staying clear

of the fan area, make sure there are no leaks; if there is a leak, reposition, and retighten clamp until it is no longer present.

If an inspection of the cooling system reveals any cracks, bulges, brittleness, or any other signs of aging or damage to a hose, it should be replaced. It is a risky practice to stretch the life of a hose. Since hoses are not very expensive, avoid having a hose fail at an inconvenient time. Replacing hoses is not a difficult procedure. However, have some extra antifreeze on hand, since some coolant may be lost when changing a hose.

How to Replace Cooling System Hoses

Tools required

Screwdriver, knife. (If the hose at the bottom of the radiator is to be changed, a large clean pan, or container is also necessary.)

Procedure

Note: For the sake of comfort, and the avoidance of accidental burns, it is best to change hoses when the engine is cool.

1. If you are changing the lower radiator hose, a lot of coolant will be lost when the hose is removed. To minimize this loss, place a pan or large container under draincock, and turn it counter-clockwise to allow coolant to flow into the container.
2. No matter which hose is being replaced, turn the clamp screw corresponding to either clamp counter-clockwise, until clamp is very loose; remove clamp, or slide it out of the way.
3. Slide hose off its connection. If it is stuck, it may be necessary to use a knife, and make a lengthwise cut in the hose to free it (but be sure to cut only the hose).
4. Examine the connection and make sure it is clean. If necessary, wipe it with a rag, or gently scrape it with the knife.
5. Turn clamp screw on the other clamp counter-clockwise, until clamp is very loose. Slide clamp along the hose to remove it.
6. Repeat steps 3 and 4 for this end of the hose.
7. Slide a clamp onto the hose at either end, and move it about 8 inches from the end of the hose.

8. Using the screwdriver, turn screw clockwise until the clamp doesn't move.
9. Slide the hose over its connector, until it covers it completely.
10. Again, using the screwdriver, turn the clamp screw counter-clockwise until clamp can be moved. Then slide clamp over the portion of the hose that is over the connector, but not at the very end of the hose.
11. Use the screwdriver to tighten the clamp, by turning the screw clockwise. The clamp should be tight, but do not overtighten.
12. Slide a clamp onto the other end of the hose, until it is about 8 inches from the end (if hose is extremely short, move the clamp as far as possible).
13. Repeat steps 8 through 11 for this end of the hose.
14. If only a small amount of coolant has been lost, and the lower radiator hose has not been replaced, continue at step 15.
14a. Tighten the draincock by turning it clockwise, but do not overtighten.
14b. Test the solution in the collection pan by using an hydrometer. Insert the tapered end into the container and squeeze the ball. Read the scale or, if the floating ball type is used, the number of floating balls. If the solution is weak, add new coolant (see "How to Add Fresh Coolant"). Otherwise, use that procedure to add the coolant which has been collected in the container.
15. Any coolant which has been lost must be replaced. To do this, see "How to Add Coolant."

LACK OF MOISTURE DOES NOT MEAN LACK OF LEAKS

So far, the ispection of the cooling system has concentrated on the detection of wet spots, and the determination of potential problem areas. However, wet areas are not the only indication of the presence of leaks. A dry engine may have coolant losses.

Sometimes, coolant leaking onto a hot portion of the engine will vaporize almost immediately; thus, although a leak is present, moisture may not be evident. Fortunately, there are two indications of these problem areas. With the engine running at its normal operating temperature, and the car located in an area that is not overly bright (such as in the shade of a tree), examine the entire engine area.

The presence of white smoke in an area of the engine that is not too close to the oil filler cap, or the carburetor might mean that a "dry leak" is occurring. If a closer examination reveals that a hose, or loose or broken clamp is at fault, replace the defective part (see "How to Replace Hose Clamps" and "How to Replace Cooling System Hoses"). If the leak is in the engine itself, special skill may be required to repair it. Have your mechanic check the problem area. If the problem has been discovered early enough, it may be possible to avoid an expensive repair.

A second way of discovering a "dry leak" is by carefully observing the engine when it is cool. When coolant evaporates, a telltale white trace often remains. By following the path indicated by the white residue, the source of the leak may be found. If the engine has been cleaned occasionally by wiping it with a rag, this technique is easier to perform, and the engine will be cooled more efficiently as well.

No inspection of the cooling system is complete, without an examination of the thermostat (see fig. 4-3). This relatively inexpensive part is responsible for determining the path the coolant will take (see fig. 4-4 and 4-5).

THE THERMOSTAT—TRAFFIC DIRECTOR OF THE COOLING SYSTEM

Because of the tremendous heat generated within an internal combustion engine, it is necessary for the coolant to circulate properly within the water jacket. It may seem odd at first, but sometimes efficient cooling is undesirable. For example, your car may not perform smoothly when you first start it on a cold day. It takes some time before the engine reaches its proper operating temperature. If the efficient heat exchange process of the cooling system is inhibited, the engine will warm up faster. However, once the engine has reached its intended operating range, the cooling system should start to perform efficiently, or else damage from excess heat may occur.

The thermostat directs this activity of the cooling system, preventing coolant from passing through the radiator when the engine is cold; thus, the coolant itself is not cooled as it normally would be when it passes through the radiator and engine, and in turn, will not be cooled as efficiently by the coolant. Hence, the engine will warm up more quickly. Once the engine has reached its designed operating temperature, the thermostat will allow the coolant to flow through the radiator and efficient cooling will result.

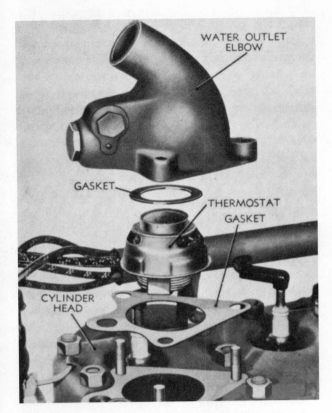

Fig. 4-3—A thermostat and its related assembly.

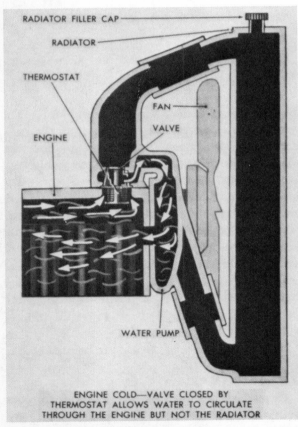

Fig. 4-4—Cooling system circulation when the thermostat is closed. This is the situation when a cold engine is first started.

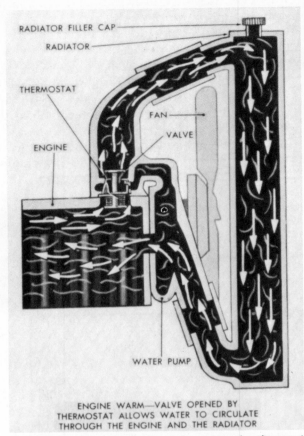

Fig. 4-5—Cooling system circulation when the thermostat is open. This is the situation when the engine has reached its normal operating temperature.

Where to Find the Thermostat

The thermostat is usually easy to locate. Simply follow the upper radiator hose, from the top of the radiator toward the engine. The thermostat can generally be found on the engine where the hose ends.

How to Inspect the Thermostat

Tools required

Regular screwdriver
Wrench
A new gasket will be needed.

Note: The only effective way to test the thermostat is to remove it from the engine. If the engine warms up quickly, and does not operate at the upper end of its operating range (observe the temperature gauge, if your car has one, or else the "HOT" warning light) and overheats, the thermostat is probably working properly.

1. Remove the upper radiator hose by loosening both clamp screws, (turn them counter-

clockwise with a screwdriver) and slide the hose off the connectors.

2. Remove the thermostat housing bolts by turning them counter-clockwise with a wrench.
3. Remove the water outlet, and gasket from the thermostat housing.
4. Visually inspect the thermostat valve to make sure it is in good condition.
5. Mix antifreeze and water in a container, (1 part antifreeze to 2 parts water) and carefully heat the solution. If a temperature is stamped on the thermostat valve, heat the liquid until a thermometer indicates 25° above this temperature.
6. Submerge the valve completely, and use a spoon to agitate the liquid thoroughly. The valve should open completely.
7. Carefully cool the mixture until it is 10° below the temperature indicated on the valve.
8. Submerge the valve, and again agitate the mixture. The valve should now close completely.
9. If each of the above tests have been met, re-install the thermostat, using a new housing gasket (reverse steps 3, 2, and 1), and continue at step 11.
10. If any of the tests fail, replace the thermostat with a new one, and install a new housing gasket as well (reverse steps 3, 2, and 1).
11. Replace any coolant that may have been lost (see "How to Add Coolant").

OTHER LEAK DETECTION METHODS

Part of the inspection of the cooling system includes checking for wet areas and changes in coloration, such as white trails (or even rust areas). Sometimes, however, coolant may be leaking from inside the engine itself. This situation may be serious, but is often easy to detect. Check the oil on the dipstick (see "How to Test the Oil Level"). If there is an internal leak, water bubbles will often appear on the dipstick. If this occurs, have your mechanic check it; one procedure is to pour a water soluble dye into the radiator. A fluorescent element in the dye turns color, when exposed to the rays of a special test lamp.

RADIATOR CAPS—SIMPLE BUT IMPORTANT

Sometimes overheating may be caused by a faulty radiator cap. On cars without coolant recovery systems, there is usually a *pressure cap*. The cap is designed to allow a certain pressure to develop within the cooling system. This has the effect of raising the boiling point of the coolant, thereby allowing the engine to operate at higher temperatures, without causing the coolant to be lost from boiling. Generally, the pressure cap contains two valves of different sizes, and which are normally closed, sealing the system. The larger valve is called the *pressure valve* and acts as a safety valve. It opens only when there is too much pressure within the system. After an engine has been operating for a while, and is then shut off, it begins to cool. As it does this, the pressure within the cooling system may drop below the outside air pressure. The higher outside air pressure forces the other valve (the *vacuum valve*) to open, which allows air to enter the cooling system by way of the overflow pipe. This permits the pressure inside the cooling system, and outside it to be the same. (The entrance of air into the cooling system can promote rust formation and corrosion; coolant recovery systems reduce the amount of air in the system.) Often, radiator pressure caps will have a pressure release mechanism, usually a button or lever on the top. This allows for manual releasing (equalization) of the pressure, so the coolant can be checked after pressure has been built up within the system. Figure 4-6 shows a pressure radiator cap.

Defects in the radiator cap prevent the cooling system from operating efficiently. Many service station mechanics overlook checking the cap, even though it takes just a minute and requires no tools.

How to Inspect a Radiator Pressure Cap

Tools required

None

Procedure

1. Remove the pressure cap (see "How to Check the Coolant Level")
2. Look for any cracks that might be present in the seals.
3. Check to make sure the springs are working properly, and are not broken or loose.
4. If the cap has a pressure release mechanism, (usually a button or lever) press the button, or lift the lever and check to see that the pressure release mechanism is functioning.
5. If any defects are discovered, replace the cap with a new one. Otherwise, reposition the cap on the radiator.

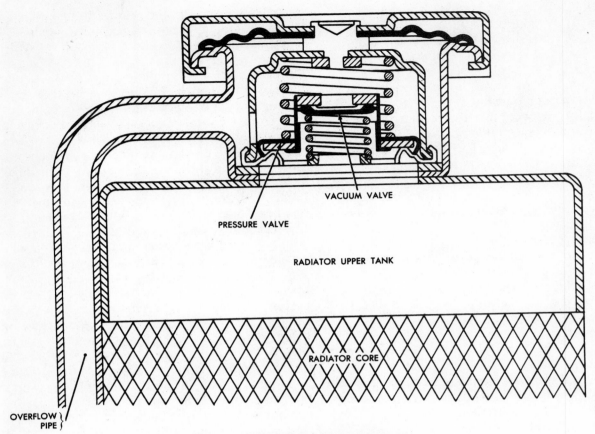

VACUUM VALVE

PRESSURE VALVE

RADIATOR UPPER TANK

RADIATOR CORE

OVERFLOW PIPE

Fig. 4-6—A radiator pressure cap.

TRAFFIC CAN CAUSE OVERHEATING

Automobile engines are designed to move cars. When the car is in gear, but is not moving for extended periods, a situation exists which your car was not intended to handle. Unfortunately, this situation happens all too frequently on congested highways where traffic jams, often compounded by high summer temperatures, put additional strains on engines. Even a well maintained car can overheat under this stress. However, there are some measures that can be taken to prevent overheating, or to cool the engine if overheating occurs but there is no mechanical or cooling system malfunction.

A Driving Tip To Prevent Overheating

If you are stuck in traffic, and the weather is warm, place the car in neutral gear occasionally, and momentarily accelerate the engine. This will increase the speed of the fan, and aid in drawing cool air through the radiator. Do not race the engine for more than brief periods, however. Doing so can damage the engine. This is also useful for air cooled engines.

Tips for Cooling an Overheated Engine

If your engine overheats, pull off the road as soon as it is safe to do so. Let the engine run while you open the hood (with the car in neutral or park and the parking brake set). Staying clear of the fan, make sure there is no obvious mechanical problem (such as a leak or broken hose). If none exists, accelerate the engine momentarily. If you have a water cooled car and this does not help, try turning the heater and fan to their maximum on positions. This will help cool the coolant (and thus, the engine), but the passenger compartment will become warmer. If there is no mechanical problem, and you have sufficient coolant, this should cool the engine, and eliminate the overheating condition.

TROUBLESHOOTING THE COOLING SYSTEM

Regular inspection, and maintenance of the cooling system can help prevent the need for troubleshooting the cooling system, or for expensive road calls due to mechanical breakdown. However, despite careful and frequent inspections, a problem may develop. The most common problems associated with the cooling system are overheating, and loss of coolant.

Problem:—The temperature gauge or warning light is indicating an overheating condition.
Possible Cause:—Insufficient coolant.
Solution:—Check for leaks, especially from hoses. Any leaks should be stopped as soon as possible, and coolant should be added (see "How to Add Coolant"). It is normal for some cars to occasionally require additional coolant, but regular checks of the coolant level, as described in this chapter, should prevent an overheating condition from insufficient coolant.
Possible Cause:—Fan belt slipping. Sometimes a high-pitched squeal can be heard, if the fan belt is slipping. To test for a loose fan belt, shut the engine off, and press firmly between the pulleys. If the fan belt moves more than about ½ inch, it should be tightened. If any part of the fan belt appears worn, frayed, or cracked, replace the fan belt.
Possible Cause:—The water pump may be defective. Since a faulty pump will not enable the water to circulate properly, efficient cooling will not take place. To check for this condition, remove the radiator cap with the engine off (see "How to Check the Coolant Level") and, with the engine operating, observe if the coolant is moving. (Catn: Stay clear of the moving fan, and do not bend over the radiator filler area.) If the coolant is not circulating, the water pump is probably defective.
Solution:—Have your mechanic check the water pump, and replace it if necessary.
Possible Cause:—The thermostat may be stuck closed. This will cause the coolant to circulate through the engine, but not through the radiator.

Since the coolant itself will not be cooled properly, its ability to cool the engine will be impaired.
Solution:—See the procedure "How to Inspect the Thermostat." If it is found to be defective, it should be replaced.
Possible Cause:—The radiator air flow may be restricted. If, for any reason, the air flow through the radiator is restricted, the coolant may not be cooled properly and, in turn, may not be cooling the engine efficiently.
Solution:—Check the radiator, and make sure debris is not obstructing the air passages. Examine the fan. If any of the blades are badly bent or broken, it will hinder the proper flow of air; replace it.
Problem:—The engine fails to reach its normal operating temperature.
Possible cause:—The thermostat may be defective.
Solution:—Consult the section on "How to Inspect the Thermostat." If it is defective, replace it, as described.
Problem:—The engine warms up too slowly.
Possible cause:—The thermostat may be defective.
Solution:—Check the thermostat, (see "How to Inspect the Thermostat") and replace it if necessary.
Possible cause:—The automatic choke may not be closing properly. Although not directly related to the cooling system, the automatic choke helps control efficient combustion, and does affect the rate at which the engine warms up.
Solution:—Refer to the section on the carburetor. Remove the air cleaner, and check to see that the choke is opening and closing properly. If necessary, your mechanic can adjust the choke, or make any needed repairs.

CHAPTER 5

TIRES

One part of a car or truck often taken for granted (until something goes wrong) is the tires. Yet, it is the tires that carry the entire weight of the vehicle, absorb road shocks, and provide the necessary traction for the wheels. Different types of tires on otherwise identical vehicles can significantly alter the handling characteristics of the vehicle, and can even effect gas consumption. Worn tires can cause accidents. Tires that may be acceptable for local driving may not be suitable (or safe) for highway or turnpike travel. Knowing about tires not only affects your safety, it can also save you money—the most expensive tires may not necessarily be the right ones to buy.

HOW TIRES ARE CONSTRUCTED

Not too long ago, tires consisted of a rubber shell enclosing a balloon-like membrane, called an *inner tube*. Air could be pumped into the inner tube by means of a tire valve, thus inflating the tire. If the tire was punctured by an object such as a nail, the casing could generally be patched, and the inner tube repaired or replaced, thus extending the service life of the tire. However, just as a balloon deflates suddenly when punctured, an inner tube puncture can cause a sudden "blow out," making it difficult to control the vehicle, and bring it to a safe stop.

Late model cars no longer use tires that have inner tubes. Instead, *tubeless tires* are standard equipment. Tubeless tires consist of three major components: the *beads, cord body,* and the *tread* and *sidewall.*

The beads are actually two wire hoops made of a tough steel wire. They are tied into the cord body, anchoring the tire to the wheel rim, and causing the cord body to have an airtight seal. The cord body is made up of several layers (called *plies*) of rubber coated fabric, usually nylon or polyester, which are bonded together to form one unit. Enclosing the plies is the tread and sidewall. The tread is the part of the tire that is in contact with the road surface, and is made of tough rubber compounds molded into a pattern; different tires have various tread patterns designed for varied driving conditions (for example, rain or snow), and particular handling characteristics. A different rubber compound is used for the sidewalls (the sides of the tire), since they must be flexible. There are three different types of tires in general use today.

TYPES OF TIRES

The *bias ply tire* has been used since the 1920's. The plies (layers) comprising the body of the tire criss-cross at an angle called the *bias angle*, which is usually about 30-40° to the center line. Cords are arranged in two or more plies (an even number), determined by the strength desired in the tire. This type of construction gives rigidity to the sidewall and tread. However, bias ply tires "squirm" more, and tend to run hotter than the other types of tires described below. Figure 5-1 shows the construction of a bias ply tire.

Like the bias ply tire, the cords in a *belted bias tire* are arranged in a criss-cross manner. However, they also have an additional two or more layers of fabric, or *belts*, under the tread.

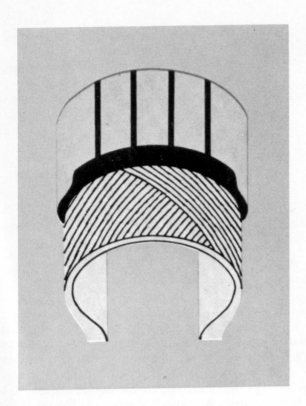

Fig. 5-1—The construction of a bias ply tire.

The cords in the belts run at an angle of about 25° to the center line. The construction of a belted bias tire yields a sidewall stiffness, comparable to that of a bias ply tire, but it also results in increased strength, and stiffness in the tread. Generally, the body cords are made of rayon, nylon, or polyester, while the belt cords are made of fiber glass, rayon, or steel. Belted bias tires "squirm" less than bias ply tires, run cooler, and give more mileage than that type of tire. The construction of this type of tire is pictured in figure 5-2.

The third type of tire in wide use is the *radial tire*. Here, the cords in the body run at right angles (90°) to the centerline, and are arranged in from one to three plies. This is the *radial section*. A belt consisting of up to four plies is placed over the radial section. The cords in the belt are at an angle of about 15° to the centerline. Tires with this type of construction have flexible sidewalls, and at the same time have great stiffness and strength in the tread area. Because of the flexibility of the sidewalls, radial tires generally look like they need air, even though they may be fully inflated. The belt is generally made of steel, fiberglass, or rayon. Radial tires have minimal

"squirm," run cool, and offer long wear. Figure 5-3 shows the construction of a radial tire.

TIRE PROFILE CAN EFFECT HANDLING

How a tire looks in a cross-sectional view is called its *profile*. The trend in tires designed for use on passenger cars has been from a high, narrow profile to a low, wide one. In fact, some passenger car profiles are almost twice as wide as they are high. Many cars have wide tires, which offer wider "footprints" (the impression a tire might leave on the ground) than those of conventional tires. Wide tires provide better cornering, while extremely wide tires can present some problems. They may not fit the tire rims the car is designed to use, they are harder to steer on cars which do not have power steering, they take up considerable room in the trunk when they are used as spares, and they can give a harder ride. Cars which do not normally come equipped with very wide tires may have fender wells, which are not wide enough to permit turns without rubbing. Thus, before replacing the tires on any car with wider ones, check to see if the new ones will fit. Figure 5-4 shows the profiles, and footprints of conventional tires versus those of low profile tires.

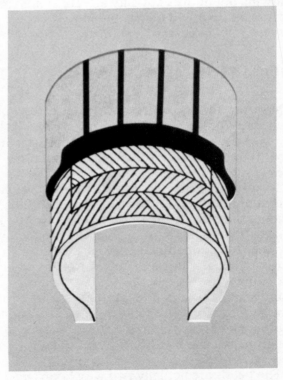

Fig. 5-2—How a belted bias tire is constructed.

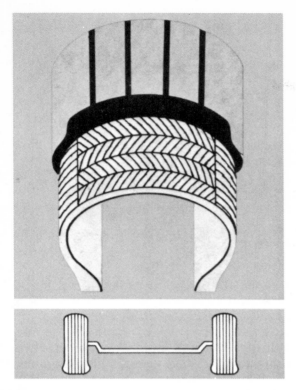

Fig. 5-3—The construction of a radial tire. Because of the flexibility of the sidewalls, a properly inflated radial tire gives the impression of needing air.

tion. Fig. 5-6 demonstrates the appearance of a tire after a blow-out has occurred.

Since punctures and blow-outs cause accidents, tire manufacturers have developed different types of puncture-and blow-out-resistant tires. These range from having a steel safety belt beneath the tread, an "inner tire" separated from the main tire by an air space, or using a sealant to prevent or slow the escape of air in the event of a puncture. Increased safety is a strong selling point for these tires. However, some of these tires exhibit a heat buildup, and others are difficult to balance satisfactorily. Fig. 5-7 shows a puncture-resistant tire.

Puncture-resistant tires are designed to reduce the possibilities of sudden loss of air or flat tires. If the tire has been penetrated by a nail or other object, repait it or replace it as soon as possible. Do not rely on the sealing property of the tire as a permanent repair. Because of the continual flexing that occurs in the sidewalls of tires as they are run, it is sometimes difficult to make a safe, permanent repair to a tire that has had this part damaged. A tire that has been repaired may be suitable for low-speed local travel. But, that same tire might not be safe for high-speed use or on rough roads, or under heavy loads.

PUNCTURES AND BLOWOUTS CAUSE ACCIDENTS

Punctures are caused when an object penetrates the tire and permits air to escape. Usually, punctures do not cause extensive damage to the body of the tire. However, if the tire remains in use while flat it may be ruined. This sometimes happens when it is not immediately possible to safely pull off the road, and the tire must be driven on until a suitable spot is found. Fig. 5-5 shows a tire with a tread that has been penetrated by a nail.

Blow-outs result when the cord gives way, and the tire deflates suddenly. Often, tires which have had blow-outs can no longer be used. Blowouts are generally caused by a slow weakening of the cord due to the flexing that occurs when the tire is used, or by impacts with rocks, pot holes, curbs, or other objects. They can be extremely dangerous, and can cause serious accidents, particularly if they occur at high speed, or on a curve. When a front tire has a blow-out, a strong, steady pull results, while a blow-out in a rear tire can produce a difficult to control weaving mo-

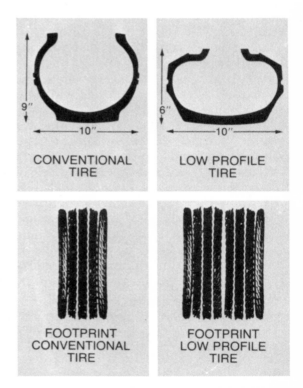

Fig. 5-4—Profiles and footprints of conventional, and low profile tires.

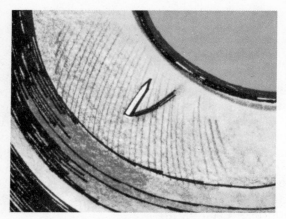

Fig. 5-5—A tire that has been punctured.

Fig. 5-6—When a tire has a blow-out, the cord gives way, and the tire deflates suddenly.

SNOW TIRES AND STUDS

Snow tires are designed with special tread patterns to give better traction on snow than regular tires. This pattern prevents snow from packing in the grooves and preventing traction. Snow tires come with many different tread patterns designed for different driving conditions. For example, for use on snowy, dry roads, the tread design is a cross between one to be used in deep snow, and that of a regular tire. While a snow tire may have a tread pattern that appears rugged, it may wear quite rapidly if it is continually driven on dry pavement. Fig. 5-8 shows a snow tire tread pattern that might be used on roads that are intermittently snowy and dry.

If you expect to drive in an area which has considerable rain, select a tread design with an open channel along the tread, to minimize the accumulation of water that can occur. Otherwise, it is possible that the tire will *hydroplane*, that is, ride on the water and lose traction. This can happen even at relatively low speeds. Fig. 5-9 shows a tread pattern containing water channels.

Most snow tires are designed to be used with small pieces of metal, called *studs*. These dig into ice or packed snow, and considerably improve traction. However, they do wear rapidly on dry pavement. Because they damage road surfaces, some states do not permit their use, and others restrict usage to certain months. If you are contemplating the use of studs, check the local laws and regulations concerning their use. Many dealers charge extra for studs, depending on the number of studs added. Usually, 100 studs per tire are sufficient; 150 are the maximum. Using more can decrease traction on wet and dry pavements. It is the rubber tread that grips the dry

pavement and makes a path through the water film on wet pavement. Fig. 5-10 shows a snow tire tread to which studs have been added.

No matter what type of snow tire you use, expect it to wear more rapidly than regular tires on dry pavement. Some types are not recommended for high-speed driving.

Note: If radial tires are mounted on your car, and you wish to use snow tires, they must also be radial tires. Mixing conventional tires with radial tires causes poor handling, and is dangerous.

SELECTING THE RIGHT TIRE

Tires with treads that are so badly worn that the tread pattern is not discernable are called *bald*. Bald tires are dangerous to drive on, and should be replaced. In fact, tires with a tread of 1/16 inch or less should be replaced. Even if your

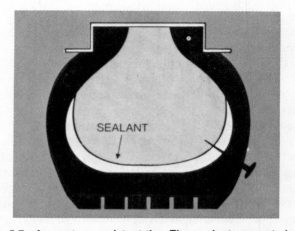

Fig. 5-7—A puncture-resistant tire. The sealant prevents loss of air when the tire is penetrated.

Fig. 5-8—A typical tread pattern for a tire designed for roads which are sometimes snowy, but are also often dry.

Fig. 5-9—A tread pattern containing water channels. These channels eliminate water accumulation, and reduce hydroplaning.

tires are practically brand new, you may want to consider changing tires. The conditions under which you drive may change, you may be carrying heavier loads or pulling a trailer, or you may be dissatisfied with the handling characteristics of the car. Sometimes just a different appearance is desired. Whatever the reason for buying new tires, the proper selection of tires is an important decision affecting your safety.

How to Select the Right Tires

1. Choose a tire strong enough to support the maximum load you carry. Be sure to include the weight of the car, and its passengers in this consideration, as well as additional anticipated weight. Family cars, for example, may carry just the driver one day, but on other occasions may be used to carry the entire family plus baggage; consider the latter case when buying tires for a family vehicle.
2. Consider the type of roads over which you generally expect to drive. The handling and wearing characteristics of different tires varies depending on road conditions. Tires designed for use on rural roads or rocky terrain react differently from those intended for highly abrasive surfaces.
3. Choose a tire that will maintain its footprint through curves and corners, at the maximum speeds at which you drive. As you go around a curve, or make a sharp turn, the mass of the car tends to continue in the direction it was going. When this happens the tires hold their footing, thereby obeying the driver.
4. Select tires that are designed to give the best over-all performance under the various conditions that you are likely to encounter. For example, a tire that is fine for driving at moderate speeds may not be able to survive

turnpike speeds. Since tire flexing increases at high speeds, this flexing generates heat that can destroy a tire that is not designed to handle it.

5. Select tires that will satisfy your driving needs, even if the cost is slightly higher or lower than expected. Buying tires on the basis of price alone can be a serious mistake. Safety, convenience, and performance must all be taken into consideration, as well as the potential cost from tire failure.

It is not necessary to buy more tires than you will use. If you do not drive at high turnpike speeds, you needn't bother with tires designed for a speedway. And small, light cars do not need tires that can handle loads normally carried by a larger, heavier car.

Note: If you decide to buy radial tires, make sure all the tires on the vehicle are radials, preferably the same type. Mixing radial tires with conventional tires will result in dangerous handling characteristics.

It is possible to mix bias tires and belted tires, but do not use different types together on the front or rear. Better handling results when the bias tires are mounted on the front, and the belted tires are placed in the rear.

Fig. 5-10—A snow tire tread to which studs have been added.

BREAKING-IN NEW TIRES

Many car manufacturers recommend certain driving patterns, and maintenance procedures that should be followed when their cars are new. This is called the *break-in period* of the car. What many people do not realize is that new tires also need a break-in period. This allows the various components of the tires to seat together. When using new tires, do not exceed 60 miles per hour for the first 50 miles.

MAKING TIRES LAST LONGER—SAFELY

Although tire life expectency depends upon the way the tire is designed and manufactured, other factors play a large role in determining its service life. Perhaps the most significant factor, is the way you drive.

In general, the faster you drive, the hotter your tires get, and heat increases the rate at which tires wear. Thus, driving at moderate speeds increases the life of your tires. Fig. 5-11 shows how the temperature in a "typical" tire increases as the speed at which they are run increases.

Accelerating rapidly can cause the wheels to spin, particularly on wet or sandy pavement. This results in increased tire wear. Make it a point not to accelerate too quickly.

When a corner or curve is taken too quickly, the forces on the tire increase, and the tire will often give a squealing noise. This tends to reduce tire life. Avoid letting the tires squeal as you drive around corners or around curves.

To further insure a long tire service life, drive at moderate speeds, avoid sudden and rapid acceleration, and reduce your speed to avoid squealing. Thus, not only will you increase the service life of the tire, you will increase the gas mileage as well.

Using brakes more often than necessary reduces tire life. Where possible, reduce speed gradually, rather than stopping quickly. If a sudden stop is necessary, avoid locking the wheels. When the wheels are locked in a panic stop, not only do the tires wear but, more importantly, stopping ability may be reduced, and loss of control may result.

One important factor concerning tire wear that is not directly related to driving habits is tire pressure. Tires are designed to carry specific loads, but only at the intended design pressure. Max-imum tire performance depends upon maintaining the proper pressure. When tires are run with pressures lower than intended, they flex more. This means they will run hotter and wear faster, particularly on the edges of the tread pattern. If, on the other hand, the tires carry too much pressure, there will be excessive wear at the center of the tread. Either too much pressure, or too little pressure reduces traction, and can result in a loss of control of the car. If the tires carry unequal pressures, a different problem may arise: Unequal pressure, especially in the front tires, can result in uneven braking, making it difficult to control the vehicle—especially in emergency situations. Fig. 5-12 shows how you only ride on a portion of the tire when the tire is either under- or over-inflated. Examining this figure indicates how the uneven wear patterns shown in fig. 5-13 are produced.

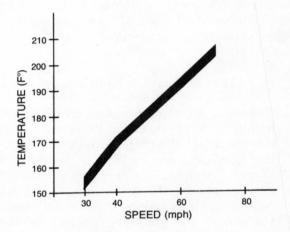

Fig. 5-11—Speed is related to tire temperature.

How to Tell Whether Tires are Over-inflated

1. Check for excessive wear in the center of the tread.
2. Too much pressure will cause a hard ride.
   If either of the above conditions are observed, while periodic checks of tire pressure indicate that the recommended levels are being observed—double check the pressure, using a different gauge. The one you are using may be faulty.

How to Tell Whether Tires are Under-inflated

1. Examine the tires for excessive wear on the outside of the tread.

Fig. 5-12—Cross-sections of under-inflated and over-inflated tires.

2. Too little pressure tends to produce a mushy ride.
3. If the pressure is too low, the tires will squeal when rounding curves or on corners. Since taking corners or rounding curves too quickly can also cause squealing, see if this situation continues at lower speeds.

Many cars are designed with uneven weight distributions. Often, manufacturers recommend different pressures for the front and rear tires of these vehicles. Your owner's manual should indicate recommended front and rear tire pressures. Car manufacturers and tire producers sometimes recommend that tires be inflated to higher pressures, if unusually heavy loads are to be carried or if considerable high-speed driving is planned. Your owners manual or tire dealer can

Fig. 5-13—Too much pressure causes excessive wear in the center of the tread (above), and results in a hard ride. Too little pressure results in wearing on the outside of the tread, and is accompanied by a mushy ride and a tendency for the tires to squeal on corners and curves.

indicate the proper pressures in such cases. However, *never* exceed the maximum pressure rating of the tire.

Note: Do not rely on the pressure settings found on air pumps in most service stations. The National Bureau of Standards conducted tests which showed that about one third of these gauges are wrong by 4 or more pounds per square inch, and three fifths of these gauges had errors of at least 2 pounds per square inch. Only one pocket gauge in 10 was found to have an error of 2 or more pounds per square inch. The purchase of a good quality pocket tire pressure gauge is a sound investment. Use it at least once a month, and always before long trips. For accurate readings, the tires should be cool. Test the tires before you have driven more than a mile, or when the tires have had a long time to cool.

ALIGNMENT CAN AFFECT TIRE WEAR

The angle of the wheels relative to the direction the vehicle is traveling is called the *wheel alignment*. Although the wheels are generally aligned when a vehicle comes from the factory, bumps, pot holes, rocks, curbs, and the normal action of the tires on the road surface can eventually cause the wheels to be out of alignment.

To provide for good steering control and vehicle stability, the front wheels are arranged at various angles to the frame. For example, *caster, camber, kingpin inclination, toe-in,* and *toe-out* all involve wheel positioning, and affect tire wear.

It is caster which causes the wheels to align themselves in the direction in which the car is moving. If the caster is too large, steering will be difficult and "shimmy" will occur at low speeds, while too little caster will cause weaving at high speeds, and erratic steering when the brakes are applied.

The angle between a vertical line, and a line drawn through the center of the wheel is called camber. Since the top of the wheel is inclined away from the car, this angle is not zero. Camber places the center of the tire in such a position as to make steering easier. Often, cars are designed with minimum camber to reduce uneven tire wear.

Kingpin inclination provides steering stability by raising the front end of a vehicle during a turn or while cornering. It is often called *steering axis inclination,* since many cars have ball-joint suspensions and such a suspension does not have kingpins.

Because the front wheels tend to turn away from each other due to compression of some of the parts in the steering mechanism, the front wheels are aimed "pigeon-toed," that is, as if they would meet each other if they were not attached to the car. Actually, the wheels move parallel to each other. Fig. 5-14 shows the affect on tire wear from too much toe-in; the inside edge of the tread pattern appears feathered.

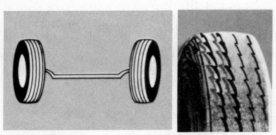

Fig. 5-14—An exaggerated picture of toe-in, and the effect of too much toe-in. There is a feathered edge on the inside of the tread pattern.

The outside wheel on a curve moves at a greater arc than the inside wheel. In order to prevent excessive tire wear, and possible scuffing, the inside wheel must turn at a sharper angle. To provide this angle, the steering arms are set at an angle to the wheels. The arms move an equal distance, but the angular movement is unequal; the wheels toe-out. Too much toe-out causes a feathered edge on the outside of the tread pattern, as shown in fig. 5-15.

Fig. 5-15—An exaggerated picture of toe-out, and the effect of too much toe-out. There is a feathered edge on the outside of the tread pattern.

BRAKES AFFECT TIRE WEAR

The purpose of the brakes is to slow or stop a moving vehicle. To do this, they change the speed at which the wheels turn. Because they act on the wheels, and the tires are connected to the wheels, the brakes affect the tires.

Brakes which are not adjusted properly cause tires to wear unevenly. For example, many cars have a breaking system which employs components called *brake drums*. As the brakes wear, these drums become "out-of-round." When this happens, excessive wearing of the tire tread in one spot can occur, as shown in fig. 5-16.

Fig. 5-16—Excessive tread wear in one spot. This is one result of brakes that are not adjusted properly.

TIRE BALANCING

In order to ensure uniform tire wear, the wheels should rotate uniformly. Unfortunately, this is generally not the case, for, in order for this to occur, the wheel rims, and the tires which are mounted on these rims would have to be manufactured and installed perfectly. And, even if this were the case, when the tires had to be replaced, these,too, would have to be perfect and installed accurately. Even dents, scrapes, bends, and scratches on the rim would have to be repaired in this manner. Instead, it is far more practical to *balance* the wheels, that is, to compensate for these imperfections of manufacturing and installation.

Wheel balancing is especially important in small cars, because these vehicles tend to have smaller wheels. Smaller wheels must rotate more quickly than larger ones in order for the vehicles they are mounted on to travel at the same speed. As an unbalanced front wheel rotates, it causes the entire front-end of the vehicle to vibrate, and shake in time with the wheel. The faster the wheel turns, the greater the frequency of vibration. The result is often shimmy, or steering wheel vibration.

There are two types of balancing—static and dynamic. Static balancing is performed when the wheel is not moving, while dynamic balancing is performed while the wheel is revolving. Accurate dynamic balancing must be preceded by static balancing. Often, tire distributors will only balance the tires statically. If your vehicle has a noticeable front-end shimmy, or steering wheel vibration, particularly at high speeds, have the tires statically and dynamically balanced; a front-end repair may not be necessary.

While tire imbalance is most noticeable on the front tires, all four tires should be balanced for minimal tire wear. Cars with independent suspension systems should always have all four tires balanced.

Note: Uneven or excessive wear on any of the tires may be an indication of worn wheel bearings or shock absorbers, or of loose or damaged parts.

Have the car inspected, and make any needed repairs or adjustments.

TIRE ROTATION

Although four identical tires may be placed on a car, their effective service life will usually differ. A major factor in the determination of this difference is the location of the tires on the car.

Different driving conditions result in different wearing conditions at each tire position. For example, in normal city driving, the front wheels usually wear more than the rear tires. This is because of the greater amount of cornering that occurs in city driving, as compared to highway travel. Turnpike and highway driving usually results in greater wear on the rear tires. Cars with

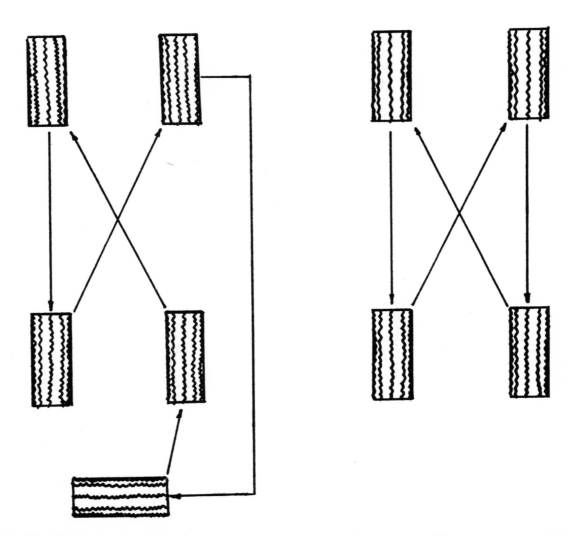

Fig. 5-17—Tire rotation patterns for bias ply and belted bias tires. The diagram at the left should be referenced when the spare tire is to be used.

front wheel drive generally show more wear on the front tires.

To distribute tire wear more evenly, tires should be *rotated* regularly, that is, their position on the car should be changed. Four types of tire rotation patterns are recommended, two for use with conventional tires, and two with radials. Rotating the tires at 5,000 mile intervals extends the lives of the tires, and thus tends to save you money. It also has the additional and more important benefit of being a good safety practice. Figs. 5-17 and 5-18 indicate recommended rotation patterns for conventional and radial tires.

For convenience, tips for extending tire life are listed below.

How to Increase Tire Life

1. Break-in new tires properly. Keep speeds under 60 miles per hour for the first 50 miles.
2. Keep your speed down.
3. Avoid rapid and sudden acceleration.
4. Reduce your speed when cornering, or going around curves.
5. Do not use brakes more than necessary. If a sudden stop is necessary, avoid locking the wheels.
6. Maintain proper tire pressures.
7. Make sure the front end of the vehicle is properly aligned.
8. Have all new tires balanced.
9. Rotate tires at recommended intervals.
10. Do not carry loads above those specified for the tire.

TREAD DEPTH INDICATORS

As a safety aid, modern tires have built-in tread depth indicators. When the tread depth is reduced to about 1/16 inch, the safe service life of the tire is ended. To indicate this situation,

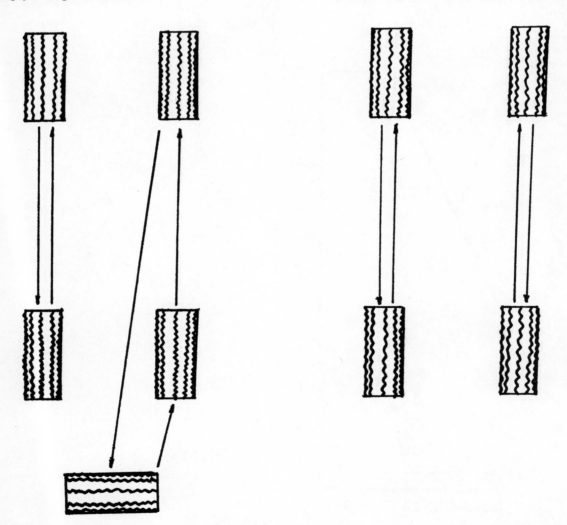

Fig. 5-18—Tire rotation patterns for radial tires. The diagram at the left should be referenced when the spare tire is to be used.

smooth narrow bands appear across the tread pattern, often similar to that shown in fig. 5-19. Using a tire after this warning indication appears is extremely dangerous, particularly on wet roads. Do not take any chances. Replace the tire. If the tire wears unevenly so that a portion of the tread is less than 1/16 inch, determine the cause of the uneven wear, correct the condition, and replace the tire.

Fig. 5-19—A modern tire with a tread depth indicator. When this pattern appears, the tire is no longer safe. Replace it.

CHAPTER 6

BRAKES

If you rub your hands together very rapidly, they will become quite warm. This is because friction has been used to turn motion into heat. This same principle is in evidence when you slow or stop a car. The parts of the car responsible for this comprise the *braking system.*

There are various types of braking systems, but the same principle mentioned above is used in each automobile braking system. Each uses a rotating unit, and a non-rotating unit, which contain the braking surfaces which rub together to produce the braking action.

For best braking action, the drums should be as perfectly round as possible, and have a uniform surface. As brakes are used, the brake drums tend to become "out-of-round" or scored. Brake drums which are too out-of-round, or badly scored should be replaced, reground, or "turned down" in a lathe until smooth and round. However, care must be taken to ensure that the drums do not become too thin, or they may become distorted when used, or a severe squeak may result.

The brake drum is attached to a part called a *hub,* which rotates around a wheel *spindle.* The

DRUM BRAKES

The most common type of braking system makes use of *drum brakes.* In this system, the non-rotating unit is placed inside a rotating *drum.* The drum not only provides a rotating braking surface, it also acts as a cover, protecting the braking mechnaism from dust, dirt and water. Since heat is produced when the brakes are applied, a well-designed braking system generally uses the brake drums to transmit much of the heat away from the braking surfaces. To provide for the best combination of strength, weight, response to friction, and heat resistance, the drums are generally made from a combination of metals, usually steel with a cast iron liner for the braking surface. For additional strength and better heat dissipation, cooling ribs are sometimes added to the outside of the drums. Figure 6-1 shows the construction of a typical brakedrum with cooling ribs.

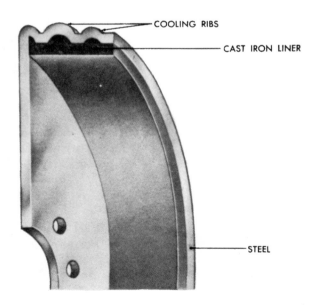

Fig. 6-1—A typical brakedrum with ribs for cooling.

wheel itself fits over the brake drum, and is bolted to the hub; thus, the hub, drum, and wheel rotate as if they were one unit (fig. 6-2).

Attached to the chasis is a rod-like part called the *steering knuckle spindle*. It is fixed and does not rotate. Bolted to it is a circular *backing plate.* Two curved components called *brake shoes* are

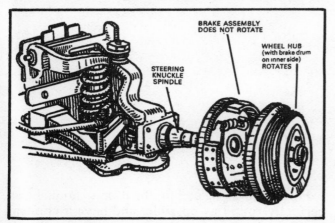

Fig. 6-2—A drum brake assembly, showing the parts that rotate and are stationary.

attached to the backing plate. To connect the two brake shoes, an anchor pin is used. Below this pin, there is a *wheel cylinder* (see fig. 6-3) containing two pistons, one at either end, such that each piston bears against one of the brakeshoes. The bottom end of the shoes is attached to an *adjustment screw.* A *brake lining*, a heat resistant strip usually made of asbestos and other materials, is attached to the outer surface of each brakeshoe.

When you slow or stop the car, you press on the brake pedal. *Hydraulic force* (see "The

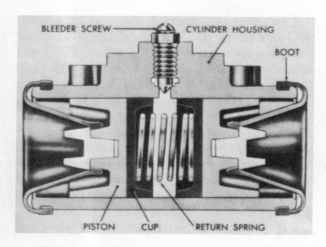

Fig. 6-3—A cross sectional view of a wheel cylinder.

Hydraulic System") causes the two pistons in the wheel cylinders to move outward, moving the brakeshoes against the inner side of the brake drums, thereby slowing or stopping the wheel from rotating.

The components of a drum brake are shown in fig. 6-4. The insert shows the affect of hydraulic force.

The regular operation of the brakes might not be sufficient for positive braking action. To increase the braking effect, the brakes are designed so that the rear shoe tends to wedge against the anchor pin. Brakes designed with this feature are called *self-energizing* or *servo.*

As the brakes are used, the linings tend to wear. The brakes on most late-model cars are designed to automatically correct for this wear. Systems with this feature are called *self-adjusting.*

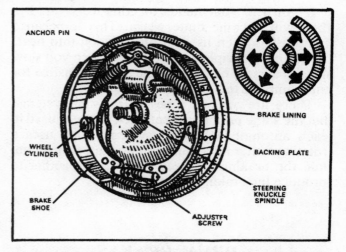

Fig. 6-4—The components of a drum brake. Hydraulic force results in the wheel pistons moving outward, and the brakeshoes move against the drum, as demonstrated by the insert.

DISC BRAKES

While drum brakes have been used on modern vehicles for many years, another type of brake system has been gaining increasing popularity. Called *disc brakes*, they, too, use friction to stop the wheels from rotating. If you were to take the lid of a jar, and rotate it between the thumb and forefinger of your hand, you would have a simple demonstration of the principle of disc brakes; bringing your fingers together in a pinching motion on the sides of the lid makes it very difficult for the lid .o be turned. Disc brakes work by clamping two sides of a disc between two flat brakeshoes.

The *caliper* is the part of the braking mechanism that supplies the "pinching." The caliper is bolted to the fixed rod-like steering knuckle. Two steel brake shoes are attached to the caliper, each one with a brake lining that is usually asbestos.

As with drum brakes, the wheel hub fits over the spindle and rotates around it. However, instead of using a drum, a steel *disc* is attached to the hub, and this disc is positioned within the brakeshoes on the caliper, just as the lid of the jar in the example above was placed between your fingers. The wheel is bolted to the hub, so that the hub, disc, and wheel rotate as if they were one unit (fig. 6-5).

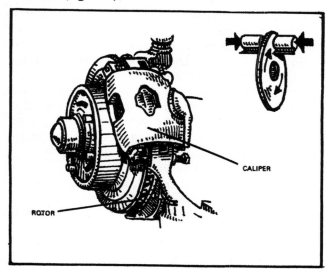

Fig. 6-5—A disc brake. The insert illustrates how the brake pads move against the disc to stop the wheel.

When the driver depresses the brake pedal, hydraulic force (see "The Hydraulic System") acts on one or more pistons in the caliper, which cause the brakeshoes to "pinch" the disc and the wheel slows or stops.

Disc brakes dissipate heat faster than drum brakes, and are more efficient. Since greater force is required to stop the front wheels of a car than the rear ones, many cars have disc brakes in front and drum brakes in the rear.

THE HYDRAULIC SYSTEM

Originally, motor cars had very simple braking systems. The driver operated a lever, and a system of rods would cause a shoe to rub against the wheels, stopping the vehicle. Eventually, cables served the same purpose, but a mechanical linkage was still used. In the modern automobile, pressure applied at the brake pedal is transmitted to the brakes by a liquid. The components which

are used in this transmission of pressure comprise the *hydraulic system.*

To fully understand how an hydraulic system works, it is necessary to mention four basic facts:

1. Liquids do not compress easily.
2. Liquids can transmit force and motion.
3. If liquid is in a container, and pressure is exerted on that liquid, that pressure is transmitted in all directions.
4. If pressure is transmitted through a liquid to a piston, the force at the piston can be changed by changing the size of the piston.

Because of these properties, the pressure of a foot on the brake pedal is transmitted from the pedal to the four wheels, activating the wheel cylinders in systems using drum brakes, and the pistons in a disc brake system.

There is a wall separating the engine from the passenger compartment. A *master cylinder* is mounted on the engine side of this wall. On older cars this master cylinder contains a single piston which is linked by a push rod to the brake pedal (see fig. 6-6). To provide greater safety, late model cars have a *dual master* cylinder. Here, the push rod from the brake pedal operates a *primary piston* in the cylinder; the primary piston activates a secondary piston. Since one piston controls the front brakes, and the other piston the rear ones, greater safety is provided in case of failure.

A means must be provided to link the master cylinder to each of the wheel cylinders. This is the purpose of the *brake lines.* (Do not confuse brake lines with brake linings. Brake lines join the master cylinder with each wheel cylinder, while brake linings fit on the brakeshoes.) Brake lines are built to withstand high pressures, and are actually steel tubes coated with lead. The entire system is filled with a special liquid called *brake fluid.*

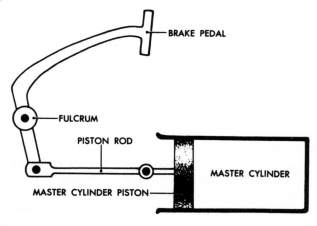

Fig. 6-6—The foot pedal is linked to the piston in the master brake cylinder.

When the driver presses the brake pedal, the push rod transmits the motion of the pedal to the piston (or pistons) in the master cylinder. Pressure is exerted on the fluid, and, because the fluid isn't compressed (fact 1 above), the pressure is transmitted to the brakes via the brake lines. At the wheels having drum brakes, the pressure forces the pistons in the wheel cylinders outward, and the brake shoes are forced against the inner surface of the brake drum. At wheels having disc brakes, the pressure moves the pistons, and the brake "pads" in the calipers press against the disc.

Drum brakes have return springs to pull the shoes away from the drum; this forces the pistons back to their original positions in the wheel cylinders, and causes the fluid to return to the master cylinder. Fig. 6-7 is a diagram of an hydraulic braking system.

It is important to make sure that air does not enter an hydraulic brake system. This is because air can be compressed. Air in the hydraulic brake system can result in a "spongy" feeling when the brake pedal is depressed. Sudden brake failure may also occur.

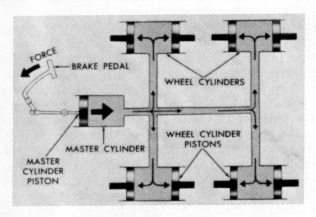

Fig. 6-7—How an hydraulic braking system works.

POWER BRAKES

Power brakes is the term applied to systems which allow the driver to use reduced pressure on the brake pedal to slow or stop the car. To supply the power for this system, a power booster which uses engine *vacuum* is added between the brake pedal and master cylinder. A vacuum is nothing more than an area from which air or gas has been removed. As the pistons move up and down in an internal combustion engine, a vacuum is created.

Air has weight, and this weight exerts **pressure on all objects it comes in contact with.**

If a container has air removed from it, the pressure inside it will be less than that of the air outside. This difference in pressure is used to perform work; this is the principle used to operate power brakes.

When the car is driven, very little air enters the intake manifold of the engine, and the pumping action of the pistons results in a reduced pressure in the manifold. The driver removes his or her foot from the accelerator pedal when the brakes are applied. The difference between the vacuum pressure and the atmospheric pressure that results operates the brakes.

The power booster contains a piston. There is a valve inserted between the booster and the manifold to control its operation. There are various designs for the power booster, but fig. 6-8 demonstrates the basic principle used. When the valve, (which is operated by the brake pedal) is opened, air is removed from the chamber ahead of the piston. The pressure from the air on the other side of the piston (atmospheric pressure) exerts a force; the amount of this force depends on the area of the piston.

When the valve is closed, the area ahead of the piston is disconnected from the manifold. Air enters through the valve, and the pressure in front of the piston is raised to atmospheric pressure. This is depicted by the lower picture in the figure. Since the pressure on both sides of the piston is the same, no force is exerted on the

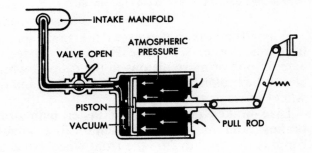

PRESSURE APPLIED

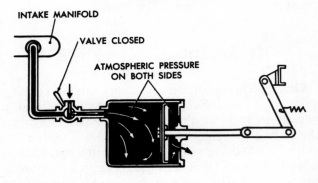

PRESSURE RELEASED

Fig. 6-8—How a vacuum brake piston operates.

pull rod, and so it remains in the release position.

Vacuum power brake systems are designed so that in the event of failure, the brakes will still operate; however, it requires considerably greater force on the brake pedal.

PARKING BRAKES

Parking brakes are designed to activate the rear brakes, by using a linkage which is separate from the hydraulic system. They are usually activated by pulling a lever, or pressing a small foot pedal.

MAINTAINING AND INSPECTING BRAKE SYSTEMS

Modern braking systems do not require a great deal of maintenance to assure trouble-free performance. However, the few minutes required for regular inspection can help to detect any trouble before a serious (and expensive) difficulty develops. One important step is to regularly check the fluid level in the master brake cylinder; a low level may be indicative of a leak in the hydraulic system or a defect in one of the brake system components. The fluid level should be checked when the engine oil is changed, or if the brake pedal appears low.

How to Check the Brake Fluid Level

Tools required

Wrench or screwdriver (depending on the design of the master cylinder).
Procedure

1. If the master brake cylinder has a bolt on top, use a wrench to loosen this bolt; if it has a clip, raise it, using a screwdriver if necessary.
2. Carefully lift the top of the master brake cylinder. Avoid spilling any fluid.
3. The fluid level should be approximately ¼ inch from the top of the container.
4. If the fluid level is low, *slowly* add a top quality brake fluid, until the level is about ¼ inch from the top. Consult your owner's manual for the specific type of brake fluid to be used. Adding fluid too quickly can cause air to enter the system, which could result in serious problems or brake failure.
5. Replace the top of the cylinder. Tighten the bolt firmly (do not overtighten), or reposition the clip.

Most modern braking systems have self-adjusting features to compensate for the wearing of the brake linings. However, if you notice that the brake pedal is low, or that the brakes are not responding as they should, have your mechanic check the brakes. He can check the self-adjusters to see that they are working properly. By removing a wheel (usually the front-left) he can examine the brake linings to determine if they have to be replaced. Have the linings checked every 30,000 miles, or if the brakes do not seem to respond properly.

The best test for brakes is the *dynamic brake analyzer*. This equipment is usually found in any good diagnostic center.

BARGAINS CAN KILL

Except for minor adjustments, brake repairs are usually expensive. In an effort to reduce costs, many people scan newspapers and magazines looking for "bargains." While comparison shopping is recommended, beware of low-cost "specials"; they can cost you more than money. They can cost you your life.

Often the brake "bargain" is a come-on, that is, a means of getting you to take the car to the shop which placed the advertisement. Once there, you might be told (if you are fortunate) that the advertised cost was only for such items as brake linings and fluid, and that additional work must be done at extra cost. Some repair shops do the work indicated in their advertisements, and then present the customer with a bill, claiming that the car required "extra work." And some places might simply do the "cheap" job as offered, disregarding the fact that your safety is at stake.

WHAT A COMPLETE BRAKE JOB INCLUDES

Brake jobs are expensive. Because of this, you should know what to expect for your money.
1. Replace the brake linings. Often, this is all a "bargain" brake job will include. Get the best linings available. Buy reputable name linings, and be wary of parts that come in an unmarked box. Quality linings will help assure good brake performance. The difference between "unknown" linings and quality ones is just a few dollars per wheel. The linings should be the same type as those found on the car when delivered from the

factory. "Bonded" linings may not necessarily be better than "riveted" linings.

Have the linings on the car replaced pairwise at the same time, that is, have both front wheels done together, and both rear wheels together. Otherwise, balanced braking action may not occur. However, if the linings have been recently replaced on both front or both rear wheels, but those on one wheel are defective or faulty, it may only be necessary to replace the damaged linings.

2. Rebuild or replace the wheel cylinders. Although they may have been performing faultlessly, installation of new linings changes the stroke of the wheel cylinder pistons. The rubber cap may move across a pitted or rusted surface. This eventually results in fluid leaking onto the linings, which causes the brakes to "grab." The wheel cylinder will then have to be replaced anyway and, since fluid can not be removed from the linings, they, too, will have to be replaced.

3. Replace the wheel-bearing grease seals. Leaky seals are dangerous. It is a good idea to repack the wheel bearings at the same time.

4. Replace the return springs. Pulling or dragging brakes can result if these springs are weak. Despite the fact that these springs are generally not very expensive, they are generally not replaced.

5. Flush and replace the brake fluid. This is a requirement for any good brake job. The whole system should be drained and the fluid replaced with high quality fluid.

6. Check the brake lines. All lines should be carefully examined for crimps or leaks.

7. Check the brake drums. Out-of-round or scored drums must be resurfaced. New linings should be fitted by arcing them in a brakeshoe grinder.

8. Check the master cylinder. Usually, no repairs or adjustments are required, but the master cylinder should be checked for leaks. One symptom of master cylinder defects is a brake pedal that slowly moves to the floorboard.

DISC BRAKES NEED NOT BE MORE EXPENSIVE

Customers are often told that it is more expensive to repair disc brakes than conventional drum brakes. This is not necessarily true. Disc brakes cost less to maintain than drum brakes.

However, disc brakes are different than drum brakes, and since customers expect to pay more for items that are different, the service charges are sometimes higher.

DO NOT DO IT YOURSELF

If you find that you need repair work on your braking system, do not do it yourself. It takes experience to do this work correctly. The ability to stop is vital to your safety.

BRAKE SYSTEM TROUBLESHOOTING

Although it is not recommended that you do brake repairs yourself, knowing what is wrong with the brake system can help you determine what action your mechanic must take to correct the problem.

Note: Cars equipped with power brake systems also exhibit the same problems as those that do not have power units, in addition to possible difficulties with the vacuum units.

Problem—Continued or severe loss of brake fluid.
Possible cause—There is an external leak.
Solution—Clean and tighten components, and replace faulty parts.
Possible cause—There is an internal leak past the secondary seals, and into the power unit.
Solution—Rebuild the master cylinder.
Problem—Brake pedal vibrates.
Possible cause—The brake pedal free play is not adjusted properly.
Solution—Have the brake pedal free play adjusted.
Problem—The brakes grab, and the car has power brakes.
Possible cause—A broken valve spring, sticking vacuum valve, or reaction diaphragm linkage is defective.
Solution—If the vacuum valve is sticking, it should be cleaned, and lubricated with a silicone lube. If the valve spring or linkage are defective, the power unit should be overhauled.
Problem—The brake pedal is low.
Possible cause—Improperly adjusted or worn linings, or a defective adjuster.
Solution—Have the automatic adjusters checked, and if necessary, repaired or replaced. If the linings are defective a brake job should be done.
Possible cause—Air trapped in the master cylinder, or worn or damaged master cylinder.

Solution—The cause of air entering the system should be located, and corrective action taken. The air should be "bled" from the system. A worn or damaged cylinder should be rebuilt or replaced.

Problem—The brake pedal is "spongy."

Possible cause—Air in the hydraulic system, a faulty master cylinder, check valve, or damaged hoses.

Solution—Since air in the braking system can be extremely dangerous, have the hydraulic system checked as soon as possible. Damaged parts should be replaced, and air should be "bled" from the system.

Possible cause—Drums may be scored, cracked, or out-of-round.

Solution—The drums should be resurfaced, or replaced and a complete brake job performed.

Problem—The brakes grab or pull.

Possible cause—Defective shoe return spring, binding linkage, or worn brake linings.

Solution—Defective parts should be replaced and, if the linings are worn, a complete brake job should be done.

Possible cause—Uneven or worn tire treads, uneven tire pressures, poor alignment, or loose wheel bearings.

Solution—Worn tires should be replaced (see the chapter on tires), have the alignment checked, and if necessary, have the wheels aligned; loose wheel bearings should be corrected.

Possible cause—The drums, brake plate, or wheel cylinders are defective.

Solution—Any defective parts should be replaced. If the drums are resurfaced or replaced, a complete brake job should be done.

Problem—The brakes "drag."

Possible cause—The parking brake may be too tight, or the brakeshoes may be improperly adjusted.

Solution—Have the parking brake, or brakeshoes readjusted.

Possible cause—The linkage may be binding.

Solution—Have the linkage checked and freed if necessary.

Problem—The brakes squeak.

Possible cause—The brakeshoes may be adjusted improperly, or an automatic adjuster may be defective.

Solution—Have the brakeshoes examined, and readjusted if necessary. Replace any defective adjusters.

Possible cause—The linings may be worn, or parts such as the shoe return springs, drums, or support plates may be defective.

Solution—If the linings are worn, they should be replaced as part of a complete brake job. Defective parts should be replaced.

CHAPTER 7

FIVE MINUTE MAINTENANCE

While many maintenance procedures and most repairs take a while to perform, several important basics can be performed in just a few minutes. Following these procedures regularly will help to catch problems before they develop into expensive repairs. Five minutes spent every weekend, for example, can lead to a longer life for your car and continued driving pleasure.

A good way to start is by checking the oil. Observe the oil level (see "How to Check the Oil Level"). If the level is below the indicator marks, add a quality motor oil until the proper level is shown. Carefully check the condition of the oil by examining the sample on the dipstick. If it is very brown (dirty), it is time for an oil change (see "How to Change the Oil"). Remember, when adding or changing the oil, never overfill the crankcase—do not allow the level to go above the full mark. Always use a high quality oil of the proper viscosity for your particular driving conditions.

Inspect the brake fluid level by checking the master cylinder (see "How to Check the Brake Fluid Level"). If necessary, *slowly* add a top quality brake fluid, as recommended in your owner's manual. If continual addition of brake fluid is necessary, or if large amounts must be added, have the brake system examined professionally. There may be a leak or defective parts. Remember, brake repairs should always be made by a qualified mechanic—your safety depends on the brakes.

If your car has an automatic transmission, it requires a special fluid for smooth operation. The level and color of this fluid should be checked.

How to Check Automatic Transmission Fluid Level

1. Place the car on a level surface.
2. Put the gear selector in neutral, and set the parking brake.
3. For an accurate reading, the engine must be operating.
4. There is a dipstick near the back of the engine; it is usually positioned farily low. Lift out the dipstick and check the fluid level.
5. If the level is below the indicator mark, or ADD is indicated, add a high quality transmission fluid of the type recommended in your owners manual.
6. The fluid on the dipstick should be clear, often reddish in color. If it isn't, have the transmission checked by a specialist. Similarly, if the fluid smells burned, the transmission may be in need of repair.
7. Replace the dipstick.

Automatic transmission repairs are expensive. Catching a problem early enough may mean the difference between a relatively minor adjustment, and a costly rebuild or replacement.

Take a minute to examine each belt. With the engine off, press at the center of each one. If the belts have excessive "play" (that is, they move too much) they should be tightened. One indication of a loose belt is a whistling noise that can be heard when the engine is running, particularly at high speeds. Worn or frayed belts should be replaced as soon as possible. *Never* attempt to touch the belts while the engine is running, since a severe injury may result. With the engine off, examine all visible hoses. Any hoses that leak, or are cracked, worn, swollen or brittle, should be replaced. If the hoses appear to be in good shape, turn on the engine. Observe the hoses again, paying particular attention to the areas near clamps or joints. If you notice steam or liquid, it is an indication that there is a faulty hose or loose or defective clamp or connection. Any damaged part should be replaced.

If your car has power steering, check the steering action. Turn the engine on. With the parking brake set (for safety), move the steering wheel completely from one side to the other. The motion should be smooth, without stops or binding. If there are stops, roughness, or binding, have the steering checked by your mechanic. Power steering makes use of a *power steering pump*, which is driven by a belt. The pump is an hydraulic one, and for good steering action the proper oil pressure must be maintained. Checking the oil level is generally as simple as removing the cap on the power steering unit, which is usually located toward the front of the engine compartment. If additional oil is needed, use only the type recommended by the manufacturer of your car (your owner's manual probably has this information. If not, check with a dealer or parts supply store). Be careful not to overfill the reservoir.

Check the level of cooling system solution (see "How to check the coolant level"). Add additional coolant if necessary (see "how to Add Coolant"). Examine the condition of the coolant. If it is dirty, rusty or oily, have the cooling system checked. Sometimes a leaky automatic transmission results in some oil bleeding into the cooling system. If oil is noticed, have the transmission checked.

If the tires are cold, check the pressures using a good pocket pressure gauge. You will be operating a safer vehicle and extending the life of the tires at the same time.

Check the lights on the car. They are used to see and for being seen, and serve the important functions of indicating braking, backing and turning to other drivers. For safety, check to make sure that all the lights are working. Turn on the headlights, first on low beams, then high beams, and make sure they are operating properly. Walk around the car and check to see that the tail light bulbs are operating. Press on the brake pedal and have someone observe the brake lights. Turn the engine on; with your foot on the brake and the parking brake set, place the car in reverse gear. If your car has backing lights, have someone make

sure they are operating. Put the car in neutral or park, and check your turn signals. Usually, if the bulb is burned out, the turn indicator on the dash will not blink or will blink more slowly than usual. Double check by having someone observe these lights. Make sure the side lights are working and also the hazard lights ("flashers"). Because the replacement procedures differ with different makes of cars, a general replacement procedure is not presented here. Some lights are designed for ease of replacement, while others require some degree of manual dexterity. Since you can save money by replacing bulbs yourself, examine the light that needs attention. Sometimes all that is required is to twist and pull off the old bulb. This type of lamp is called a *bayonet* type bulb. Others require screws to be removed and a lens or reflector to be lifted or pulled.

Although each light may be working, there may still be a problem. Sometimes a bad connection or faulty "ground" (a common connection, usually the car body itself) can result in a flickering, or in different lights having uneven brightness. Check for loose wires or poor connections in the vicinity of the bulb and, if any are found, make the necessary adjustments. If none are apparent or if making adjustments does not solve the problem, have the car's wiring system checked by the service department of a dealer. Often, even excellent mechanics do not have the expertise or manuals and equipment necessary to trace the complicated wiring and circuit boards used in modern cars.

Even if every component in the car is working perfectly, there are two procedures that should be performed frequently for safety. Signal lights are most effective when they can be seen clearly, and headlights are intended to give off a certain amount of light. To ensure maximum effectiveness of the lighting system, and for safety, make sure that all lights, and reflections are cleaned often. Similarly, windows are designed for looking through. If they are dirty, visibility, and hence safety, is reduced. Clean all windows thoroughly and frequently. Often, people clean only the outside of the windows, neglecting the inside areas. Not only can this eventually affect visibility, but misting in bad weather will occur more easily on dirty windows than it will on clean ones.

For safety, make sure the windshield washer container is full. To avoid freezing lines and a possibly damaged motor, be sure the proper amount of windshield washer antifreeze is used in cold weather. Having a properly functioning windshield cleaning system is particularly important in very dusty or muddy areas and in those regions where slush and road dirt are often kicked up onto the windshield.

While you are checking the windshield washer, examine the wipers as well. These consist of a long section called the *wiper arm*. At the end of the arm, and at an angle to it is the *wiper blade*. The blade holds the rubber part that sweeps over the windshield to clear it of rain and snow. This rubber part is called the *wiper element*. On most cars it is replaceable and, if so, is also referred to as a *refill*. On those cars that do not have refills, it is necessary to replace the wiper blade if the element is worn.

How to Replace Windshield Wiper Elements

Tools required

None

Procedure

1. There are two types of wipers that are in general use; those that have a push button to release the element, and those that have springs in the blade.
1a. If the wiper assembly has a button, pushing it will release a link holding the element to the blade. Lift the arm from the glass without rotating it, and slide the element from its grips.
1b. If the blade has a spring, lift the arm from the glass, without rotating it and bend the blade backwards to aid in element removal. At one end of the blade there is generally a pair of vertical grips. Press them towards each other to release the element and slide the element from its grips.
2. Carefully slide the new element into position starting at the end from which it was removed. Make sure it is postioned in the same way that the worn refill was.

Caution: Be sure the refill is placed properly within its grips. Otherwise, damage to the wiper or glass may result.

3. If the refill has a notch or lock, make sure it is engaged with the corresponding part of the blade. This keeps the refill from working loose during operation of the wipers.
4. If the blade is the button type, reposition the link so that it clicks onto the blade.

Wiper elements become cracked and brittle as they age. If they exhibit these signs, or if the wipers streak or smear instead of cleaning

thoroughly, replace the elements. If you live in a very dusty or polluted area, occasionally cleaning the elements with some cotton which is dampened with a little rubbing alcohol may extend their life.

In order for the wipers to perform efficiently, the wiper arms must position the blades properly. Sometimes the spring in the wiper arm itself loses its tension or breaks. When this happens, the element will not stay against the glass as intended. The element may even pass over water on the windshield. If this situation is occurring, the arm itself must be replaced.

How to Replace Windshield Wiper Arms

Tools required

Wrench

Procedure

Note: The exact procedure may differ slightly, depending on the type of replacement arm used or if the car has "hidden" wipers. However, the procedure will be approximately the same.

1. Using the wrench, loosen the nut at the base of the arm beneath the windshield. Slide the old arm off its mounting.
2. Some arms have blades attached, others do not. If necessary, attach a blade and element to the new arm.
3. Slip the new arm onto the mounting and tighten the nut "finger tight." Make sure the arm is engaged properly with the mounting, then tighten the nut more firmly.
4. Some arms have the spring tension holding the blade and element to the glass pre-adjusted at the factory. However, some means of adjusting the tension is usually provided, generally in the form of a screw. Adjust the screw until the element makes good contact with the glass, but is not too tight. If there is insufficient tension, the blade may lift from the glass in a strong wind or at high speeds.
5. Some means of adjusting the sweep area of the wiper is usually provided. Often, this just involves bending the arm slightly near the blade so that the blade is in the same relative position as it was on the old arm.

Always allow the windshield to become sufficiently wet before turning on the wipers. Otherwise, the elements will wear faster and, if any sand or grit is present on the windshield, it may be scratched.

For convenience, a "five minute" checklist is listed below.

Inspection Checklist

1. Check the oil level. Add oil if necessary.
2. Check oil cleanliness on the dipstick. Change oil if necessary.
3. Inspect the level of the brake fluid in the master cylinder. Add top quality brake fluid if necessary.
4. If the car has an automatic transmission, set the park brake, turn on the engine, and with the car in neutral or park on a flat surface, check the transmission fluid level. Add a quality transmission fluid if necessary. Examine the color of the transmission fluid to see that it is a "clean" color (usually red) and that it does not have a burned smell.
5. Check the belts for tightness and have worn or frayed belts replaced. (The engine should be off).
6. Examine hoses for cracks, brittleness or damage, and make sure all connections and clamps are tight.
7. If the car has power steering, check the level of the fluid in the power steering reservoir. With the engine on, turn the wheel from full right to far left, and make sure the steering is smooth. Have it checked if roughness or binding occurs.
8. Check the coolant level. Add radiator mixture if necessary.
9. Make sure the cooling system fluid is "clean." Dirt, rust or oil in the system may mean cooling system problems or difficulties with an automatic transmission.
10. With the engine off and the parking brake set, check for proper tire pressures. Add air if necessary.
11. Make sure all lights are working. For safety, any burned out bulbs should be replaced as soon as possible. Clean all lenses and reflectors to aid in seeing and being seen.
12. Clean all windows both outside and inside if necessary.
13. Examine the wiper elements for cracks, brittleness and wear. Replace them if necessary.

CHAPTER 8

EMISSION CONTROL SYSTEMS

Recently, there has been considerable concern about the environment and the health hazard created by unclean or contaminated air. Automobiles are powered by internal combustion engines, wankel rotary engines, and occasionally by diesel engines. Each type operates by a burning fuel (gasoline or diesel oil). The end products of this combustion are various gases. Previously these exhaust gases were released directly into the atmosphere. Although the amount of gas released by each car is relatively small, there are millions of cars in the United States. Large numbers of automobiles are concentrated in major cities. Here, the gases and pollutants from each car accumlate, creating smoke, haze and smog. To alleviate this problem, there has been a trend

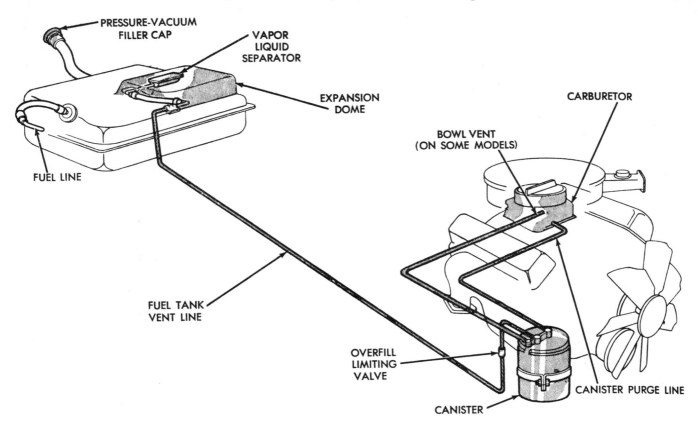

Fig. 8-1—A diagram of the evaporation control system of a car. As its name implies, this system is designed to control the evaporation of gasoline.

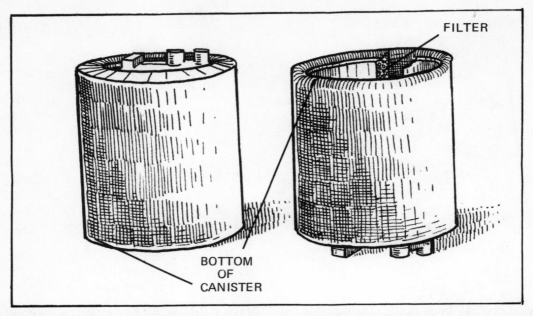

Fig. 8-2—A carbon canister used in the evaporation control system. The bottom of the canister generally has a fiberglass filter.

since 1968 to require each car to reduce its level of output of these contaminants. This is the job of the *emission control system*. An improperly adjusted emission control system can affect smooth operation of your car, costing you money.

GASOLINE EVAPORATION

Gasoline evaporates unless it is prevented from doing so. Left unchecked, much of this evaporation will occur in the fuel tank. To prevent this, vapor is passed through a *vent line* (fig. 8-1) to a canister which contains carbon granules (fig. 8-2). These absorb the vapor until the engine is started. The engine sucks the gasoline vapor into the carburetor. The canister generally contains a fiberglass filter which should be replaced at 25,000 mile intervals. If you live in a dusty area, or use gasoline that contains lead, it may be necessary to replace it more frequently. (Do not use leaded gasolines in cars which are not intended to operate using these fuels.)

Special pressure-vacuum gasoline filler caps are usually part of the evaporation system. Relief valves in the cap operate only in the event of a system malfunction. They prevent excessive pressure or vacuum in the tank. They have a special design which allows pressure to be relieved without actually removing the cap from the filler pipe. Removal is accomplished by turning the cap through an additional angle, usually about 90°. This prevents pressure build up in the tank or vapor line from forcing fuel out of the tank.

Figure 8-3 is a diagram of this type of cap. Gasoline also evaporates from the float bowl in the carburetor. In order to reduce this, it is necessary to modify the carburetor.

TEMPERATURE AFFECTS POLLUTANTS

When the proportion of gasoline is reduced in the fuel-air mixture, the mixture is *leaned*. Leaning the mixture reduces two types of emissions, *hydrocarbons* and *carbon monoxide*. To get this leaner mixture, a thermostatically controlled air cleaner is used. Air passes over the exhaust

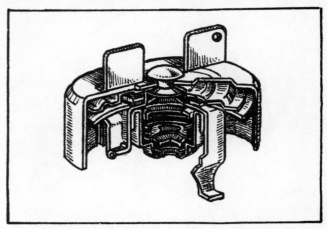

Fig. 8-3—A pressure-vacuum filler cap is generally part of the evaporation system.

manifold and passes into the carburetor at about 100°F. The warmer air and the modified carburetor provide a uniformly lean mixture for the combustion chambers.

The amount of unburned hydrocarbons is reduced when the temperature of the fuel-air mixture is raised, since the mixture burns better. To help get these higher temperatures, various modifications are employed. One important modification includes changing the timing of the engine.

The distributor directs the spark and controls the time at which the spark occurs; this depends on the speed and load of the engine. An *electronic* or *controlled spark advance system* is used to *retard* (delay) the spark. This delay causes the exhaust gases to have a higher temperature. This results in the reduction in the level of unburned hydrocarbons. Unfortunately, it also results in one unwanted effect-the fuel consumption increases.

EXHAUST GASES AND POLLUTION CONTROL

No matter how good an internal combustion engine is, some exhaust gases pass the piston rings and enter the crankcase. These gases, called *blow-by*, must be removed or else the engine may be damaged. A *positive crankcase ventilation* system (abreviated PCV) is used for this purpose, rather than letting the blow-by gases be exhausted into the atmosphere.

When the engine is running, a vacuum is created within it. This vacuum sucks air through a hose which connects to the air cleaner and the crankcase. The air flow carries the blow-by gases, and passes through the crankcase. It then exits through another hose and enters the intake manifold via a *PCV valve*, whose purpose is to regulate this flow according to the engine's speed and load. The exhaust gases are reburned and pollution is reduced.

For the proper operation of the crankcase emissions control to occur, each component must work as intended. Often, the PCV valve will get clogged or stuck, and will not operate freely. It should be checked every 10,000 miles; most simply unscrew from the cylinder head cover. (see "How to Inspect PCV Valves".) Figure 8-4 is a drawing of a closed crankcase ventillation system showing a detail of the PCV valve.

EXHAUST GAS RECIRCULATION

Certain gases, called nitrogen oxides, are formed during combustion at the extremely high temperatures that are present. Thus, reducing the temperature of combustion reduces the amount of these gases. Only a relatively small temperature drop is required. The purpose of the *exhaust gas recirculation system* is to produce this temperature reduction. It works by feeding small quantities of the exhaust gases into the intake manifold. An *air injection system* aids in "purifying" exhaust gases. Air is forced, or injected, into the cylinder exhaust ports as the hot gases exit from the combustion chambers. The additional oxygen in the air allows the gases to burn more completely. This reduces the levels of hydrocarbons and carbon monoxide.

CATALYTIC CONVERTERS

In a further attempt to reduce air pollution, many 1975 cars have *catalytic converters* (see fig. 8-5). They are part of the exhaust system and can be found between the exhaust manifold and the muffler. A catalyst is something that speeds or promotes a chemical reaction, so it is not surpris-

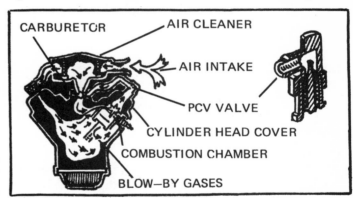

Fig. 8-4—A closed crankcase ventillation system.

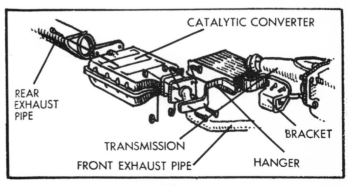

Fig. 8-5—A catalytic converter.

ing that this device contains a catalytic material. The eventual result of the chemical reaction that occurs is "cleaner" exhaust. The catalytic material is replaceable and normally should last for approximately 50,000 miles. The catalytic converter (figs. 8-6 and 8-7) is designed to reduce hydrocarbon and carbon monoxide pollutants in

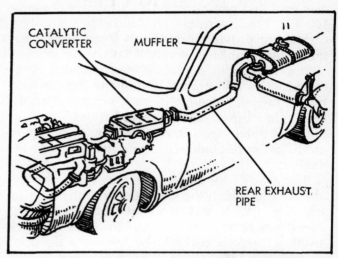

Fig. 8-7—The exhaust system of a car with a V-8 engine and having a catalytic converter.

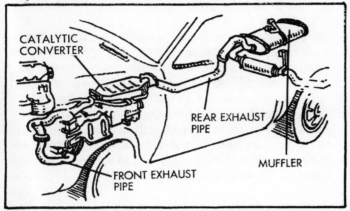

Fig. 8-6—The exhaust system of a car with a 4-cylinder engine, showing the placement of the catalytic converter.

the exhaust gases. It consists of a container filled with beads, coated with platinum and polladium. Since the presence of lead can severely shorten the life of this material, cars equipped with catalytic converters should never be operated with gasoline that contains lead. They should use only unleaded gasoline.

INSPECTING THE EMISSIONS CONTROL SYSTEMS

Many states require periodic inspection of cars. An examination of the exhaust pollutant level is mandatory in a number of these state required inspections. Although most adjustments to the pollution control systems should be performed by qualified mechanics, there are some checks that should be made regularly to ensure that the vehicle has an emissions control system that is performing properly.

Caution: Check any warrantees that come with your car. Unauthorized replacements or adjustments may void these warrantees.

It is good practice to inspect the emissions control systems prior to every tune-up. Since the PCV valve is usually easily accessible, it is good place to start.

How to Inspect PCV Valves

Location

PCV valves are generally located on top of the cylinder head cover, and have a hose connected to them.

Tools required

None

Procedure

1. Loosen and remove the hose connected to the PCV valve. It is connected to either the carburetor base or intake manifold.
2. Remove the PCV valve by unscrewing it.
3. Check to make sure the valve is free to move. If it isn't, spray it with choke cleaner until it is. If the valve still doesn't move freely, replace the PCV valve assembly.
4. Replace the PCV valve by screwing it into position.
5. Re-attach the hose.

After checking the PCV valve, examine the hoses in the emission control systems. Replace any that are worn, cracked, or damaged. Use a hose of the same type or its equivalent. This is very important because these hoses are made of a special material designed to withstand high temperatures.

Check the hose routing. Any interference with the hose may cause wearing.

AIR INJECTION PUMPS

Air injection pumps provide fresh air to help in the combustion of unburned exhaust gases. It compresses the air and forces it through the air manifolds in the area of the exhaust valves. Since the injection of air results in a "richer" condition, backfiring could occur. A valve is used to prevent this. It works on a vacuum principle and blocks the air injection. This *diverter valve* also contains a check valve which prevents exhaust gases from entering and damaging the air injection pump. This is necessary since "back flow" can occur under normal conditions.

If your car has an air injection pump, you will find it towards the front of the engine. It is run by a pulley. Since a belt is involved, it should be checked for cracks, fraying or wear. If any defects are found, have the belt replaced. When replacing it, care must be taken to avoid prying on the pump housing, since distortion of the housing can result in damage to the pump.
Note: Some emissions control systems may be slightly noisy. Often, this noise will rise in pitch as the speed of the engine increases. If your car makes a great deal of noise, the drive belt can be disconnected temporarily. If the noise continues, the emission control system is probably not the cause.

EMISSION FILTERS

Injection pumps generally contain a filter. To get at the pump filter, it is necessary to remove the belt and pump pulley. Since some experience in the use of tools and some knowledge of the construction of the pump is required, it is not recommended that you replace this filter yourself. The emission filter should be checked if a test of exhaust emissions indicates an unacceptable level of pollutants, or as part of a regular maintenance procedure by an authorized mechanic as indicated in your owner's manual.

THE CARBON CANISTER

The carbon canister is an important part of the evaporation control system. Its purpose is to absorb gasoline vapor until the engine is started. Under normal circumstances, it should not need replacing for 25-50,000 miles. It is cylindrically shaped and is usually located near the fender wall, inside the front of the engine compartment. If there is an odor of gasoline before the engine is started, have the canister checked. Sometimes a clogged canister can be responsible for an engine racing, since gasoline vapor can be sucked into the carburetor. The carbon canister should be checked at every tune-up.

EXTENDING EMISSION CONTROL LIFE

Since 1972 most cars have been designed to use either low-lead or no-lead gasoline. Use of these fuels prolongs the life of spark plugs, mufflers, and emission control components. In fact, cars with a catalytic converter must use unleaded gasoline or it will be damaged. The use of low-lead or unleaded fuels also extends the service life of other components.

It is particularly important to make certain that cars with pollution systems are kept in tune. Otherwise, vehicle performance will be affected and emission "purity" will suffer.

CHAPTER 9

THE CAR BODY

Most people enjoy driving a car that not only runs well, but also looks good. Even if your car engine is maintained properly and long mechanical life is expected, full service life will not be attained if the body is not kept in good condition. There are two basic considerations in assuring a long lasting, good looking car body. Maintaining the body, and repairing any dents, scratches or imperfections that may develop.

MAINTENANCE-THE FIRST STEP

The finish of your car is not only intended to look good, it is also a defense against the wearing affects of sun and weather. Cars are usually made of steel (there are some made of fiberglass) and steel will rust when it comes in contact with air and moisture. The finish protects the steel from rain and moisture. It consists of two parts-paint and primer. The purpose of the primer is to seal the metal from the air and moisture, and to provide a special surface for the paint. It is the primer that does the most to prevent rusting. However, primers are not intended to stand up to the rigors of sun, sleet, and abrasive dust. Besides looking attractive, the paint protects the primer, and it further protects the body. Although the paint eventually wears, regular care can slow this process considerably. Owners manuals generally indicate the best way to care for the finish. However, there is a regular procedure you can follow.

How to Care for the Finish

1. Wash the car regularly with plenty of *cold* water, using a garden hose if available. Sponge off stubborn dirt or mud. If you wish, a special mild soapy solution may be used, but only use a soap (sometimes called *wash liquid*) prepared for this purpose. Detergents can scratch the finish-*never* use them. Dry the finish using a clean, soft cloth, or, preferably, a *chamois*. A chamois is a special "cloth" made from animal skins.

   Note: Never sponge a dry surface. Dust, grit, and even the sponge itself can scratch the paint.

2. Although some manufacturers contend that the finish on some of their models only needs occasional washing to retain its new appearance, most finishes will last longer and look better when they are waxed. Use a wax which is marked "safe for all finishes," or is safe for the specific finish on your car. There are several different types of waxes and cleaners available. Most major brands are excellent, but different products should be used for different purposes.

CLEANERS AND WAXES

The major products for cleaning finishes are called *rubbing compounds*. As their name implies, a certain amount of work is required in using them. Usually they are applied with a damp cloth to a small area at one time, rubbing in a circular or back and forth motion. The cleaner is removed by wiping with a clean cloth. There are three types of cleaners:

1. Coarse cleaners. Coarse cleaners should be used on badly weathered finishes, usually as a first step in refinishing the car.
2. Fine cleaners. Fine cleaners should be used to remove minor scratches from the paint or to remove tar, bugs, or other deposits.
3. Medium cleaners. This variety is a cross between fine and coarse compounds, and is intended for moderately weathered finishes.

For best results, the car should be waxed (or refinished) as soon as possible after compounding.

Note: Never use cleaning compounds on bumpers, chrome, or plastic trim unless the package specifically indicates it is safe to do so. The chrome plating on bumpers may be removed by them, and chrome can be scratched. Plastic trim may also be scratched or discolored.

Once the car has been washed and, if desired, compounded, the next step is to wax it. There are various types of waxes available. Choose the one that best meets your needs.

1. Paste waxes without cleaners. These waxes generally give the most protection to a car and tend to last longer than other types of waxes. However, they are also usually the most difficult to use, since they generally require a great deal of rubbing and buffing. For best results, the wax should be applied to a clean surface. If you use a cleaning compound, paste wax should be used immediately afterward.

   Paste waxes are generally applied to a small area at a time, using a soft, clean, damp cloth in a circular motion. Wipe the section with a different soft, dry cloth and then do another portion. When you complete the whole car, rubbing it vigorously with a clean, dry cloth (the process is called *buffing*), a brilliant shine will be evident.
2. Pre-softened paste waxes without cleaner. This product is similar to the traditional paste wax, except it is easier to apply. However, it probably will not last quite as long as regular paste wax and may be more expensive. This wax can also be used following compounding.
3. Paste wax with cleaner. This type of wax is usually pre-softened paste wax, which contains special fine cleaning compounds. They are generally fairly easy to use and do not re-

quire considerable "elbow grease." They usually do a good job in removing tar, bugs, sap and other deposits. Although application techniques may differ slightly (follow the directions on the can), they are usually applied with a clean, damp cloth using a circular motion. Sometimes an applicator pad comes with the wax. If so, use it instead. After applying it to a small section, allow the wax to dry to a haze and then wipe using a new cloth. Since cleaner is already included in the wax, it is not necessary to compound the car before using it, thus saving one step (and considerable time). This wax is really intended for the individual who waxes his car several times a year, but not more often then about once a month. Compounding a car too frequently promotes paint wear.

4. Liquid wax without cleaner. This is an extremely easy wax to use and an entire car can usually be done in a short period of time. However, liquid waxes generally do not last as long as paste waxes. They really should be used to "freshen the shine" between waxings, and to provide additional paint protection. However, as with any wax, never use it on a car that has not been washed.
5. Bumper wax. As the name implies, it is a wax specially formulated to protect bumpers. This is not as easy as simply protecting paint, because bumpers may take considerable abuse, especially in areas where curbside parallel parking is customary. The wax applied to bumpers must be capable of withstanding this abuse, and at the same time it should not remove the thin chrome plating, which makes the bumper look attractive.
6. Chrome polish. Chrome and metal trim can be made very shiny by the application of chrome polish. This is usually a specially formulated liquid cleaner/polish that is extremely easy to apply. Since it is meant for chrome and metal, avoid spilling any on the paint. Follow the directions on the can.
7. Vinyl cleaner. Unless otherwise indicated on the package, cleaners and waxes are not meant to be used on vinyl tops. Use special cleaners that are intended for this job. They are very easy to use.
8. Spray wax. This type of wax is sprayed on the car with a garden hose. This wax should be used between regular waxings to lengthen the shine and provide additional protection. Since it can be used as the car is washed, it is a fast way to get a shine and wax protection.

COMMERCIAL CAR WASHES

The best way to wash and wax your car is by hand. Only you can provide the care your car deserves. However, there are times when this is not possible. For example, in cold weather or in urban areas where personal car washing is not practical, commercial car washes can be used. They are relatively inexpensive and usually have spray waxing facilities. However, scrubbing brushes in automated facilities can scratch the finish if they are not maintained properly by the management. Also, the management usually does not take any responsibility for damage to radio antennas, trim or finish.

TOUCHING UP THE PAINT

Despite careful attention, the paint may chip or be scratched. Minor blemishes can be repaired without taking the car to a body shop. Usually, all that is required is some fine sandpaper and a small jar of touch-up paint. However, it is important to use paint that exactly matches the color of the car. The manufacturer's code generally appears on a tag on the dash, door frame, or elsewhere on the body. If in doubt, check with a dealer or the store where you buy the paint.

How to Touch Up Minor Paint Scratches

Tools required

Fine sandpaper.
Fine rubbing compound.

Procedure

1. If the scratch is light and superficial, it can generally be removed by rubbing the area lightly with a *small* amount of fine rubbing compound applied with a damp cloth. After compounding, wash the area with plain cold water and then wax it.
2. For chips and deep scratches, make sure the area is free of dirt, grease, and wax. Wash the area several times if necessary. Allot sufficient time for the area to become *thoroughly* dry.
2a. Very lightly and carefully sand the scratch or chip. Wipe the area with a clean rag to remove any dust from the sanding.
2b. Make sure the paint in the touch up jar is mixed thoroughly so that the color is uniform throughout.
2c. Apply the paint *sparingly* to the chip or scratch, using the brush that comes with the paint. If for some reason the brush is not available, use a fine, soft brush. If the imperfection is not completely covered, wait a few minutes and apply some more paint. Repeat this step until the scratch or chip is completely covered and the paint is as thick in the damaged area as it is in the surrounding region. Never apply thick quantities of paint. There is a tendency for large quantities to run, bubble, or dry improperly.
2d. Allow the paint to dry overnight and then apply wax.

Using a touch up paint with a built in brush is fine for repairing minor scratches, but covering large areas with such an applicator can be extremely tedious, and the results would not be as good as desired. A different technique is used to cover large areas. This method uses paint in spray cans. This procedure can only be used in those areas which allow the sale of spray products.

How to Touch Up Large Painted Areas

1. Make sure the area to which the paint is to be applied is clean and free of wax and grease. Wash it several times if necessary, and be certain the area is thoroughly dry before applying paint.
2. Roughen the area slightly by lightly sanding with fine sandpaper. Wipe the region with a clean cloth to remove any sanding dust.
3. Cover adjacent areas with newspaper and tape. This process is called *masking* and protects these regions from accidentally being sprayed with paint.
4. Shake the can thoroughly to be sure the paint is well mixed and uniform throughout.
5. Spray a piece of paper with the can about 15 inches from the paper. This will give you a "feel" for spray painting and help in keeping you from applying the paint unevenly.
6. Hold the can about 15 inches from the surface to be sprayed and move the can back and forth pressing the valve. Avoid spraying too much paint in any one area as the paint may run. Apply several light coats, allowing the paint to dry between coats.
   Since the color of paint may change with time, it is sometimes very difficult to exactly

match the color of the portion of the panel being sprayed with that of the surrounding area. Trial spraying on a piece of paper gives a good indication of the final color (but it is probably not exact) and enables an easy comparison with the surrounding paint. Be sure to shake the can until as exact a match as possible is obtained. If difficulties are encountered in obtaining a suitable match, better results may be achieved by spraying an entire panel, rather than just a small part.

INSPECTING FOR RUST

Despite careful attention to the paint and trim, moisture may still combine with the steel to form rust. This is due to condensation, imperfections in the paint, weakening of the finish due to the corrosive nature of road salt, and other factors. It is extremely important to counteract the affects of rust as soon as possible. This can prevent a minor situation from becoming an expensive body repair. It is important to occasionally inspect the body for rust and to eliminate it as soon as possible.

How to Inspect for Rust

1. Examine the paint for dark brown or red spots. Unless this is the proper color of the vehicle, rust may be forming underneath the finish. Similarly, pitting paint is an indication of the formation of rust. Minor pitting can be slowed by compounding and then waxing.
2. Using a flashlight, check underneath body, side chrome and molding. Because of the confined space between molding and the body itself, there is a tendency for moisture and corrosive agents, such as road salts to accumulate. Often, people who wash their cars using buckets of water rather than garden hoses neglect to clean these areas thoroughly. If any rust is detected beneath the trim, touch up the paint as soon as possible. If it is not tended to, the rust will get worse, making it necessary to remove the trim to affect repairs. Those without experience in this area often find it difficult to replace the trim after it has been removed.
3. Examine the fender wells (the area of the body surrounding the tires). Mud, road salt,

sand, pebbles and other objects are often thrown against these areas by the rotating tires. This continuing assault can cause the eventual wearing of the protective coatings in these areas. If not checked, rusting soon follows. It is sometimes difficult to detect the presence of rust in these areas until it has become severe. This is due to the dirt and mud that accumulates and masks the damage. Wash these regions thoroughly with a garden hose. After allowing the areas to dry, inspect them with a flashlight. (*Caution:* When working near the wheels or underneath the car, be certain that the vehicle will not roll. If necessary, block the wheels.) If any rust is detected, sand it away or gently use a stiff brush. Spray the area with undercoating, a thick paint-like product available in spray cans. Undercoating is sold in areas where sales of spray products is permitted. Avoid getting any undercoating on the exterior paint or trim. (*Note:* To avoid the possibility of accidentally getting spray in your eyes, wear safety goggles when you use any automotive spray product.)

4. After making sure that the car can't roll, or the next time the car is on an hydraulic lift, examine the underside of the car. Although most cars have undercoating (either at the factory or as an option), sometimes this protection is not applied carefully to the entire underside of the body, or it wears with time. Either sand rusted areas, or use a stiff brush to remove rust from the body or frame. Wipe the affected areas with a cloth and then spray undercoating over them (see previous note). Be sure to spray only the underside of the body or frame and not any cables or components on the underside of the car, since spraying a cable could cause it to stick, and applying paint or undercoating to the muffler or exhaust pipes can result in a terrible odor as high exhaust heat burns it away.
Note: Vapors from spray paints can be harmful . Always use spray products in well ventillated areas.
5. Check the area around the windshield and back window. Water often accumulates in the trim that generally surrounds the glass, particularly on slant-back body styles. If any rust is present, sand it away and touch up the paint as soon as possible. Severe rusting in these areas may result in an expensive body repair.

REMOVING RUST

If you have been neglecting the car body and it is beginning to show large areas of rusting, restoration is still possible. However, once the body has started rusting from within, little hope exists. Thus, it is important to attack rust spots immediately.

Minor rust areas can be removed by sanding and touching up the paint. Use a stiff brush on badly rusted areas that are still solid. Follow up by sanding and then repairing the paint. To assist in removing rust from large areas, or difficult to reach places, there is a wide variety of rust removing products on the market. Some of these, such as jellies, are designed to be brushed on. After they are applied, for the specified time indicated on the package, they are then thoroughly washed off the affected areas taking the rust with them.

Other products are intended for use on badly corroded areas. One class of products are various paints that are specially formulated to bond with rust. These slow or stop additional rust formation. However, it is hard to find colors that will exactly match your car, and areas of severe corrosion may still be visible after application.

UNDERCOATING PREVENTS RUSTING

Although most people think of the painted areas when body rusting is mentioned, the underside of the vehicle is also subject to corrosion. It is splashed by puddles and mud, and pebbles are often thrown against it. To protect the under portion of the vehicle, most cars have an undercoating. This is a special paint-like substance that is sprayed on the undercarriage. If your car has never been undercoated or if it is showing signs of minor rusting, the car should be undercoated. It is not difficult to do and does not take very long. Usually, it can be done by using spray cans, which are available in those areas where the use of spray products is permitted.

It is applied in a manner similar to spray paint. Use a garden hose to remove dirt from the undercarriage. After allowing sufficient time for the car to *thoroughly* dry, follow the procedure mentioned in step 4 of "How to Inspect for Rust" and carefully spray the underside of the car.

Undercoating the car has an additional benefit besides rust prevention—it helps to deaden sound so the vehicle rides quietly.

REPAIRING DENTS

Accidents often result producing bends or tearing in the sheet metal. Major bending generally requires the use of specialized equipment and experience in body work to restore the car. In some circumstances, removing the damaged section and welding a replacement panel into position is more economical. However, unless you are familiar with welding techniques and have the necessary facilities, have the work done by a reputable body shop. If the damage is severe, be sure to get estimates for the cost of necessary repairs and a list of what the cost includes. By obtaining estimates and dealing only with reliable shops, you could be minimizing the cost of the repair. When getting estimates, find out if there is a charge for this service. If there is a charge for the estimate, it can often be applied to the cost of repairs.

Although major repairs should be made by experts using specialized facilities, many dents and bangs can be fixed by anyone with patience. Often, a little skill in sanding and soldering, or using a putty knife, is required. There are two common methods for filling dents and hand holes in the body: soldering and "plastic" filling.

How to Fill Dents and Holes Using Soldering Techniques

1. Make sure the area is clean of rust, dirt, wax, and grease.
2. Roughen the area by sanding with a coarse sandpaper. If the area to be repaired is large, a power sander will produce better results.
3. Use a torch to heat the cleaned surface slightly.
4. Apply flux.
5. To tin the area, hold a bar of solder against it, and use the torch to melt the solder.
6. Spread the solder by using a paddle. The solder should be kept soft, but not liquid.
7. Overfill the area.
8. Sand with an abrasive paper, such as a number 24 open coat paper, in order to even the surface.
9. Remove some of the paint around the area with a number 24 paper.
10. Smoothe the entire area, using a fine sandpaper.

11. Apply a special paint called *primer* (see steps 2 through 6 of "How to Touch Up Large Painted Areas"). If additional protection is desired, apply a second coat of primer after allowing sufficient time for the first coat to dry thoroughly.
12. Following steps 2 through 6 of "How to Touch up Large Painted Areas," apply fresh paint. Be sure to let the paint dry thoroughly, before applying additional coats.

Although soldering works well in filling large areas, it does require some experience in soldering techniques in order for best results to be obtained. In the last several years, the use of "plastic" and fiberglass fillers has become popular. They are easier to use than soldering large areas and do not require the use of specialized tools, such as torches. All that is needed is an applicator, such as a putty knife.

How to Fill Dents and Holes Using Plastic Fillers

Tools required

Putty knife.
Fine and medium sandpaper.

Procedure

1. Clean the area so that it is free of rust, dirt, grease, and wax.
2. Sand the area using the medium sandpaper.
3. If the damaged area has a hole, it is necessary to place a backing on it. A piece of fiberglass screen is generally used for this purpose, and is available at most well-stocked auto supply departments or hardware stores.
3a. Plastic fillers generally come in two tubes or containers. Mix part of the contents of the two containers, according to the directions on the package, using only enough to hold the screen backing in position. Once the contents have been mixed, any mixture that is unused is wasted. It can not be saved. Be sure the desired amount from the two containers is mixed thoroughly to ensure proper hardening. Use a putty knife to apply the mixed substance to the edges of the screen, and the area being repaired, to hold the screen backing in position. Let the mixture holding the screen dry for several hours before continuing with step 4.
4. Mix a portion of the two containers according to the directions on the package. Use a putty knife to apply a little at a time. If the dent is deep or a hole is present, fill in the area in layers, allowing several hours between each application. The area should be filled until it is a little higher than the surrounding region.
5. After letting the filled portion dry for several hours, sand the repaired region until it is flush with the surrounding area.
6. Follow steps 2 through 6 of "How to Touch Up Large Painted Areas" to apply fresh paint.

WEATHERED FINISHES

As a car gets older, rain, moisture from condensation, humidity, sunlight and heat, and abrasive particles slowly wear away the paint. Usually, this happens unevenly. When it does occur, the results can generally be seen as dull streaks or flat, wavy patterns in the finish. This dull pattern is often called *weathering*, and the dull spots on the paint are referred to as *dead pigment*. Cars that are waxed regularly (see "Cleaners and Waxes") do not show weathering as readily as cars which are left unprotected. Thus, waxing the vehicle not only makes it look better, it protects it as well. However, if the finish has become weathered, it can often be restored by applying rubbing compound.

If the finish has been neglected for quite a while (several years), much of the paint may be dull and weathered with numerous scratches. For severe weathering, course rubbing compound is recommended (see "Cleaners and Waxes"). It is excellent for removing dead pigment and for "evening out" the finish, that is, making it look uniform. However, it may be too severe for cars with large areas of good paint. If compounding does not signficantly help, it may be necessary to refinish the car (see "How to Touch Up Large Painted Areas"). For best results and increased protection, wax the car with a good quality paste wax as soon as possible after compounding. Then buff the finish using a very soft, clean cloth. Repeating the waxing and buffing process several times will result in a more lustrous shine and compensate, in part, for the loss of paint pigment. Once the weathering has been fixed, it is important to keep the finish protected with wax to prevent or slow its reccurrence.

If the car is several years old but is showing noticeable signs of weathering, use either fine rubbing compound or medium compound, depending on the severity of the weathering. If the paint is generally good, but there are several areas where it is noticeably worn, dull, and scratched, use the medium compound. If the paint is just beginning to wear or has minor scratches, use fine rubbing compound. As with the use of coarse compounds, immediate waxing with a quality paste wax is recommended, and buffing the wax results in a better shine. Repeating the waxing and buffing several times gives increased protection and a better shine.

It is worthwhile repeating a caution mentioned in ''Cleaners and Waxes.'' Never use cleaning compounds on bumpers, chrome, or any plastic trim unless the package specifically says it is safe to do so. The cleaning compounds may remove the thin chrome plating on the bumpers, and can damage chrome trim and scratch or discolor plastic.

ELIMINATING RATTLES

The development of rattles is an annoying nuisance to car owners. They are often difficult to locate, and make you feel as if the vehicle is ''falling apart.'' Actually, most rattles are caused by nothing more than a loose bolt or screw. Bolts and screws in the doors, hood, and deck lid should be checked and tightened occasionally. Sometimes foreign objects such as nuts, bolts, small sections of body deadener, or even pebbles, or small twigs find their way into door wells, pillars, and quarter panels. To see if any objects have gotten into the door wells, simply strike the underside of the door carefully with a rubber mallet. Loose items will usually vibrate or move when the door is hit.

Weatherstripping and antisqueak material that have moved out of position are another prime source of squeaks and rattles. If necessary, apply adhesive or a suitable cement and install this material in its proper position.

A small pebble that has worked its way into a wheel cover can sound as if the whole car is rattling or falling apart. Before taking any drastic steps, remove and check each wheelcover. Check the metal underpanels behind each wheel well. Sometimes small pebbles thrown by the wheels lodge in areas where the metal bends. Although they generally do no damage and soon fall off the vehicle, a rattling sound is heard as they vibrate as the car is driven.

Check the bolts holding add-on trim, such as bumper guards, in place. Occasionally they will come loose and vibrate. Be sure to examine the license plates. Sometimes they vibrate and the noise is transmitted by the car body to the interior.

Examine for loose screws in the passenger compartment. For example, a loose assembly in the glove compartment can cause the glove compartment door to vibrate. Check small screws on the dash or holding interior trim in place, to see if they are tight and that the trim is secure. A check of door handles, push locks and window crank assemblies might prove helpful in solving the problem. Even a loose knob on a radio can cause an annoying vibration.

Sometimes an object in the car that is not part of the vehicle itself can cause the problem. For example, keys placed in the glove compartment or loose change normally kept in the passenger area (perhaps to pay tolls) may rattle. Their presence is rarely considered as a potential source of noise. Hence, they are often overlooked as a source of rattles.

One factor that makes locating the exact source of a rattle very difficult is that the sound can be transmitted by the body, so that it appears to be coming from a different direction. Considerable patience is often necessary in tracing the source of the noise. If tightening of nuts and bolts does not cure the problem, the difficulty may be due to misalignment of the doors, hood, or deck lid. If this is the situation, it is necessary to have them realigned in order to eliminate the rattles.

CHAPTER 10

THE CAR INTERIOR

Most people like to travel in a car that not only runs well and looks good on the outside, but is clean, comfortable, and quiet on the inside. By taking care of the interior of the car you also help it to retain more of its new car value. There are several easy things that can be done to keep the interior looking new longer.

Just as with the exterior of the car, regular cleaning of the interior is necessary for maintaining the car's attractiveness. A clean interior not only is more attractive than a dirty one, it is actually safer; if the interior is untidy with loose objects not stored properly, a dangerous situation exists in the event of a sudden stop or accident. Innocent looking objects such as pencils can become deadly missiles in unexpected situations. Thus, the first step in maintaining the interior is to be sure that all non-essential items are stored properly. For example, large objects such as packages should be stored in the trunk and small items such as pencils or map markers should be kept in the glove compartment or map pockets. Putting small items in their proper places also helps to make the car interior look better longer as well. This is because sharp objects can tear upholstery and markers can stain both upholstery and carpeting. Other articles, such as food and beverages, can leave ugly stains if they accidentally leak on the carpet or seats; try to place them in the trunk or, if you must carry them inside the passenger compartment, place them on the floor mats in such a way that bags and containers will not move or tilt as a result of the car's motion.

GENERAL CARE OF THE INTERIOR

Dust and dirt on the carpets, seats, and interior trim should be removed by frequent vacuuming and, if necessary, the use of a wisk broom or soft brush. Clean vinyl or leather trim by wiping with a damp cloth. Many spots and stains can be removed by the proper use of trim cleaners. However, determine as accurately as possible the type and age of the spot or stain before attempting to remove it. Some substances, such as lipsticks, certain types of ink, grease, mustard and others, are often extremely difficult to remove; sometimes it is impossible. One problem in attempting to remove stubborn stains is that care must be taken to avoid enlarging the soiled area. Although you may want to completely restore the fabric or trim, it may be better to have a small spot or stain than to widen the soiled region by inexperience or carelessness. Fortunately, many such spots can be removed with water or a vary mild soap solution. Suggestions for removing specific types of soil are given in "Hints for Removing Stains."

Unless specifically recommended, never use volatile cleaning fluids on soft interior trim, upholstering or carpeting. Some of the items that should be avoided unless specifically mentioned include lacquer thinners or enamel reducers, acetone and nail polish removers, harsh laundry soaps, bleaches, or reducing agents. Do no use gasoline, naptha, or carbon tetrachloride for cleaning. Such chemicals may be toxic (poisonous) or flammable; they may even damage soiled areas rather than cleaning them.

CLEANING SEAT BELTS AND SHOULDER HARNESS

Seat belts and shoulder straps should always be kept clean and, except when being cleaned, should always remain dry. To clean them use a mild soap solution and lukewarm water. Never bleach or dye seat belts or shoulder harnesses. To do so may cause a severe loss of strength. It is better to have dirty or faded belts and straps than to have them fail in an emergency.

USING CLEANING FLUID

Stains containing grease, oil, or fats can often be lessened or removed by the use of cleaning fluid. The use of a tool which can be used for scraping (such as a dull knife) is helpful. However, care must be taken to avoid the formation of a cleaning ring.

How to Clean Fabrics With Cleaning Fluid

Tools required
Tool for scraping.
Cheese cloth or absorbent towel.

Procedure
1. If possible, "test" the fabric by applying a very small amount of cleaning fluid to a region that doesn't show, and then wipe the area vigorously with a piece of cheese cloth or absorbent towel. If a ring forms, it might be better to leave the soiled section alone, rather than attempting to remove the spot or stain and leaving a visible ring.
2. Use a clean scraper or dull knife to remove any excess stain. Be careful not to damage the material by using too much pressure or scraping too vigorously.
3. Apply a very small quantity of cleaning fluid to a section of cheese cloth or towel.

4. Start with the outside of the stain and clean towards the center. Frequently rotate the cleaning cloth to a fresh section.
5. After applying cleaning fluid to the fabric and removing the stain, be sure to wipe the area vigorously *immediately* with a section of fresh cheese cloth or absorbent towel. This will dry the area and help prevent a ring from forming.
6. If a ring should form, the entire area should be cleaned immediately. Detergent foam cleaners are often good for removing minor rings; however, consult with package directions to determine if its use is recommended for your particular type of fabric.

CLEANING GENERAL SOILAGE

Although cleaning fluids often give good results in removing grease, oil, or fat stains, general stains and dirt can frequently be "lifted" with the use of a detergent foam cleaner. They can also be used to clean areas where a minor ring has formed as the result of using cleaning fluid.

How to Clean Fabrics With Detergent Foam Cleaners

Tools required
Vacuum cleaner.
Clean sponge or soft bristle brush.
Dry towels.

Procedure
Note: When using detergent foam cleaners always clean a full panel or complete section of trim.
1. Vacuum the area to remove loose dirt.
2. Mask (cover) adjacent areas along weld or stich lines.
3. Carefully follow the mixing directions on the package.
4. Apply the cleaner with a clean sponge or soft bristle brush. Be sure to avoid wetting the fabric excessively.
5. If a brush is being used as an applicator, do not rub the area too vigorously and avoid using too much pressure. Use care to avoid wearing the fabric.
6. Use a *slightly* damp cloth or towel to wipe the area clean, turning or replacing the cloth frequently.
7. Use additional dry towels or cloths to dry the

fabric; these should be applied immediately after the fabric is cleaned.

8. Use a fresh, dry absorbent towel or cloth to rewipe the fabric. This helps to remove any dried residue and restores the appearance of the trim.

In addition to cleaning fluids and detergent foam cleaners there is also available a wide assortment of easy-to-use upholstery cleaners. These are usually spray foams and, although they can be used on some types of stains, they are really intended to clean stubborn dirt and grime from the seats and fabric. Many of these products can also be used to help remove soil from interior carpeting; check the package.

TAKING CARE OF CARPETS

Just as taking care of the upholstery can preserve the attractiveness of the seats and fabric trim, occasionally cleaning the carpets and mats maintains or improves the appearance of the entire passenger compartment. Carpeting should be vacuumed regularly. Not only will this make the carpets look better, but is also protects them; grit and other forms of dirt can cause matting and damage to the fiber used in some interior carpets. Stained carpets can ruin the appearance of an otherwise attractive interior.

There are many carpet cleaning products on the market. They are usually sprayed onto the carpet or applied with a damp sponge. The dirt is then wiped off or removed by vacumming; follow the directions on the package of the product you choose.

FLOOR MATS

Floor mats serve several purposes. Firstly, they are attractive. Since there is no installation involved in their use and are relatively inexpensive, they can be changed easily when worn or faded; it is easy to "redecorate" a car interior by changing the color or style of the mats, thus giving the passenger compartment a slightly different appearance. (Try placing a matching carpet section on the rear shelf or hatchback floor; this can "spruce up" the interior of an older car and can help make a new car interior more attractive.)

Car mats protect carpets from mud or snow, rain water, slush, and other forms of moisture

and dirt brought into the car on the shoes of its passengers and driver. It is much easier to remove dirt from the mats than it is to clean the carpets (see "How to Clean Car Mats").

If the carpeting in your car is worn, badly faded, or deeply stained, attractive floor mats can cover these areas. If you want the beauty of your carpeting to be visible, but wish to protect one particular area, for example, the region near the brake and accelerator controls, or wish to cover only a localized stain, small mats are readily available. For covering large areas, full mats can be used.

Mats can actually be a safety factor. Since they can be cleaned easily, it is a good idea to get into the habit of wiping wet shoes on them before placing them on the control pedals. This reduces the chances of accidentally having your feet slip off the pedals.

If your car does not have carpets, floor mats make the interior more attractive and easier to clean. Since quality floor mats are usually made of heavy rubber, they can help to reduce road noises and unwanted sound. This is especially useful if the car does not have interior carpeting.

HINT: If you have mats that may have worn with time or have become faded and no longer look attractive, or if you have decided to "redecorate" and use new mats, do not throw out the old ones. Place the old mats in the trunk (or on the hatchback floor for that style vehicle) to protect that area from accidental spills from oil cans, anti-freeze containers or other packages that are often stored in that area. In addition, full mats will tend to make the car quieter by reducing road noises.

STAIN REMOVAL

Despite occasional cleaning and regular care of the interior of the car, spills and other accidents can occur which result in stains or deep soil. Some suggestions for the removal of specific types of soil are given here. However, it is a good idea to check with your owner's manual and follow the specific recommendation of the manufacturer of your car.

Hints for Removing Stains

Blood—Wipe the area with a clean, damp cloth. The water should be cold. Do not use soap.
Shoe polish—Paste or wax types of shoe polish can generally be removed by a light application of

cleaning fluid. However, whenever cleaning fluid is used there is the possibility of a ring being formed. Dry the area immediately using a clean, absorbant cloth or towel and rubbing vigorously. If a ring does form, immediately using a detergent foam cleaner (see "How to Clean Fabrics With Detergent Foam Cleaners") may help to remove it.

Candy—If the candy deposit has chocolate, use a cloth that has been soaked with lukewarm water. For other types of candy deposits, use a cloth that has been dampened with very hot water. Use absorbant towels or cloths to dry the area. If additional effort is necessary, a very light application of cleaning fluid (see *"How To Clean Fabrics With Cleaning Fluid"*) may help; be careful of ring formation.

Chewing gum—A good trick is to harden the gum with an ice cube. Then scrape the gum with a dull knife. Moisten any residue with cleaning fluid and repeat the scraping.

Foods and beverages—Certain food stains such as fruit, wines and liquors and milk **can be removed** by using a cloth soaked in cold water. **Do** not use soap; it might set the stain. If it is still necessary, a light application of cleaning fluid may help.

Catsup—Use a clean cloth that has been soaked in cool water. Rub the area several times. If additional effort is required, refer to the section on detergent foam cleaners.

Grease and oil—Grease, oil, butter or margarine, and crayons can be removed as described in the section on cleaning fabrics with cleaning fluid.

Tar—Any excess tar should be removed with a dull knife or scraper. Apply cleaning fluid to moisten the material; then scrape the area again. Using additional cleaner, rub the area lightly. Be careful that a ring does not form; if one does form, immediately, apply a detergent foam cleaner as described in "How to Clean Fabrics With Detergent Foam Cleaners."

Urine—Use a mild soap to create soap suds in a bucket containing lukewarm water. Apply the suds with a clean cloth. Wipe several times with a cloth soaked in clean, cold water. Mix 1 part household ammonia water with 5 parts regular water. Soak a clean cloth in this solution and then apply it to the affected area for 1 minute. Use another clean cloth that has been soaked with cold water to rinse the area.

Vomit—Wipe the area with a cloth that has been made very damp with cold water. Then use another cloth that has been placed in a solution of lukewarm water and mild soap suds to lightly wash the area. Mix one teaspoon of baking soda

to one cup of water which is at room temperature. Apply this mixture with a fresh cloth, and then lightly rub the region with a cloth that has been placed in cold water. If necessary, further cleaning can be made by the application of a very small amount of cleaning fluid.

RESTORING WORN INTERIORS

As a car ages, the interior usually wears despite regular attention. In getting in and out of the car people slide across seats, wearing the fabric. Packages may spill, creating stains that may not have been removed completely. Restive children pull and hide knobs and trim. Accidental pokes with umbrellas leave small holes in upholstery and headliners. Even if the car interior has no people-induced wear, the sun tends to fade fabric, and vinyl dashes, while heat tends to make vinyl dry and brittle with cracks. These and other factors can leave the passenger compartment with an aged appearance. However, there are certain procedures that can be followed to make the interior look more attractive.

How to Make a Worn Interior Look Attractive

Seats—If the seats are not badly worn, a thorough cleaning may be all that is necessary. However, if they are badly worn it is probably best to cover them. Place cloth or plastic tape over any cuts that might be present. If you wish, place some foam padding over the seat cushion; this will give a more comfortable and quieter ride. Cover the seats with the proper style seat cover for your car; there is a vast selection available, ranging from relatively inexpensive to costly—comparison shop in different stores. Packaged seat covers are usually easy to install and do not require special tools. Better fitting and fancier covers are available at special stores which also custom install them; these are generally considerably more expensive but usually have a much better appearance and last longer.

Dash—If your car is older, it may not have a padded dash; use a damp sponge to clean it, rubbing badly soiled areas. Wax bright painted areas with a paste wax with a cleaner in it. However, do not wax "chrome" trim on the dash or door panels; usually these are actually finished plastic and the wax should not be used on them.

Wash padded dashes with a cloth that has been dampened with cold water, rubbing badly soiled areas if necessary. If the dash has deep soil or grime, a spray foam product can be used if the label indicates that it is safe to do so.

Use window cleaner on the glass areas of the instrument panel, but be careful to avoid getting any on the padding or painted areas.

Steering column—Use a damp sponge to clean painted and plastic areas of the steering column, rubbing vigorously to remove accumulated grime. Padded areas can be cleaned by rubbing with a damp sponge and then using a spray foam cleaner.

Headliners—Clean headliners using a damp sponge. If the fabric is badly soiled, use a mild soap suds solution and rub. Rinse the material using a cloth that has been soaked in cold water.

Some newer model cars have "solid" headliners rather than material ones. Using a mild soap suds solution and a cleaning sponge generally removes most dirt; follow by rinsing with a cloth soaked in cold water and dry the headliner with an absorbent towel.

Carpeting—Clean the carpeting using a spray foam cleaner that is widely available in most automotive departments or specialty stores. If the color is badly faded, there are some color sprays that may be used to freshen or change the color. Choose a product that is recommended for the type of carpet you have. Floor mats may be used either to enhance the carpeting or to cover badly worn areas.

Floor mats—Use floor mats to cover badly worn carpets. If you already have them, clean them outside the car as follows:

Vinyl—Immerse the mats in a sink or wash tub filled with cold water and soap suds. Let them soak for several minutes and then rub with a cloth to loosen packed dirt. Scrape off tar or chewing gum with a dull knife or scraper. Rinse the mats with cold water.

Rubber—Follow the same procedure as for vinyl mats to wash rubber mats. However, lightly rubbing with a steel wool pad or kitchen scouring pad helps to remove stubborn or ground-in dirt. Rinse the mats with cold water.

Rear shelves— Usually, rear shelves become faded or start peeling as they age. Usually, the best results are obtained by covering them with fabric, rugs, or towels. Unless fastened down, however, fabric or towels tend to blow when the windows are open; hold them in place with carpet tape or glue. Never use heavy objects to keep them in place; besides obstructing your view through the rear window (which may be illegal in your state), they can be very dangerous in the event you are involved in an accident.

CHAPTER 11

AUTOMOBILE INSURANCE

Not only is automobile insurance required in most areas, it is actually vital protection if you are involved in an accident. However, since mechanical and body repair expenses have risen and the costs of hospitalization and medical treatment has increased sharply in recent years, automobile insurance rates have also climbed, even though you may not have submitted claims. Yet, most of us do not know much about this subject other than what advertisements and insurance salesmen tell us. Knowing a few basic facts can save you considerable money on this insurance.

COMPETITIVE SHOPPING

Contrary to a widespread belief, insurance costs are not the same for comparable coverage with different companies. It is important to shop around and compare prices before purchasing any automotive insurance plan. Check the prices of several companies—compare at least four to six. Different companies have various plans and options that could amount to a difference of quite a few dollars for the particular coverage you need.

TYPES OF COVERAGE

Part of being able to shop competitively consists of knowing exactly what coverage is best for you. You may not need certain types of coverage, or you might require additional protection in another area.

Liability Insurance

This type of coverage is absolutely essential. Without it, an accident could result in the loss of your home, savings, or future earnings. The bodily injury and property damage liability provisions pay part of the costs you legally become responsible for when someone else is injured in an accident, or his property is damaged. But be careful! Your policy probably will limit the amount the insurance company will pay; you are responsible for the remainder. How great this maximum liability is determined by how much you are willing to pay for increased protection. The legal minimum in many states is $5,000 for property damage, and $20,000 for injuries with at most $10,000 going to any individual. Since you are liable for any amounts over the limits of your policy, get as much liability insurance as you can afford—do not try to save on this portion of your insurance.

For a few dollars more, protection against property damage can be increased to up to $25,000! That's five times the protection. For example, if you pay about $43 for the $5,000 property protection, from $3 to $5 will buy $25,000 worth of protection. Similarly, additional protection for bodily injury claims can be obtained for relatively small increases in the amount you pay for the additional coverage. This increase will be slightly higher than that for increased property damage protection.

Collision Insurance

It is difficult to quote figures here for what you can expect to pay for protecting you vehicle against mechanical repairs and body work required as the result of an accident. There is a wide variance in the rates, depending on your accident record and the area in which you live. If you must save money on insurance, this is the place to do it, since your liability (the amount you stand to lose) is limited by the cost of the car and any charges involved in disposing of it if necessary. To protect themselves against the cost of numerous small claims, insurance companies usually set a minimum damage amount over which they will pay. This amount is called a *deductible* and what it really means is that you must pay this amount in the event of damage to your vehicle; the insurance company pays anything over this amount up to the limit specified in your policy, usually the value of your car.

You can save a considerable amount of money by increasing the deductible amount. For example, if you pay about $100 for the collision insurance provision of your policy and are responsible for any damage up to $50 (that is, $50 deductible), you can probably save $16 to $18 by increasing the deductible to $100; this means that you are responsible for paying the first $100 dollars worth of damage to the car rather than just $50, but you pay about $82 to $84 rather than $100 for this reduced protection.

Since the insurance company is generally responsible only for the value of the car, it may not pay to have collision insurance on an older vehicle. However, with the increases in new car prices, used car prices have also risen; thus it probably pays to protect your car for a longer period than previously. There is no clear cut cutoff point for this type of coverage, but most "ordinary" cars lose enough value that it probably does not pay to carry this provision if the car is over 5 years old. Since the value of certain "prestige" cars reduces more slowly with age, it may pay to continue this coverage for a longer period. Other factors to consider is car usage and its condition. It probably does not pay to continue coverage on a car that has been abused and is about ready for "recycling."

Medical Payments

The purpose of this provision is to provide immediate cash in case of an injury to you or any of your passengers in the event of an accident. Often, people carry minimum protection because they don't understand its advantages or because they were urged to do so by their insurance agent. However, it is generally one of the most valuable forms of insurance protection while at the same time is also inexpensive. Since only a small increase in the premium can result in a big increase in protection, it is worthwhile increasing your coverage if you can afford to and are not carrying adequate protection. For example, if you are covered for $1,000 and are paying $17 to $20 for this protection, an additional sum of about $3 to $5 can bring your coverage up to $5,000 per person.

Comprehensive Insurance

This is a combined policy; that is, it covers such things as fire, theft, vandalism and other items which depend on the specific policy. Usually this type of coverage is expensive, but, in spite of its cost it may still be worthwhile. For example, if there have been a number of car thefts in the area where the car is usually parked, it probably pays to have this insurance rather than paying for a new car if your vehicle is selected.

Uninsured Motorist

As its name implies, this type of insurance protects you from an individual who has no insurance, or from an individual who damages your car and does not stay at the scene long enough to be identified. The insurance company pays all bills up to the maximums as described in your policy. This coverage is usually vey inexpensive.

SAVING ADDITIONAL MONEY ON CAR INSURANCE

There are various plans that can save you money on part or all of your automobile insurance. While some companies do advertise the availability of some of these plans, many do not. Insurance is a product; before buying it compare and ask questions.

How to Save Money on Car Insurance

Non-resident student driver plan—Suppose you have children of driving age who are students living at a school which is at least about 100 miles from your residence. You probably qualify for a discount of up to 20%. Insurance companies figure that if an individual is 100 miles from the car, he or she is not going to drive it very often.

Safe driver plan—Approximately 70% of all drivers have not had an accident or serious driving violation within the last 3 years. If everyone in your family who drives the car is in this category, you can qualify for a discount of up to 20%.

Driver education plan—A discount of up to 20% can be applied if any children of driving age who drive the family car have successfully completed a recognized driver education course.

Multiple car discount—Discounts of about 15% are available to families with two or more cars that insure them with the same company.

Compact car discount—If your car is classified by the insurance companies as a compact model, you may be eligible for a discount. Check with different companies to see if they have this reduction.

Bumper discount—Owners of cars with bumpers designed to withstand impacts of at least 5 miles per hour are eligible for special discounts. Although many insurance companies offer such a reduction, few advertise this fact.

Age graduation plan—In general, those drivers in the 16 to 24 year age bracket pay considerably more for insurance than older persons. There is generally a sharp decrese in the rate when an individual turns 25. However, some companies have a plan which offers a graduated reduction in the rates for each violation-free and non-accident year. Thus, a driver at the upper end of this age bracket (for example, 24 years old) might save a large amount of money by shopping for a company offering this plan.

Although there are many discounts available for those that shop for them, there are also some surcharges that many companies tack on the premium of certain individuals. For example, if you drive to work regularly and the distance is 10 miles or more, you can expect to pay a generally higher insurance rate than those who do not drive to work or live close to the job. If the car you insure is classified as a high performance vehicle, you may be charged an additional 25 to 30% more; some cars prior to 1970 can cost an additional 70% to insure! If you drive a car model that has a history of being attractive to car thieves or if you live in a high car theft area, you may be charged an additional sum for theft insurance or the company may refuse to give you this type of coverage.

NO-FAULT INSURANCE

When an accident occurs, it is often necessary to establish who caused the accident before much of the covered payment is awarded. Delays of several years have been experienced while court battles and delays occur. This means that part of the insurance company's expenses are for court costs and legal fees; while the legal profession benefits, you as the consumer pay for these costs through your premiums even if you never have an accident. *No-fault insurance* is designed to reduce these costs considerably and the time involved in waiting for payment by reducing or eliminating the need to establish fault for the accident.

There are two basic types of no-fault insurance—pure no-fault and partial no-fault. In the pure no-fault version, payment is made for losses and costs as a result of an accident. Suits to recover additional damages are generally not permitted. Under partial no-fault (also called modified no-fault) bringing suit is permitted once the damages have exceeded a certain amount.

CHAPTER 12

USED CARS

When new cars were relatively inexpensive, it was customary to trade in the old vehicle and start paying for the new one. Because most people did not keep a car for more than a few years, many did not concern themselves with rigorous adherence to maintenance schedules. Often, the term "used" really meant "abused."

Today, people are keeping their cars for longer periods and maintaining them better. A life expectancy of 100,000 miles or more is no longer uncommon. Thus, although used car prices are higher than before, "used" does not necessarily mean "worn." According to the U.S. Department of Transportation, it is actually cheaper to drive a car for a life span of 10 years than it is to replace it with a new car, even though an older car may have increasing maintenance costs.

Age and Condition Affect the Purchase Decision

Contrary to the widely held belief, the age of a car should not be the primary consideration when purchasing a used car. Its condition is far more important. A fairly new car that has been driven hard, abused, or neglected is a worse buy than an older one that has been maintained and possibly garaged. However, age does play an important role in the *depreciation* (that is, how much value a car loses as it is used) of a vehicle. From a financial point of view, cars that are about two years old make the best purchases. This is because the major depreciation of the car has already taken place; its trade-in value will decrease more slowly than previously.

If you are considering both a late model used car that originally had a low sticker price and an older car in the "luxury" class, the later model is probably the better buy. The reason that you are purchasing the car also plays an important part in determining how old the car should be. If the vehicle is going to be the primary one you own (that is, given the most use and relied upon more often than any others) or if it is to be the only one you own, it is a good idea to consider automobiles that are 2 to 5 years old.

Body Types

Another important factor to consider when purchasing a used car is its body style. Often, the sportiest cars are not the best ones to buy. For example, hardtops generally have higher price tags than other used cars. The elimination of body pillars and window frames adds to the appearance of the automobile, but also makes the car structurally weaker and gives the car a tendency to develop rattles as it gets older. In an attempt to make these cars safer, the Federal Government has issued regulations requiring the use of pillars on hardtops. Remember, you are paying for the looks of this type of car in addition to other factors.

If a sporty looking car is not an absolute must for you, you probably should consider sedans. Sedans have pillars, are usually boxed shaped, generally have more room than hardtops, and are less expensive than used hardtops. It is a more practical car, with greater room and body strength.

Convertibles are nice-looking cars, usually with high sticker prices when they are new. Although their used car prices are also high, they offer a considerable number of drawbacks as used cars. The plastic rear windows of these cars generally require frequent replacement, and the top itself will need to be changed occasionally; besides wearing, convertible tops are often damaged by vandals and are attractive to thieves desiring to steal items from inside the car. Because of inherent dangers in a roll-over situation, the Federal Government regulations concerning pillars for hardtops are also applicable to convertibles. These factors are the reasons the convertible body style appears to be passing from the car scene.

Station wagons should probably be considered only if considerable room for people is an absolute requirement. They are much heavier than conventional styles, and usually offer considerable air resistance when driven at highway speeds; this means that fuel economy will be lower with station wagons than with other cars. They are also noisier, especially as they get older; the floor vibrates and its large area reverberates the sound. Rattles are a common complaint by those who own older wagons. The large area inside these vehicles poses an additional problem—it makes it difficult to heat the interior in cold weather and to effectively air condition in warm months. In addition, by having the storage area in the passenger compartment, a safety problem is introduced; in the event of an accident, items can be thrown against people. Because objects which would otherwise be stored in the trunk of a car are plainly visible, station wagons are often tempting targets of thieves. If carrying large and bulky items (such as ladders or lumber or panelling) is a capability your car must have, you may do well to consider a pickup truck instead. Despite their large areas, wagons are still cars, not trucks, and can carry only about 100 pounds more than a large sedan.

The highest risk category for used cars consists of the so-called high performance vehicle. Also known as muscle cars or factory modified stocks, these cars come with special engines and drive trains. They are intended to be driven hard and fast, and most people who buy them new drive them that way. Because of stricter mechanical tolerances in the mechanical parts of these cars, repairs and maintenance intervals are usually more frequent, and the needed parts are more expensive to insure, and are often checked closely by police watching for speeders and for drivers who treat highways and local streets as if they were racing courses.

Glamour and Appearance

The appearance of the car often has a large ef-fect on the price. Glamourous paint such as "racing green" or "fire engine red," or the presence of special trim can result in a higher price. However, it also means that you may be able to save some money by buying a car which, although mechanically and physically sound, is not attractive to other buyers. For example, a car with an unusual or unappealing color might sell at a lower price than comparable models. If, in addition, the interior is plain or not properly color coordinated the price may be reduced further; use these disadvantages as bargaining points to reduce the asking price.

Some cars are considered less glamorous or less appealing than others, and therefore they sell for less. For example, cars produced by American Motors often have a lower resale value than comparable automobiles produced by their competitors. However, they appear to age as well as other American cars. Thus, you can probably get as much service life from such a car as from one made by Chevrolet or Ford, but at a lower purchase price.

Sometimes a major car manufacturer will discontinue a model. Usually, this is not because of major problems with the car but rather due to marketing considerations. A car with a design that does not appeal to the general public can usually be purchased for less money than comparable popular models. In most cases, obtaining replacements parts poses no problem since parts used on the discontinued line are generally used on other models.

How To Shop for a Used Car

There are two basic places to obtain a used car—from a dealer or a private individual. When purchasing from a dealer it is important to deal with reputable businesses. Often, the best place to go is a new car dealer. Since he has a considerable investment in his lots, cars, and service facilities he usually can't afford bad word-of-mouth publicity which could result from his being deceptive. Bad publicity could result in his losing new car sales which is his main business. Because his image is very important to this business, the new car dealer generally tries to sell only the best of customer trade-ins; other used cars are generally sold to wholesalers and to independent used car lots. Since he has a service facility, he can do any repair work or reconditioning that is necessary. New car dealers generally handle late model cars since these generally require the least reconditioning and can be sold more quickly.

Another type of dealer is the independent used car lot. Since many of them deal with the same banks as the new car dealers they are often as reputable as the new car dealer. However, the cars they sell may come from different sources. The cars sold by new car dealers generally come from trade-ins, while those from an independent lot may be purchased from wholesalers or at auctions. This means that he is more removed from the original purchaser of the car, and so their's is a greater risk to the used car buyer.

It has been estimated that nearly 10 percent of all used cars once served as rentals. Many, many others were once cabs, delivery vehicles, or police cars. Even though these cars may be late models, they often have high mileage; 100,000 miles is not uncommon. Since independent lots do handle fleet cars, it is not uncommon for them to sell this type of used vehicle. These cars are usually intermediate or standard size, generally with a plain color, and tend to have few options. Be careful if you see such a car and it has a new headliner or holes drilled under the dash or elsewhere on the body; fleet vehicles such as police cars and taxi cabs had original equipment not found on ordinary vehicles (roof lights and signs, sirens, meters and other items) and unused drilled holes or new fabric may indicate that the vehicle was once used for this purpose.

To many people, the used car business does not have a good reputation. If so, this is probably due to the image created by salesmen for independent lots which are not very reputable, and it is unfortunate that they affect the image of the entire used car business. These independents buy worn vehicles (often referred to as *sleds* or, more aptly, as *iron*), and use many gimmicks to disguise the true condition of the cars. Some of this "reconditioning" includes the use of thick oil, wire, and even wooden wedges. They generally do not work with banks; rather, they sell to people who have difficulty getting credit elsewhere, even though the dealer knows that such people may well default on their payments (that is, they won't have the money to pay the credit installments). The dealer insists upon a down payment of an amount that is the same as his investment; thus he can't lose money. He makes a profit through any payments that are made by the customer. When payments are not made, a collection agency is used. He does not even mind repossessing the car, since he can sell it again under the same conditions. The unscrupulous dealer may also offer "easy financing". What this term actually means is easy money for him when he offers financing terms. Various gimmicks can be used such as providing low interest rates but substituting hidden charges or "carrying charges" or "a small service charge just to cover the paper work". Recent laws that require disclosure of the actual rate of interest on loans have helped protect the consumer against many of these tricks.

Buying From Owners

Some individuals prefer not to deal with professional used car salesmen; they often feel that it is too much of a bother to evaluate a dealership as well as a used car, and so they would rather buy from an owner. Yet, there are often many risks involved in this type of transaction as well. While many dealerships will offer some kind of guarantee or warrantee, an individual owner who is selling his car will rarely do this; he wants to sell the automobile and forget about it. Since an owner is selling only one car, he may mislead potential buyers or lie about the car's faults in order to make the sale; unlike the reputable car dealer, he need not be concerned about his reputation or worry about repeat business.

Sometimes there is a lien against the car that an individual is trying to sell. This means that somebody else has a prior claim to the car and this lien must be paid. If you buy a car that has a lien, you also must pay it off. It is a good idea to make sure that there are no undisclosed liens; this can usually be done by checking with the appropriate state office, generally the Secretary of State.

While there are some pitfalls to purchasing a car from a private individual, there are certain advantages to this as well. Since the individual is not in the car business, he does not need to cover large overheads or make profits; as long as he owns the car he may even have various expenses to be met, such as insurance, fees or taxes, and parking or garage costs. Thus, he may be willing to sell the car at a lower price. Since the private owner generally is not an expert on car body and engine repairs and most likely does not have special tools and equipment, he is less likely to disguise faults effectively.

Some people feel intimidated by car salesmen. They feel that because he does sell cars for a living, he is experienced in all aspects of sales, including bargaining over prices, and so the salesman has an unfair advantage over the customer. Such individuals would probably feel a little more at ease negotiating with a private seller rather than a professional salesman.

Guarantees, Warranties and What They Mean

There are various types of guarantees or warranties that often come with cars purchased from dealers. Usually, these are limited in the time that protection is offered—30 days or 1000 miles, whichever happens first. Be careful of dealers who assure you that the car is under a guarantee but do not tell you the terms of the protection; it may be limited to parts installed as part of the reconditioning process. Since these parts are probably guaranteed by their manufacturers anyway, this type of guarantee is essentially meaningless.

There is another guarantee that is often used. This type, often called the partial or half guarantee, says that if repairs are necessary the dealer will do the necessary work but the buyer must pay half the cost. Keep in mind that the dealer can claim that the work cost twice as much as it actually did and you can wind up paying the full amount anyway.

Many other guarantees have disclaimers that can severely reduce their effectiveness and protection to the buyer. For example, guarantees that cover only parts are very common. Under this type of "protection" the dealer will pay for parts and you pay for labor. Since it is the labor involved in the installation of parts that costs the most money, this type of guarantee offers little.

A disreputable salesman can actually use a guarantee to protect himself rather than the buyer. For example, he realizes that the car he is selling may be dangerous to operate; operating this type of vehicle could result in an accident. To protect himself, the dealer may put in a clause that excludes consequential damages. This means that if a defect in the car causes an accident, he is not liable for the damages that result.

Salesmen will often indicate that a new car warranty is still in effect for a used car that they are trying to sell. Even if the car is fairly new and has sufficiently low mileage to qualify, only new car dealers generally have the right to transfer a warranty. Since an inexperienced or overzealous but honest salesman can make this mistake, be sure to read any warranties that are involved.

Most buyers of any product feel that they are getting some degree of protection when they are offered a guarantee with an item they are buying. While this is true to a certain extent, guarantees are really meant to limit the manufacturer's or seller's liability. Thus, in general, guarantees are really meant to protect him, not the buyer. However, while limiting the manufacturer's or seller's liability, guarantees can still offer some degree of protection to the buyer; at least items mentioned in the guarantee are covered. Without a written statement, the seller can claim that the car (or other product) was sold in an "as is" condition—that is, what he saw is what he bought.

Finally, be careful in buying a car that is "unconditionally guaranteed". Since a guarantee is a written document that indicates specific items that are covered and terms for repair or replacement, there is no such thing as an unconditional guarantee. Honest dealers and manufacturers sometimes use the term to mean that they stand behind their products and are very concerned about your being satisfied with them. The "shady" dealer will use the term to lower your guard so he can make a sale. Be sure to read and understand all guarantees and warranties that come with a car.

The Right Time to Shop

When you have decided what type of car best suits your needs and where you are going to shop for it, the next thing to consider is *when* to do the shopping. Buyng a used car at the wrong time can result in major headaches; purchasing it at the right time can save a great deal of money.

Often, buying a used car at the end of any month can result in a cash saving. Salesmen are often given sales *quotas*, that is they are told how many cars they must sell in a given month. Often, if they sell more than this assigned number, they receive a bonus. A salesman who has not met his monthly quota or is anxious to receive a bonus may be willing to give concessions in order to make the sale.

December is probably the best month to buy a used car. Dealers generally sell the greatest number of new cars during September, October and November when the latest models appear. Since they often take used cars as trade-ins, the number of these cars that they have available is generally greatest following this peak period. Since there is a larger number of cars to choose from, the price is generally lower. And there is an additional incentive to the dealer to lower his used car prices—many areas levy a tax on business inventories on hand the last day of the year, December 31. If the dealer can reduce his inventory, he can lower his taxes as well; lowering prices is probably the best way of making a used car attractive to potential customers.

The Time of Day is Important

While the time of the year or portion of the

month that a used car is purchased affects the price, it is the time of the day that is important in determining the type of car that will be obtained for the money. Shopping for a used car at night can be a mistake. Dealers will display their car to best advantage by special placing of lights or bright signs. Artificial lighting tends to soften the seriousness of defects and disguises the true appearance and color of the automobile. Defects such as poorly matched paint or touch-ups, rusting, scratches or dents, or even obvious signs of body work can often be overlooked in artificial light.

Weather Plays a Part

Buying a car in bad weather can be risky. Inclement weather makes it difficult to see many defects in the car and can even disguise the operating smoothness and condition of the engine; this is because some engines may run better in damp weather. Thus, avoid buying a used car during a rain or snow storm. If you do see a car during bad weather and feel that it could be the right one for you, arrange to see the car when the weather changes. Chances are that it won't be sold to someone else while the weather is bad, and seeing it when the weather changes might reveal conditions that could change your mind about the car.

Although it is generally a bad practice to buy a used car during poor weather, the day after a storm can be ideal. Bad weather means that customers don't feel like shopping and salesmen with quotas to meet and dealers with few opportunities for sales will be more inclined to offer better terms. The longer the bad weather lasts, the more **anxious** these individuals will be to complete a sale. This can place you in a very good bargaining position; with few other potential buyers around, he would rather make some concessions than lose a sale. This means that you can offer a lower price for the car than you might otherwise. If the dealer does not care for your offer he probably will not try to raise the price as much as he ordinarily would since he knows that you can always go somewhere else.

Inspection is Necessary

Before you buy a used car it is a good idea to have it inspected by a professional mechanic. Although there is generally a charge for his labor, this is a wise investment. Only someone who is thoroughly familiar with cars can determine the actual mechanical shape of the vehicle. Be sure

that you are the one that selects the mechanic, not the dealer. Most reputable dealers will agree to let you take the car to your mechanic, or else to allow him to inspect the car on his lot. Since you probably will not want to pay a mechanic to look at every car you see, be sure to pre-inspect the car yourself for obvious faults. In this way you can reduce the number of cars under consideration to just one or two.

How to Pre-Inspect Used Cars

Note: Wear old clothes since they may end up dirty.

Procedure

1. Inspect the paint for ripples, bumps, and uneven texture. Paint spots on chrome or metal trim or on the glass may mean that the car has been repainted or touched up. Check the color of paint on the car body exterior and compare it to an area of paint that is protected, such as inside the trunk. Although a slight degree of diffeence in an older car (due to fading) is acceptable, a marked difference is another sign of a touch-up. A well-kept late-model car rarely needs large touch-ups unless it has been banged up or has rust problems.

2. Check the metal and chrome trim. If they are pitted but the paint looks good, the car may have been repainted to cover bad rusting.

3. Check for any bumps in the paint, and for any signs of rust on the rocker panels or inside the wheel wells. Rust usually starts in "hidden areas" such as under the paint or behind bumpers. Press any bumps that are encountered. If you can push through them with a fingernail, the car is suffering from a severe rusting problem.

4. Check underneath the car for signs of rust. Be sure to examine the exhaust pipes and the muffler at the same time. Although replacing an exhaust system on a car without a catalytic converter is generally not expensive, it is an additional cost which you will have to pay for and you may be able to lower the purchase price accordingly. Exhaust systems of cars with catalytic converters can be expensive to replace.

5. Examine the frame. A bent frame means that the car was probably in an accident. Such a frame can seriously affect the way the car handles; straightening a bent frame usually costs hundreds of dollars.

6. While you are inspecting underneath the car, check the ground. Signs of oil from beneath the engine, transmission, or rear end could indicate a serious leak. Since cars often have small leaks that could result in innocent accumulations on the pavement beneath the car, ask to move the car to a clean area and check it again later. Leaks can sometimes be very expensive to repair.

7. Look at the general appearance of the car. If it sags or leans in any direction and it is parked on a level surface, there may be something wrong with its springs.

8. Firmly press down on each fender; the car should move downward and return. If it keeps moving or rocking the shocks are probably worn.

9. Using both hands, firmly hold the top of one of the front wheels. Shake it as vigorously as you can. If it moves very freely or makes clunking or thudding noises then there may be a problem with the suspension or wheel bearings.

10. Examine the tires for bulges, cracks, tears, flat spots, and "feathering". Remember, problems with the tires may indicate other difficulties such as bad alignment, worn brakes, or other weak or worn mechanical parts (see the chapter on tires). Tires with insufficient tread depth must be replaced, and additional cost for you unless the seller agrees to replace them or reduces the purchase price accordingly. While you are checking the condition of the tires, check the tire brands as well. A car that is only one or two years old should have the same tires on all the wheels, including the spare. Different tread designs or brands of tires on different wheels may mean that the car had some unusual problem or that the mileage shown on the speedometer is not correct.

11. Check the windows and front and rear windshields. Fogging or chalking of the windows could mean that they may not pass inspection in the state where the car will be registered, and so will have to be replaced. Sometimes pit marks in the windshield can mean that wiper blades may streak in wet weather; this could be merely an annoyance or it might be a safety hazard if it is severe enough. Windows should have mechanisms which work properly; not being able to open or close a window is not only annoying, it can be a safety problem as well. Cracked windshields must be replaced.

12. Check the outside mouldings and the mouldings and trim around the doors and windows. Damaged moulding around the outside of the windows could mean that water will leak into the passenger compartment in inclement weather. The moulding around the windows and vents should be in good condition and be firmly in place; if it is not, air at highway speeds will cause a whistling or whining noise. Loose weatherstripping means a drafty and uncomfortable interior in cold and windy weather.

13. Move the car to a shady or dark area and check the lights. If one light appears brighter than another, there may be a problem with some of the wiring.

14. Open and close each door or hatchback. The doors should open and close freely with no grinding noises. The doors should not rub against their frames, and their locking mechanisms should work properly. The trunk lid should close firmly and not rattle when it is locked; press down and release several times to check this.

15. Examine the seats for tears. While this does not affect the performance of the vehicle, torn seats (if you are willing to put up with them) can be used as a factor in bargaining for a lower price. Bounce up and down on the seats a few times to check the condition of the seat springs and construction. If the seats are badly worn, the car may have been driven more than it otherwise appears, or else the car may have been mistreated. If the back seat is worn much more than the front, this might mean that the car was used commercially as a cab or delivery vehicle.

16. Look for worn steering wheels, floor mats and carpets, and control pedals. If the car being examined is a late-model one and the foot pedals and mats are brand new, the car has probably seen considerable use; the old ones were probably too worn to be displayed. One way to check this further is by removing and checking the underneath side of the ash tray. If it is discolored and shows considerable signs of use, the car has probably been driven considerably more than average. (Of course this test does not indicate anything if the previous owners either did not smoke or rarely used the ash tray).

17. Check the **odometer**, the mileage indicator on the speedometer. Most drivers put 10,000—12,000 miles per year on their cars. First figure out how old the car is in years,

then divide the number of miles indicated on the odometer by the age. The result represents the average number of miles driven per year. If the number is considerably higher than 12,000 then the car has been used much more than average. If the number is considerably less than 10,000 then either the car was not used too much or someone tampered with the odometer. Make sure all the numbers on the odometer are aligned with the one next to it. When you test drive the car, make sure the odometer does not vibrate; pay particular attention to the right-most digit. If it vibrates or moves unevenly the mileage may have been set back. Double check by examining the lubrication sticker that is generally placed on the door panel each time your car is greased or its oil changed by a service station or dealer. If the numbers on the sticker are greater than those on the odometer, the odometer has been tampered with.

18. Every switch and gadget in the car should be tried before you purchase the vehicle. A device which does not work should be replaced or a credit given. Pay particular attention to any electrical appliances in the car—radios and stereos, defrosters, power windows and door locks, air conditioning and lights; tracing car wiring to locate electrical problems is tricky and expensive. Be sure that all the lights work by actually getting out of the car and observing them. Close the windows and turn on the engine and the air conditioner, making sure that it is working properly. Check the heater and defroster by operating them, too.

19. Operate the windshield wiper. It should be quiet and work smoothly. If they make noise other than the usual scraping sounds, there may be a defect in the linkage mechanism or it may be loose. The wipers should operate at all wiping speeds, so move the switch to each position and check it out. Sometimes noise or uneven wiping patterns may be due to only a loose linkage or wiper arm, or the wiper motor may need replacing.

20. Check the gauges and instrument lights with the engine off. Gauges should be in their off positions or else they may be indicating false readings when operating. Turn the key to the on position. If the car has warning lights, they should come on; failure to do so may mean only that a bulb is burned out (in which case it should be replaced) or that something

is wrong—have the mechanic check it when he is examining the car.

21. Press on the brake pedal and hold it down for at least one minute. It should not go lower; if it does there is a problem with the brakes, and the car may be dangerous to drive until repairs are made.

22. Turn the steering wheel in each direction; if the car has power steering the engine should be operating when this is done. The steering should be smooth and quiet without more than a little "play".

23. Check the exhaust system while the engine is on and the car is parked. If there are dark gray, blue, or black gases coming from the exhaust the cars burning oil and needs expensive engine work. Sometimes a car that has only begun to start burning noticeable amounts of oil will have a discoloration around the tail pipe opening. In more severe cases, deposits may be found on the under side of bumpers.

24. As long as the engine is running, place the car in neutral or park and set the park brake. Gently press down on the accelerator pedal and listen to the engine. No rattling or other strange noises should be heard. Rattling may mean problems with engine bearings and there is the chance of expensive repair.

25. Shift the car through each of its gears; there should be no problems in changing from one gear to another. If the car has a standard transmission, the clutch should engage easily.

26. Examine the engine. If you are buying the car from a dealer, he has probably reconditioned the car. Part of this process usually involves steam cleaning the engine, a way to clean the engine of accumulated grease and grime. If he has not done this, he may not have done any other work on the car either.

27. Check for any discoloration on the engine. If they have not been removed in the cleaning process, oil around the cylinder head gasket or in the vicinity of the spark plugs usually means an oil leak.

28. Check the wires in the engine compartment. They should be clean and free of cracks and fraying. Many people often look only at the ignition wires, the thick wires leading to the distributor, coil, and spark plugs. However, these wires are relatively inexpensive to replace even though they do have an important effect on the car's performance. It is the smaller wires on the firewall that should be looked at more carefully. These wires lead to

the instrument panel and the switches and controls on the dash. Replacing or troubleshooting these wires is very expensive, often running into hundreds of dollars.

29. Examine the cooling system with the engine off. Check for traces of anti-freeze leaks from te radiator. If the radiator has a greenish color, seepage may be occurring. The radiator core should be dry; moisture in the core is a sign of a leak. If silver spots are present on the radiator, white lead was used to repair the radiator. Examine the hoses; they should be free of cracks and bulges, otherwise they will need replacement. Although they are not very expensive, hoses that need to be replaced mean and additional expense.

30. Check the radiator coolant; it should be clear and clean. If it is discolored, the cooling system may be need of repair, or else it may have been patched.

31. Check the oil. If it registers more than full or appears to be diluted, forget about the car—coolant is draining into the oil, a sign of a cracked block. If the oil on the dipstick appears to be very thick and perhaps even a gray color, then it may have been treated in an attempt to disguide a cracked block or an engine that burns oil. Your best bet is to drop the car from further consideration.

If you are still interested in the car after making a pre-inspection, the next step is to actually drive the car. This is important since many problems will not show up while the car is not moving. Even if there is nothing wrong with the car mechanically, its performance or handling characteristics may not be what you want. After the road test, some of the pre-inspection examinations should be made again to check if moving the car has revealed disguised engine problems.

How to Road Test a Car

1. Have a friend actually drive the car away from you at a slow speed; kneel behind the center of the car and observe if the car tends to move down the street at an angle; if the pavement is straight and level, and the care has a tendency to move this way, then it may have been in an accident.

2. One purpose of this test drive is to listen for any noises the car might make. Therefore, make sure that "noisemakers" such as radios, stereos, and tape decks are off; you can turn them on to check them when the ride is over.

3. To check if the engine operates smoothly, drive the car at different speeds. If the car has an automatic transmission, increase your speed to the point where the transmission just shifts into high; let the car lose some speed without allowing the transmission to downshift. Then, rapidly increase the speed of the car, but again do not let the transmission shift. If the car has a shift, place it in high gear and, starting at about 15 mph accelerate rapidly to about 40 mph. Whether or not the car has an automatic transmission, it should accelerate smoothly and evenly. If it shows any signs of hesitation or bucking, or makes any mechanical noises, the car may need adjustments, a tune-up, or perhaps even an expensive overhaul.

4. Check the transmission next. Although this was done as part of the pre-inspection, it is worthwhile repeating. Shift the car through its forward and reverse positions several times (in a safe area, of course), and let the car move in both directions. If the car has a shift, the clutch should not grab or bind, and it should not chatter. Cars with automatic transmissions should have shifts which are smooth; jerks or slamming should not occur and the engine should not race when the transmission shifts. Any strange noises, and in particular, howling or whining, should be investigated further by a mechanic.

5. Part of the pre-inspection process was checking the brakes while the car was not moving; now is the time to check them when the car is in motion, which, of course is the time when they are needed most. Be sure to make this test in a quiet area, that is, one where you can change speeds and stop suddenly and safely without worrying about traffic or pedestrians. At about 45 mph, step hard on the brakes, but do not lock the wheels. Repeat this test two or three times quickly. The car should stop evenly and smoothly without veering off course; the brakes should not grab or fade and the brake pedal should not feel soft or spongy.

6. Check the steering while the car is moving. The car should move where you want it to. Make a few left and right turns at different speeds. The steering should not be loose or sloppy, nor should it be too tight.

7. If there is a long hill nearby that does not have heavy traffic, the condition of the rings can be checked. If it is safe to do so, drive down the hill without pressing the accelerator pedal. Before reaching the bottom

of the hill, press the accelerator hard. A cloud of heavy blue smoke from the tail pipe means that the engine needs an overhaul, usualy an expensive proposition. Black smoke is only an indication that the carburetor is out of adjustment. If there is not a suitable hill nearby, allow the car to get up to a fairly high speed, and then let it slow down; press hard on the accelerator and look for smoke from the exhaust.

8. Although the suspension was checked when the car was static, that is, when it was not moving, as part of the pre-inspection examination, now is the time to see how well it can perform when under actual driving conditions. Find a rough roadway and drive the car over it. If you have trouble steering, or the car bounces when small bumps are encountered, or there are loud rattles and squeaks, then the suspension is probably worn.

9. After the car has been driven for a while, check for overheating. If the car has a temperature gauge, examine it from time to time while you are driving; it should not be reading in a high position. If the car has a temperature warning light, it should only come on when the car is first started as an indication that it is working; it should not light when the car is operating. If it is lit, pull over when it is safe to do so and shut off the engine. A hissing sound or steam or coolant escaping could mean cooling system troubles which may be expensive to correct. (*Caution:* Do not remove the radiator cap.)

Once you have driven the car and are still interested in it, have a mechanic check it out. If he uncovers any problems ask him to estimate the cost of repairs. These costs should be mentioned to reduce the price of the car if you decide you still wish to purchase it.

What a Mechanic Should Check

1. Observe the compression of each cylinder. This check can reveal valve and piston ring problems.

2. Examine the brakes and wheel bearings. All four wheels should be removed, and an examination made to discover scored drums or discs, worn linings, hydraulic leaks, and worn or damaged front wheel bearings. With the wheels removed, it is also easier to check for rusting within the wheel wells.

3. The car should be placed on a lift and the engine and transmission examined. A check should be made for rear-axle leaks. With the car raised, a thorough examination of the exhaust system is possible, and its condition should be checked. Any damages or repairs to the frame should be noted, and a check for underneath body integrity should be made. Suspension components should be examined and the tires and rims checked.

Getting the Best Price

Once the car has been examined and you are still interested in it, the next step is determining its price. Do not feel that a listed price is the actual selling price. Dealers generally list a price that is $100—$200 above what they expect to get, so if you decide not to discuss price you are in effect giving them a gift of this amount. Do not be afraid to negotiate. Since the dealer feels free to raise the price over what he expects to get, there is no reason why your initial price offer should not be less than you expect to pay; also remember that the dealer isn't going anywhere and he doesn't want you to go away and perhaps buy from a competitor. Although he may act shocked and insulted by your offer, he really isn't. Mention any flaws or defects in the car that you or your mechanic have discovered; use the cost of repairs as a bargaining point to reduce the price.

If you are buying the car from a private individual, you should also bargain. It will still cost you money to make any needed repairs and the seller may also be asking for a price above what is actually expected. If circumstances are such that a quick sale is a necessity, then a low purchase offer may actually be accepted. Remember, if the seller says no, then a counter offer can be made.

Appendix A
ENGINE STARTING AND EMERGENCY TROUBLESHOOTING

When an engine stops or refuses to start, there is always a reason. Sometimes minor incidents can give the impression of being major problems. Before you try the emergency procedures described here, check the following:

1. Has the ignition key accidentally been turned to the off position? Although it may be surprising, it does sometimes occur.

2. If your car has an automatic transmission, is it in neutral or park? Cars with automatic transmissions will not start in gear. Attempting to start while in "DRIVE" or "D" has resulted in a number of needless emergency service calls.

3. Is the vehicle out of gas? If the engine has been running, it may sputter, that is, start and stop, several times before finally quitting. If the engine has not been running and you turn the key, it may start and then "die." When you add gasoline under such circumstances, do not be surprised if the car does not start immediately; it can sometimes take a minute or more for fuel to reach the carburetor. Do not operate the starter for more than about 30 seconds at one time; instead, operating it 2 or 3 times should cause the engine to start.

4. Is the battery dead? If the engine does not turn over, turn on the lights; if they don't work, the problem is most likely a dead battery or loose cables. If the engine turns very slowly and then stops, the battery is weak. To check for loose battery cable connections, turn off the ignition switch and then tap the terminals with a rubber mallet. If the engine still does not start when the key is turned, switch it off again and carefully insert a heavy bladed, *insulated* handle screwdriver between the positive terminal and the cable clamp. Twist the screwdriver slightly while someone attempts to start the car. If that does not work, the battery is probably dead; use jumper cables as described elsewhere in this book.

5. Does the engine refuse to start but the lights and electrical accessories work? The car may have a defective transmission safety switch; it is this switch which allows cars with automatic transmissions to start only in "PARK" ("P") or "NEUTRAL" ("N"). Try moving the shift lever between the "PARK" and "NEUTRAL" positions while attempting to start. If this does not work, the starter switch may be defective. Try turning the key several times to see if a good connection can be made.

Emergency Procedures

1. Car does not start and there is a strong odor of gasoline:
The carburetor is "flooded,' that is, too much gasoline is being delivered to the engine. Wait several minutes and then hold the accelerator pedal to the floor (do not pump the gas pedal!) and attempt to start. If this doesn't work, remove the cleaner cover and insert a screwdriver in the carburetor to hold the choke valve open, and try to start the engine. If the ignition system is working properly, the car should start.

2. The engine cranks strongly but will not start and there is no odor of gasoline:
The carburetor may not be supplying sufficient gasoline. Try pressing the accelerator pedal to the floor 3 or 4 times and then hold the pedal half way down while attempting to start. If this does not work, take off the air cleaner cover and tap the choke a few times; it may be sticking. Try to start again. If this still doesn't work, have someone press the gas pedal several times while you look down the carburetor from a safe distance to avoid accidentally getting gasoline in your eyes. If no fuel spurts from the jets, the fuel pump may be defective or the gas lines or filter may be clogged.

Caution: Never smoke while working near the fuel lines or carburetor.

3. The engine turns over but does not start and a check of the carburetor indicates that it is getting fuel:
There is an ignition problem causing loss of spark. If your car does not have a high energy ignition system, this can be checked by removing each spark plug wire one at a time and holding it about half way between the ends, place the end removed from the plug near the block of the engine. (Be sure to stand on dry ground when performing this check and do not allow the spark plug wire to move near the carburetor.) Have someone try to start the engine; lack of spark with any wire indicates an ignition problem. Sometimes, a loose cable may be the cause of the problem; push each ignition and distributor and coil wire connection to make sure that they are making good contacts.

4. The car will not start in very wet weather or stops operating properly after driving on very wet roads:
The ignition system may be too wet to perform properly. Turn the ignition switch to the off position. Use a clean, dry cloth to dry the ignition cables. If you can, remove the distributor cap and dry the inside; then replace it. Make sure all wires are making good contacts and then try starting again.

Appendix B
TUNING AN ENGINE

Experts, mechanics, newspaper and magazine articles, and even advertisements constantly remind us to have cars tuned. Often, they mention some of the benefits—increased gas mileage, faster starts, better starting in cold weather and better pollution control. Unfortunately, they generally fail to explain exactly what a tune-up entails.

WHAT TUNE-UPS ARE

Constant motion, temperatures hot enough to melt ordinary steel, large temperature changes, components in gasoline, and friction are some of the factors which cause engine parts to wear. The replacement or adjustment of worn parts, particularly in the ignition system, combined with various tests and inspection procedures constitutes a tune-up. Specific procedures to be followed in a tune-up vary; what is done depends upon the mileage interval between examinations, and the rate of wear of various components. However, the following items are usually checked, replaced, or adjusted:

1. Battery—since the battery plays a vital part in supplying electrical power, it is usually checked using a *voltmeter*. If the battery is weak and cannot be charged effectively, it should be replaced.

2. Engine compression—compression plays an important role in determining the power that can be delivered by an internal combustion engine. For this reason, the compression should be checked using a *compression gauge*. Low readings are often an indication

of necessary adjustment or repairs to rings and valves. This type of work is generally expensive.

3. Spark plugs—spark plugs begin wearing as soon as they are installed and the engine is started. They are either cleaned and adjusted or else replaced at every tune-up. Since it is easier and less time consuming for mechanics to replace spark plugs rather than reconditioning them, this is usually done.

4. Points and condenser—in cars that do not have electronic ignition systems, the points and condenser play an important part in the smooth operation of the ignition system. The points, which are constantly opening and closing, wear relatively quickly and are generally replaced. To ensure smooth operation of the ignition system, the condenser is usually replaced at the same time.

5. Ignition wires—these wires carry the electrical current needed for the ignition system. Engine heat and air tend to cause them to become brittle, corroded, or to develop worn insulation. They should be replaced at the intervals recommended in your owner's manual or if these conditions are noticed.

6. Timing—in order for the engine to operate most efficiently, the sparks must occur at the right time. This adjustment is made by using a *timing light* and a *tachometer*, a device for measuring engine speed. The electronic timing light is used to align special marks on the engine.

7. Distributor spark advance—the vacuum advance which is attached to the exterior of the

distributor and the centrifugal advance, which is inside the distributor and which advances or retards the occurrence of the spark, depending on the load on the engine and its speed, are tested and adjusted. The distributor spark advance is important to the emission control systems on late model cars.

8. Fuel and air filters—these filters are checked and, if necessary, replaced.

9. Carburetor—the idle mixture on the carburetor is checked and adjusted if necessary.

10. Automatic choke—the automatic choke should be checked to see if it is free and performing properly.

11. Belts—all belts are checked for the proper tension; if available, a tension gauge is used.

12. Emissions control—a check of the emissions control system is made on those cars that have one. Parts such as the PCV valve are inspected and cleansed or replaced.

Exact tuning procedures and specifications vary with the make, model, engine, and year of manufacture of the car. For a complete tune-up, some accurate gauges and tools are required; for example, a good electronic tuning light, compression gauge, voltmeter, and tachometer are important. The shop manual prepared by the manufacturer of your car is the best place to find detailed instructions on tuning and maintenance procedures, as well as exact specifications. If you have an American made car, the following rules of thumb should prove helpful:

1. In the absence of an exact spark plug gap setting specifications, use .035 inch.

2. When performing cylinder compression tests, disconnect the coil wire from the distributor and connect to a good ground to prevent the engine from accidentally starting. In the absence of other specifications, the compression for any cylinder should not be less than 100 pounds and the difference recorded between cylinders should be less than 40 pounds.

Appendix C
HINTS AND TIPS
FOR SMALL CARS

Because small cars usually have smaller engines than larger vehicles, but are often driven in the same manner by those accustomed to driving family-sized cars, regular maintenance is particularly important. Small engines work harder when operated at highway speeds for prolonged periods, and may be strained by operating under heavy loads. Certain maintenance procedures and tips will help your car to perform properly and aid in its having its designed service life.

1. Follow the maintenance schedule as indicated in your owner's manual.

2. Be sure to check the oil level regularly. When adding oil, always use a high quality motor oil.

3. Unless your car is specifically designed for such usage, avoid driving at high speeds for extended periods. This avoids unnecessary engine strain and also reduces gasoline consumption.

3. If you do a large amount of highway driving, pay particular attention to the tires. They are usually smaller than those on larger cars and, because of flexing, may run hotter. Be sure to maintain the proper inflation pressures, checking when the tires are cold. When replacing tires, make sure that they are recommended for highway and turnpike use.

4. Keep your car well timed and in tune. A spark of reduced strength in one plug on an 8-cylinder large engine may hardly be noticed, while on a 4-cylinder power plant, performance will definitely suffer.

5. Cars are designed to carry a specific maximum load. What this maximum is depends on a number of factors including engine size, tire load ratings, and the type of suspension. The maximum safe load for your car should be listed in the owner's manual or on a card or tag in the glove compartment. Never exceed this weight and, for regular usage, carry loads somewhat below this value. Remember, your little car may have a body design similar to that of a large station wagon, but appearances can be deceiving; it is probably not intended to handle the same weight.

PRICING FACTORS AND TRENDS

As the desire for increased gas mileage becomes more prevalent, many people are considering purchasing small cars. The prices of these cars have risen dramatically. As the cost of steel and other "raw materials" used in the manufacture of cars increases, so does the cost of these automobiles. However, although the quantity of these materials used in replacement parts for small cars is generally considerably lower than the amounts used in comparable parts for full sized cars, the price of small car replacement parts seems to be increasing much more rapidly than the cost for big car components. If this trend continues, it may not pay to make certain repairs to small cars.

Appendix D

CONSUMER'S GUIDE

The following information is useful to those who are thinking of purchasing the listed vehicles by providing a basis of comparison, and owners may find this material informative.

Car: JAVELIN
Year: 1967-1970
Manufacturer: American Motors

Wheelbase .... 109 inches
Length .... 191.04 inches
Weight .... 3200 lbs.
Width .... 71.89 inches
Standard Engine .... 6 cylinders
Standard Brakes .... Front: drum type
Rear: drum type
Turning Diameter..................... 38 feet
Gas mileage average
regular fuel .... 14 miles per gallon
Front leg room .... 43.05 inches
Front head room .... 37.5 inches
Rear leg room .... 30.8 inches
Rear head room .... 36 inches
Room for luggage .... 10.2 cubic feet

Car: JAVELIN
Year: 1971-1974
Manufacturer: American Motors

Wheelbase .... 110 inches
Length .... 192.31 inches
Weight .... 3300 lbs.
Width .... 75.36 inches
Standard Engine........................6 cyl.
Standard Brakes .... Front: drum type
Rear: drum type

Turning Diameter .... 36.25 feet
Gas mileage average
unleaded fuel .... 12.8 miles per gallon
Front leg room .... 42.45 inches
Front head room.................37.54 inches
Rear leg room .... 31 inches
Rear head room .... 35.49 inches
Room for luggage .... 10.2 cubic feet

Car: CAMARO
Year: 1967-1968
Manufacturer: Chevrolet — GM

Wheelbase .... 108 inches
Length .... 184.6 inches
Weight .... 3200 lbs.
Width .... 72.3 inches
Standard Engine .... 6 cylinders
Standard Brakes .... Front: drum type
Rear: drum type
Turning Diameter..................... 39 feet
Gas mileage average
regular fuel .... 16.5 mpg.
Front leg room .... 42.5 inches
Front head room .... 37 inches
Rear leg room .... 29.2 inches
Rear head room .... 36.7 inches
Room for luggage .... 8.3 cubic feet

Car: CAMARO
Year: 1969-1970
Manufacturer: Chevrolet — GM

Wheelbase . . . . 108 inches
Length . . . . 186 inches
Weight . . . . 3200 lbs.
Width . . . . 74 inches
Standard Engine . . . . 6 cylinders
Standard Brakes . . . . Front: disc type
Rear: drum type
Turning Diameter . . . . 40 feet
Gas mileage average
regular fuel . . . . 16.4 mpg.
Front leg room . . . . 42.5 inches
Front head room . . . . 36.7 inches
Rear leg room . . . . 29.2 inches
Rear head room . . . . 36.7 inches
Room for luggage . . . . 8.5 cubic feet

Car: CAMARO
Year: 1970-1971
Manufacturer: Chevrolet — GM

Wheelbase . . . . 108 inches
Length . . . . 195.4 inches
Weight . . . . 3600 lbs.
Width . . . . 74.4 inches
Standard Engine . . . . 6 cylinders
Standard Brakes . . . . Front: disc type
Rear: drum type
Turning Diameter . . . . 38.5 feet
Gas mileage average
unleaded fuel . . . . 13.5 mpg.
Front leg room . . . . 43.9 inches
Front head room . . . . 37.3 inches
Rear leg room . . . . 29.6 inches
Rear head room . . . . 36 inches
Room for luggage . . . . 6.7 cubic feet

Car: MUSTANG
Year: 1967-1970
Manufacturer: Ford

Wheelbase . . . . 108 inches
Length . . . . 183.6 inches
Weight . . . . 2900 lbs.
Width . . . . 70.9 inches
Standard Engine . . . . 6 cylinders
Standard Brakes . . . . Front: drum type
Rear: drum type
Turning Diameter . . . . 39 feet

Gas mileage average
regular fuel . . . . 19.2 mpg.
Front leg room . . . . 41.8 inches
Front head room . . . . 37.4 inches
Rear leg room . . . . 28.8 inches
Rear head room . . . . 35.9 inches
Room for luggage . . . . 9.2 cubic feet

Car: MUSTANG
Year: 1971-1973
Manufacturer: Ford

Wheelbase . . . . 109 inches
Length . . . . 193.8 inches
Weight . . . . 3230 lbs.
Width . . . . 74.1 inches
Standard Engine . . . . 6 cylinders
Standard Brakes . . . . Front: disc type
Rear: drum type
Turning Diameter . . . . 39.8 feet
Gas mileage average
unleaded fuel 13.5
Front leg room . . . . 41.7 inches
Front head room . . . . 37.2 inches
Rear leg room . . . . 28.2 inches
Rear head room . . . . 36 inches
Room for luggage . . . . 9.5 cubic feet

Car: DATSUN B210
Year: 1974

Wheelbase . . . . 92 inches
Length . . . . 161 inches
Weight . . . . 1950 lbs.
Width . . . . 61 inches
Standard Engine . . . . 4 cylinders; in-line
Standard Brakes . . . . Front: disc type
Rear: drum type
Turning Diameter . . . . 33.4 feet
Gas mileage average
unleaded fuel . . . . 29.8 mpg.
Front leg room . . . . 40 inches
Front head room . . . . 40 inches
Rear leg room
Rear head room . . . . 32.9 inches
Room for luggage . . . . 12 cubic feet

Car: DATSUN 1200
Year: 1971-1973

Wheelbase . . . . 90.6 inches
Length . . . . 152.6 inches

Weight . . . . 1750 lbs.
Width. . . . . .61 inches
Standard Engine . . . . 4-cylinders; in-line
Standard Brakes . . . . Front: disc type
                                    Rear: drum type
Turning Diameter . . . . 26.8 feet
Gas mileage average . . . . 31.2 mpg.
    unleaded fuel
Front leg room . . . . 42 inches
Front head room . . . . 36 inches
Rear leg room . . . . 33.5 inches
Rear head room . . . . 33.2 inches
Room for luggage . . . . 12 cubic feet

Car: VOLVO 142, 144, 145
Year: 1967-1974
Manufacturer: Volvo

Wheelbase . . . . 103.2 inches
Length . . . . 182.7 inches
Weight . . . . 2700 lbs.
Width . . . . .68.1 inches
Standard Engine . . . . 4-cylinder; in-line
Standard Brakes . . . . Front: disc type
                                    Rear: disc type
Turning Diameter . . . . 30.4 feet
Gas mileage average
    unleaded fuel . . . . 19.5 mpg.
Front leg Room . . . . 46 inches
Front head room . . . . 38.5 inches
Rear leg room . . . . 39 inches
Rear head room . . . . 36 inches
Room for luggage . . . . 23.6 cubic feet

Car: LEMANS - TEMPEST
Year: 1973-1974
Manufacturer: Pontiac — (G.M.)

Wheelbase . . . . 116 inches
Length . . . . 212.8 inches
Width . . . . 77.9 inches
Standard Engine V8
Standard Brakes . . . . Front: drum type
                                    Rear: drum type
Turning Diameter . . . . 40.1 feet
Gas mileage average
    unleaded fuel. 13.5
Front leg room . . . . 42.3 inches
Front head room . . . . 38.3 inches
Rear leg room . . . . 38.4 inches
Rear head room . . . . 37.5 inches
Room for luggage . . . . 15.1 cubic feet

Car: LEMANS - TEMPEST
Year: 1968-1972
Manufacturer: Pontiac — G.M.)

Wheelbase . . . . 116 inches
Length . . . . 207.2 inches
Weight . . . . 3400 lbs.
Width . . . . .76.7 inches
Standard Engine . . . . 6 cylinders
Standard brakes . . . . Front: drum type
                                    Rear: drum type
Turning Diameter . . . . .41.7 feet
Gas mileage average
    regular fuel . . . . 14 mpg.
Front leg room . . . . 42.7 inches
Front head room . . . . 38.9 inches
Rear leg room . . . . 38.8 inches
Rear head room . . . . 37.9 inches
Room for luggage . . . . 17.7 cubic feet

Car: LEMANS — TEMPEST
Year: 1967
Manufacturer: Pontiac — (G.M.)

Wheelbase . . . . 115 inches
Length . . . . 206.6 inches
Weight . . . . 3500 lbs.
Width . . . . .74.4 inches
Standard Engine . . . . 6 cylinders
Standard Brakes . . . . Front: drum type
                                    Rear: drum type
Turning Diameter . . . . .43 feet
Gas mileage average
    regular fuel . . . . 14.1 mpg.
Front leg room . . . . 40.2 inches
Front head room . . . . 38.1 inches
Rear leg room . . . . 35.7 inches
Rear head room . . . . 37.3 inches
Room for luggage . . . . 21.6 cubic feet

Wheelbase . . . . 117 inches
Length . . . . 212.4 inches
Weight . . . . 3700 lbs.
Width . . . . 78.6 inches
Standard Engine . . . . 6 cylinders

Standard Brakes .... Front: drum type
                                 rear: drum type
Turning Diameter .... 42 feet
Gas mileage average
    unleaded fuel .... 15.4 mpg.
Front leg room .... 41.9 inches
Front head room .... 38.3 inches
Rear leg room .... 36.7 inches
Rear head room .... 37.3 inches
Room for luggage .... 16.5 cubic feet

Wheelbase .... 116 inches
Length .... 204 inches
Weight .... 3300 lbs.
Width .... 76.4 inches
Standard Engine .... 6 cylinders
Standard Brakes .... Front: drum type
                                 Rear: drum type
Turning Diameter .... 44 feet
Gas mileage average
    regular fuel .... 16.2 mpg.
Front leg room .... 41.8 inches
Front head room .... 38.6 inches
Rear leg room .... 36.3 inches
Rear head room .... 37.4 inches
Room for luggage .... 15.9 cubic feet

Car: F85 — CUTLASS
Year: 1968-1974
Manufacturer: Oldsmobile — (G.M.)

Wheelbase .... 116 inches
Length .... 211 inches
Weight .... 4000 lbs.
Width .... 76.5 inches
Standard engine V8
Standard Brakes .... Front: disc type
                                 Rear: drum type
Turning Diameter .... 43 feet
Gas mileage average
    unleaded fuel .... 12.1 mpg.
Front leg room .... 42.1 inches
Front head room .... 38.3 inches
Rear leg room .... 38.4 inches
Rear head room .... 37.5 inches
Room for luggage .... 16.3 cubic feet

Car: F85 — CUTLASS
Year: 1967
Manufacturer: Oldsmobile — (G.M.)

Wheelbase .... 115 inches
Length .... 204.2 inches
Weight .... 3200 lbs.
Width .... 76 inches
Standard Engine .... 6 cylinders

Standard Brakes .... Front: drum type
                                 Rear: drum type
Turning Diameter .... 44 feet
Gas mileage average
    regular fuel .... 14 mpg.
Front leg room .... 41.3 inches
Front head room .... 38.1 inches
Rear leg room .... 36 inches
Rear head room .... 37.2 inches
Room for luggage .... 20.1 cubic feet

Car: MONTEGO
Year: 1972-1974
Manufacturer: Mercury - (Ford)

Wheelbase .... 118 inches
Length .... 219.5 inches
Weight .... 3900 lbs.
Width .... 78.6 inches
Standard Engine V-8
Standard Brakes .... Front: disc type
                                 Rear: drum type
Turning Diameter .... 41.7 feet
Gas mileage average
    unleaded fuel .... 11.9 mpg.
Front leg room .... 42.1 inches
Front head room .... 38.1 inches
Rear leg room .... 38.1 inches
Room for luggage .... 16.5 cubic feet

Car: MONTEGO
Year: 1970-1971
Manufacturer: Mercury — (Ford)

Wheelbase .... 117 inches
Length .... 209.9 inches
Weight .... 3400 lbs.
Width .... 77.4 inches
Standard Engine .... 6 cylinders
Standard Brakes .... Front: drum type
                                 Rear: drum type
Turning Diameter .... 43.7 feet
Gas mileage average
    unleaded fuel .... 14.8 mpg.
Front leg room .... 41.1 inches
Front head room .... 37.8 inches
Rear leg room .... 36 inches
Rear head room .... 36.8 inches
Room for luggage .... 16.2 cubic feet

Car: MONTEGO
Year: 1968-1969
Manufacturer: Mercury — (Ford)

Wheelbase .... 116 inches

Length . . . . 206.1 inches
Weight . . . . 3400 lbs.
Width . . . . .76 inches
Standard Engine . . . . 6 cylinders
Standard Brakes . . . . Front: drum type
Rear: drum type
Turning Diameter .44 feet
Gasoline mileage . . . . 15 mpg.
regular fuel
Front leg room . . . . 42.5 inches
Front head room . . . . 38.5 inches
Rear leg room . . . . 36 inches
Rear head room . . . . 37.5 inches
Room for luggage . . . . 15.2 cubic feet

Car: FAIRLANE — TORINO
Year: 1972-1974
Manufacturer: Ford

Wheelbase . . . . 118 inches
Length . . . . 217 inches
Weight . . . . 3800 lbs.
Width . . . . 79.3 inches
Standard Engine V8
Standard Brakes . . . . Front: disc type
Rear: drum type
Turning Diameter . . . . 41.6 feet
Gas mileage average . . . . 12 mpg.
Front leg room . . . . 42.1 inches
Front head room . . . . 38.1 inches
Rear leg room . . . . 37.6 inches
Rear head room . . . . 37.1 inches
Room for luggage . . . . 16.8 cubic feet

Car: FAIRLANE — TORINO
Year: 1970-1971
Manufacturer: Ford

Wheelbase . . . . 117 inches
Length . . . . 206.2 inches
Weight . . . . 3400 lbs.
Width . . . . 76.4 inches
Standard Engine . . . . 6 cylinders
Standard Brakes . . . . Front: drum type
Rear: drum type
Turning Diameter . . . . 45.3 feet
Gas mileage average
unleaded fuel . . . . 15.6 mpg.
Front leg room . . . . 41.1 inches
Front head room . . . . 37.8 inches
Rear leg room . . . . 36 inches
Rear head room . . . . 36.8 inches
Room for luggage . . . . 16.2 cubic feet

Car: FAIRLANE
Year: 1967-1969
Manufacturer: Ford

Wheelbase . . . . 116 inches
Length . . . . 201.1 inches
Weight . . . . 3200 lbs.
Width . . . . 74.8 inches
Standard Engine . . . . 6 cylinders
Standard Brakes . . . . Front: drum type
Rear: drum type
Turning Diameter . . . . 43 feet
Gas mileage average . . . . 16.4 mpg.
regular fuel
Front leg room . . . . 42.4 inches
Front head room . . . . 38.6 inches
Rear leg room . . . . 36 inches
Rear head room . . . . 37.4 inches
Room for luggage . . . . 16.2 cubic feet

Car: CORONET — CHARGER
Year: 1971-1974
Manufacturer: Dodge — (Chrysler)

Wheelbase . . . . 118 inches
Length . . . . 212.9 inches
Weight . . . . 3550 lbs.
Width . . . . 77.8 inches
Standard Engine . . . . 6 cylinders
Standard Brakes . . . . Front: drum type
Rear: drum type
Turning Diameter . . . . 42 feet
Gas mileage average
unleaded fuel . . . . 13.7 mpg.
Front leg room . . . . 41.9 inches
Front head room . . . . 38.5 inches
Rear leg room . . . . 36.7 inches
Rear head room . . . . 37.3 inches
Room for luggage . . . . 16.5 cubic feet

Car: CORONET — CHARGER
Year: 1967-1970
Manufacturer: Dodge — (Chrysler)

Wheelbase . . . . 117 inches
Length . . . . 209.2 inches
Weight . . . . 3400 lbs.
Width . . . . 76.7 inches
Standard Engine . . . . 6 cylinders
Standard Brakes . . . . Front: drum type
Rear: drum type
Turning Diameter . . . . 44 feet
Gas mileage average . . . . 14.9 mpg.
regular fuel
Front leg room . . . . 41.9 inches
Front head room . . . . 38.6 inches
Rear leg room . . . . 36.4 inches

Rear head room .... 37.4 inches
Room for luggage .... 17.4 cubic feet

Car: CHEVELLE
Year: 1973-1974
Manufacturer: Chevrolet — (G.M.)

Wheelbase .... 116 inches
Length .... 210 inches
Weight .... 3680 lbs.
Width .... 76.6 inches
Standard Engine .... 6 cylinders
Standard Brakes .... Front: disc type
Rear: drum type
Turning Diameter .... 39.5 feet
Gas mileage average
unleaded fuel ....
Front leg room .... 42.2 inches
Front head room .... 38.3 inches
Rear leg room .... 37 inches
Rear head room .... 37.5 inches
Room for luggage .... 15.3 cubic feet

Car: CHEVELLE
Year: 1968-1972
Manufacturer: Chevrolet — (G.M.)

Wheelbase .... 116 inches
Length .... 206.9 inches
Weight .... 3550 lbs.
Width .... 76.1 inches
Standard Engine .... 6 cylinder
Standard Brakes .... Front: drum type
Rear: drum type
Turning Diameter .... 39.6 feet
Gas mileage average
unleaded fuel .... 14.9 mpg.
Front leg room .... 41.9 inches
Front head room .... 38.3 inches
Rear leg room .... 38.4 inches
Rear head room .... 37.5 inches
Room for luggage .... 15.3 cubic feet

Car: CHEVELLE
Year: 1967
Manufacturer: Chevrolet — (G.M.)

Wheelbase .... 115 inches
Length .... 197 inches
Weight .... 3300 lbs.
Width .... 75 inches
Standard Engine .... 6 cylinders
Standard Brakes .... Front: drum type
Rear: drum type
Turning Diameter .... 44 feet

Gas mileage average
Regular fuel .... 15.5 mpg.
Front leg room .... 41.9 inches
Front head room .... 38.5 inches
Rear leg room .... 35 inches
Rear head room .... 37.5 inches
Room for luggage .... 17.1 cubic feet

Car: Special — SKYLARK
Year: 1967-1972
Manufacturer: Buick — (G.M.)

Wheelbase .... 116 inches
Length .... 206.8 inches
Weight .... 3600 lbs.
Width .... 76.5 inches
Standard Engine V-8
Standard Brakes .... Front: drum type
Rear: drum type
Turning Diameter .... 45.3 feet
Gas mileage average
regular fuel .... 12.9 mpg.
Front leg room .... 41.3 inches
Front head room .... 38.6 inches
Rear leg room .... 34.8 inches
Rear head room .... 37.3 inches
Room for luggage .... 14.2 feet

Car: SKYLARK — CENTURY
Year: 1973-1974
Manufacturer: Buick — (G.M.)

Wheelbase .... 116 inches
Length .... 209.5 inches
Weight .... 4000 lbs.
Width .... 79 inches
Standard Engine V-8
Standard Brakes .... Front: disc type
Rear: drum type
Turning Diameter .... 41.7 feet
Gas mileage average
unleaded fuel .... 11.3 mpg.
Front leg room .... 42.1 inches
Front head room .... 38.3 inches
Rear leg room .... 37 inches
Rear head room .... 37.5 inches
Room for luggage .... 15.3 cubic feet

Car: 100 LS
Year: 1967-1974
Manufacturer: Audi

Wheelbase .... 105.3 inches
Length .... 183.6 inches
Weight .... 2520 lbs.
Width .... 68.1 inches

Standard Engine . . . . 4 cylinders; in-line
Standard Brakes . . . . Front: disc type
Rear: disc type
Turning Diameter . . . . 34.8 feet
Gas mileage average . . . . 20 mpg.
Front leg room . . . . 42 inches
Front head room . . . . 36 inches
Rear leg room . . . . 42 inches
Rear head room . . . . 35 inches
Room for luggage . . . . 12.6 cubic feet

Car: MATADOR
Year: 1971-1974
Manufacturer: American Motors

Wheelbase . . . . 118 inches
Length . . . . 216 inches
Weight . . . . 3600 lbs.
Width . . . . 77.2 inches
Standard Engine . . . . 6 cylinders
Standard Brakes . . . . Front: disc type
Rear: drum type
Turning Diameter . . . . 39 feet
Gas mileage average
unleaded fuel . . . . 14 mpg.
Front leg room . . . . 41.8 inches
Front head room . . . . 39.6 inches
Rear leg room . . . . 38.6 inches
Rear head room . . . . 37.5 inches
Room for luggage . . . . 18.2 cubic feet

Car: REBEL
Year: 1967-1970
Manufacturer: American Motors

Wheelbase . . . . 114 inches
Length . . . . 198 inches
Weight . . . . 3400 lbs.
Width . . . . 77.2 inches
Standard Engine . . . . 6 cylinders
Standard Brakes . . . . Front: drum type
Rear: disc type
Turning Diameter . . . . 40 feet
Gas mileage average
regular fuel . . . . 15.9 mpg.
Front leg room . . . . 42.5 inches
Front head room . . . . 39.6 inches
Rear leg room . . . . 38.6 inches
Rear head room . . . . 37.5 inches
Room for luggage . . . . 18.2 cubic feet

Car: firebird
Year: 1971-1974
Manufacturer: Pontiac — (G.M.)

Wheelbase . . . . 108 inches

Length . . . . 192.1 inches
Weight . . . . 3300 lbs.
Width . . . . 73.4 inches
Standard Engine . . . . 6 cylinders
Standard Brakes . . . . Front: disc type
Rear: drum type
Turning Diameter . . . . 36.5 feet
Gas mileage average . . . . 12.4 mpg.
unleaded fuel
Front leg room . . . . 43.9 inches
Front head room . . . . 37.8 inches
Room for luggage . . . . 7.24 cubic feet

Car: FIREBIRD
Year: 1969-1970
Manufacturer: Pontiac — (G.M.)

Wheelbase . . . . 108.1 inches
Length . . . . 191.1 inches
Weight . . . . 3500 lbs.
Width . . . . 73.9 inches
Standard Engine . . . . 6 cylinders
Standard Brakes . . . . Front: disc type
Rear: drum type
Turning Diameter . . . . 40 feet
Gas mileage average
regular fuel . . . . 12.9 mpg.
Front leg room . . . . 42.5 inches
Front head room . . . . 37.1 inches
Rear leg room . . . . 29.5 inches
Rear head room . . . . 36.7 inches
Room for luggage . . . . 3.9 cubic feet

Car: FIREBIRD
Year: 1967-1968
Manufacturer: Pontiac — (G.M.)

Wheelbase . . . . 108.1 inches
Length . . . . 188.8 inches
Weight . . . . 3400 lbs.
Width . . . . 72.8 inches
Standard Engine . . . . 6 cylinders
Standard Brakes . . . . Front: drum type
Rear: drum type
Turning Diameter . . . . 41 feet
Gas mileage average
regular fuel . . . . 13.2 mpg.
Front leg room . . . . 42.5 inches
Front head room . . . . 37 inches
Rear leg room . . . . 29.5 inches
Rear head room . . . . 36.7 inches
Room for luggage . . . . 9.9 cubic feet

Car: BARRACUDA
Year: 1970-1974
Manufacturer: Plymouth — (Chrysler)

Wheelbase . . . . 108 inches
Length . . . . 195.6 inches
Weight . . . . 3300 lbs.
Width . . . . 75.6 inches
Standard Engine V8
Standard Brakes . . . . Front: disc type
                                          Rear: drum type
Turning Diameter . . . . 38.6 feet
Gas mileage average
  unleaded fuel . . . . 13.2 mpg.
Front leg room . . . . 42.1 inches
Front head room . . . . 37.4 inches
Rear leg room . . . . 28.9 inches
Rear head room . . . . 35.7 inches
Room for luggage . . . . 74 cubic feet

Car: BARRACUDA
Year: 1967-1969
Manufacturer: Plymouth — (Chrysler)

Wheelbase . . . . 108 inches
Length . . . . 192.8 inches
Weight . . . . 3100 lbs.
Width . . . . 69.6 inches
Standard Engine . . . . 6 cylinders
Standard Brakes . . . . Front: drum type
                                          Rear: drum type
Turning Diameter . . . . 41 feet
Gas mileage average
  regular fuel . . . . 16 mpg.
Front leg room . . . . 41.7 inches
Front head room . . . . 37.4 inches
Rear leg room . . . . 30.2 inches
Rear head room . . . . 35.8 inches
Room for luggage . . . . 5.9 cubic feet

Car: COUGAR
Year: 1971-1973
Manufacturer: Mercury — (Ford)

Wheelbase . . . . 112.1 inches
Length . . . . 199.5 inches
Weight . . . . 3600 lbs.
Width . . . . 75.1 inches
Standard Engine V8
Standard Brakes . . . . Front: disc type
                                          Rear: drum type
Turning Diameter . . . . 41.4 feet
Gas mileage average
  unleaded fuel . . . . 11.9 mpg.
Front leg room . . . . 41.7 inches

Front head room . . . . 37.2 inches
Rear leg room . . . . 28.9 inches
Rear head room . . . . 35.9 inches
Room for luggage . . . . 10.4 cubic feet

Car: COUGAR
Year: 1967-1970
Manufacturer: Mercury — (Ford)

Wheelbase . . . . 11 inches
Length . . . . 196.1 inches
Weight . . . . 3500 lbs.
Width . . . . 74.1 inches
Standard Engine V8
Standard Brakes . . . . Front: disc type
                                          Rear: drum type
Turning Diameter . . . . 41 feet
Gas mileage average
  regular fuel . . . . 13.6 mpg.
Front leg room . . . . 40.1 inches
Front head room . . . . 37.6 inches
Rear leg room . . . . 30.6 inches
Rear head room . . . . 35.9 inches
Room for luggage . . . . 10.1 cubic feet

Car: MUSTANG II
Year: 1974
Manufacturer: Ford

Wheelbase . . . . 96.2 inches
Length . . . . 175 inches
Weight . . . . 2700 lbs.
Width . . . . 70.2 inches
Standard Engine . . . . 4 cylinders; in-line
Standard Brakes . . . . Front: disc
                                          Rear: drum
Turning Diameter . . . . 33.6 feet
Gas mileage average
  unleaded fuel . . . . 19.1 mpg.
Front leg room . . . . 41.8 inches
Front head room . . . . 37.3 inches
Rear leg room . . . . 27.6 inches
Rear head room . . . . 36.4 inches
Room for luggage . . . . 6.7 cubic feet

Car: CAPRI
Year: 1970-1974
Manufacturer: Mercury — (Ford)

Wheelbase . . . . 100.8 inches
Length . . . . 177 inches
Weight . . . . 2200 lbs.
Width . . . . 64.8 inches
Standard Engine . . . . 6 cylinder
Standard brakes . . . . Front: disc type
                                          Rear: drum type

Turning Diameter . . . . 33.5 feet
Gas mileage average . . . . 23.4 mpg.
  unleaded fuel
Front leg room . . . . 41.4 inches
Front head room . . . . 37.4 inches
Rear leg room . . . . 31.1 inches
Rear head room . . . . 35.9 inches
Room for luggage . . . . 7.2 cubic feet

Car: THUNDERBIRD
Year: 1972-1974
Manufacturer: Ford

Wheelbase . . . . 120.4 inches
Length . . . . 224.8 inches
Weight . . . . 5075 lbs.
Width . . . . 79.7 inches
Standard Engine V8
Standard Brakes . . . . Front: disc type
                                         Rear: drum type
Turning Diameter . . . . 43 feet
Gas mileage average
  unleaded fuel . . . . 9 mpg.
Front leg room . . . . 42 inches
Front head room . . . . 37.5 inches
Rear leg room . . . . 36.4 inches
Rear head room . . . . 36.8 inches
Room for luggage . . . . 13.4 cubic feet

Car: THUNDERBIRD
Year: 1967
Manufacturer: Ford

Wheelbase . . . . 115 inches
Length . . . . 206.9 inches
Weight . . . . 4500 lbs.
Width . . . . 77.3 inches
Standard Engine V8
Standard Brakes . . . . Front: disc type
                                         Rear: drum type
Turning Diameter . . . . 47.2 feet
Gas mileage average
  unleaded fuel . . . . 11.2 mpg.
Front leg room . . . . 41.5 inches
Front head room . . . . 38.1 inches
Rear leg room . . . . 35.3 inches
Rear head room . . . . 36.8 inches
Room for luggage . . . . 12.8 cubic feet

Car: MONTE CARLO
Year: 1970-1974
Manufacturer: Chevrolet (G.M)

Wheelbase . . . . 116 inches
Length . . . . 218.1 inches

Weight . . . . 4430 lbs.
Width . . . . 77.6 inches
Standard Engine V8
Standard Brakes . . . . Front: disc type
                                         Rear: drum type
Turning Diameter . . . . 39 feet
Gas mileage average
  unleaded fuel . . . . 8.2 mpg.
Front leg room . . . . 42.1 inches
Front head room . . . . 37.5 inches
Rear leg room . . . . 32.9 inches
Rear head room . . . . 37.4 inches
Room for luggage . . . . 14.7 cubic feet

Car: ELDORADO
Year: 1971-1974
Manufacturer: Cadillac (G.M.)

Wheelbase . . . . 126.4 inches
Length . . . . 224.1 inches
Weight . . . . 5200 lbs.
Width . . . . 79.8 inches
Standard Engine V8
Standard Brakes . . . . Front: disc type
                                 rear: drum type
Turning Diameter . . . . 46.8 feet
Gas mileage average
  unleaded fuel . . . . 8 mpg.
Front leg room . . . . 42.5 inches
Front head room . . . . 38.1 inches
Rear leg room . . . . 35.7 inches
Rear head room . . . . 37.1 inches
Room for luggage . . . . 13.6 cubic feet

Car: ELDORADO
Year: 1967-1970
Manufacturer: Cadillac (G.M.)

Wheelbase . . . . 120 inches
Length . . . . 221 inches
Weight . . . . 4800 lbs.
Width . . . . 79.8 inches
Standard Engine V8
Standard Brakes . . . . Front: disc type
                                         Rear: drum type
Turning Diameter . . . . 45 feet
Gas mileage average
premium fuel . . . . 11.1 mpg.
Front leg room . . . . 41.4 inches
Front head room . . . . 37.5 inches
Rear leg room . . . . 36.2 inches
Rear head room . . . . 37.8 inches
Room for luggage . . . . 15.2 cubic feet

Car: RIVIERA
Year: 1974
Manufacturer: Buick (G.M.)

Wheelbase . . . . 122 inches
Length . . . . 226.4 inches
Weight . . . . 4850 lbs.
Width . . . . 80 inches
Standard Engine V8
Standard Brakes . . . . Front: disc type
Rear: drum type
Turning Diameter . . . . 43.4 feet
Gas mileage average
unleaded fuel . . . . 8.8 mpg.
Front leg room . . . . 42.2 inches
Front head room . . . . 38.1 inches
Rear leg room . . . . 35.4 inches
Rear head room . . . . 37.1 inches
Room for luggage . . . . 15.5 cubic feet

Car: RIVIERA
Year: 1971-1973
Manufacturer: Buick (G.M.)

Wheelbase . . . . 122 inches
Length . . . . 223.4 inches
Weight . . . . 5050 lbs.
Width . . . . 79.9 inches
Standard Engine V8
Standard Brakes . . . . Front: disc type
Rear: drum type
Turning Diameter . . . . 43.4 feet
Gas mileage average
unleaded fuel . . . . 10 mpg.
Front leg room . . . . 42.5 inches
Front head room . . . . 38.2 inches
Rear leg room . . . . 35.4 inches
Rear head room . . . . 37 inches
Room for luggage . . . . 14.6 cubic feet

Car: RIVIERA
Year: 1967-1970
Manufacturer: Buick (G.M.)

Wheelbase . . . . 119 inches
Length . . . . 215.5 inches
Weight . . . . 4400 lbs.
Width . . . . 79.32 inches
Standard Engine V8
Standard Brakes . . . . Front: drum type
Rear: drum type
Turning Diameter . . . . 46 feet
Gas mileage average
premium fuel . . . . 11 mpg.
Front leg room . . . . 41.2 inches
Front head room . . . . 37.7 inches

Rear leg room . . . . 36.6 inches
Rear head room . . . . 37.5 inches
Room for luggage . . . . 10.1 cubic feet

Car: MERCEDES BENZ 450 SEL
Year: 1967-1974

Wheelbase . . . . 116.5 inches
Length . . . . 199.3 inches
Weight . . . . 4280 lbs.
Width . . . . 73.6 inches
Standard Engine V8
Standard Brakes . . . . Front: disc type
Rear: drum type
Turning Diameter . . . . 37.5 feet
Gas mileage average
unleaded fuel . . . . 12.5 mpg.
Front leg room . . . . 44 inches
Front head room . . . . 38.5 inches
Rear leg room . . . . 41.8 inches
Rear head room . . . . 36 inches
Room for luggage . . . . 20.2 cubic feet

Car: CONTINENTAL
Year: 1970-1974
Manufacturer: Lincoln (Ford)

Wheelbase . . . . 127 inches
Length . . . . 232.6 inches
Weight . . . . 5500 lbs.
Width . . . . 80 inches
Standard Engine V8
Standard Brakes . . . . Front: disc type
Rear: drum type
Turning Diameter . . . . 46.7 feet
Gas mileage average
unleaded fuel . . . . 8 mpg.
Front leg room . . . . 41.7 inches
Front head room . . . . 38.8 inches
Rear leg room . . . . 41.7 inches
Rear head room . . . . 38.1 inches
Room for luggage . . . . 20.9 cubic feet

Car: CONTINENTAL
Year: 1967-1969
Manufacturer: Lincoln (Ford)

Wheelbase . . . . 126 inches
Length . . . . 224.2 inches
Weight . . . . 5300 lbs.
Width . . . . 79.7 inches
Standard Engine V8
Standard Brakes . . . . Front: disc type
Rear: drum type
Turning Diameter . . . . 50 feet

Gas mileage average
premium fuel........................9 mpg.
Front leg room ....41 inches
Front head room ....39.4 inches
Rear leg room ....40.5 inches
Rear head room ....38.6 inches
Room for luggage ....18 cubic feet

Car: IMPERIAL
Year: 1974
Manufacturer: Chrysler

Wheelbase ....124 inches
Length ....231.1 inches
Weight ....5256 lbs.
Width ....79.7 inches
Standard Engine V8
Standard Brakes .... Front: disc type
                              Rear: disc type
Turning Diameter ....44.7 feet
Gas mileage average
  unleaded fuel.....................8.8 mpg.
Front leg room ....42.3 inches
Front head room ....38.1 inches
Rear leg room ....39.5 inches
Rear head room ....37 inches
Room for luggage ....17.8 cubic feet

Car: IMPERIAL
Year: 1967-1973
Manufacturer: Chrysler

Wheelbase ....127 inches
Length ....235.3 inches
Weight ....5020 lbs.
Width ....79.6 inches
Standard Engine V8
Standard Brakes .... Front: disc type
                              Rear: drum type
Turning Diameter ....44.8 feet
Gas mileage average
  regular fuel........................9.2 mpg.
Front leg room ....41.7 inches
Front head room ....38 inches
Rear leg room ....35.2 inches
Rear head room ....37.5 inches
Room for luggage ....18.6 cubic feet

Car: CADILLAC
Year: 1969-1974
Manufacturer: Cadillac (G.M.)

Wheelbase ....130 inches
Length ....228.5 inches

Weight ....5000 lbs.
Width ....79.8 inches
Standard Engine
Standard Brakes .... Front: disc type
                              Rear: drum type
Turning Diameter ....46.4 feet
Gas mileage average
  unleaded fuel.....................8.9 mpg.
Front leg room ....41.9 inches
Front head room ....39,3 inches
Rear leg room ....44.6 inches
Rear head room ....38.3 inches
Room for luggage ....17.2 cubic feet

Car: CADILLAC
Year: 1967-1969
Manufacturer: Cadillac (G.M.)

Wheelbase ....133 inches
Length ....228.5 inches
Weight ....500 lbs.
Width ....79.8 inches
Standard Engine V8
Standard Brakes .... Front: disc type
                              Rear: drum type
Turning Diameter ....48 feet
Gas mileage average
premium fuel ....10.2 mpg.
Front leg room ....42.2 inches
Front head room ....39.3 inches
Rear leg room ....44.3 inches
Rear head room ....38 inches
Room for luggage ....17.3 cubic feet

Car: PONTIAC
Year: 1970-1974
Manufacturer: Pontiac (G.M.)

Wheelbase ....124 inches
Length ....226 inches
Weight ....4300 lbs.
Width ....79.6 inches
Standard Engine V8
Standard Brakes .... Front: disc type
                              Rear: drum type
Turning Diameter ....43.5 feet
Gas mileage average
  regular fuel ....11.5 mpg.
Front leg room ....42.6 inches
Front head room ....38.9 inches
Rear leg room ....38.5 inches
Rear head room ....38 inches
Room for luggage ....20.2 cubic feet

Car: PONTIAC
Year: 1967-1969
Manufacturer: Pontiac (G.M.)

Wheelbase . . . . 122 inches
Length . . . . 217.5 inches
Weight . . . . 4200 lbs.
Width . . . . 79.8 inches
Standard Engine V8
Standard Brakes . . . . Front: disc type
Rear: drum type
Turning Diameter . . . . 46 feet
Gas mileage average
premium fuel . . . . 11.7 mpg.
Front leg room . . . . 42.4 inches
Front head room . . . . 39 inches
Rear leg room . . . . 38.1 inches
Rear head room . . . . 37.7 inches
Room for luggage . . . . 19 cubic feet

Car: OLDSMOBILE 88, CUSTOM, DELMONT
Year: 1969-1974
Manufacturer: Oldsmobile (G.M)

Wheelbase . . . . 124 inches
Length . . . . 227 inches
Weight . . . . 4500 lbs.
Width . . . . 79.5 inches
Standard Engine V8
Standard Brakes . . . . Front: disc type
Rear: drum type
Turning Diameter . . . . 45 feet
Gas mileage average
regular fuel . . . . 13 mpg.
Front leg room 38.inches
Front head room . . . . 42.4 inches
Rear leg room . . . . 38.5 inches
Rear head room . . . . 38 inches
Room for luggage . . . . 20.6 cubic feet

Car: MONTEREY
Year: 1969-1974
Manufacturer: Mercury (Ford)

Wheelbase . . . . 124 inches
Length . . . . 226.8 inches
Weight . . . . 4550 lbs.
Width . . . . 79.6 inches
Standard Engine V8
Standard Brakes . . . . Front: disc type
Rear: drum type
Turning Diameter . . . . 41.8 feet
Gas mileage average
unleaded fuel . . . . 12 mpg.
Front leg room . . . . 41.5 inches

Front head room . . . . 38.1 inches
Rear leg room . . . . 39.7 inches
Rear head room . . . . 37.2 inches
Room for luggage . . . . 20.5 cubic feet

Car: MONTEREY
Year: 1967-1968
Manufacturer: MErcury (Ford)

Wheelbase . . . . 123 inches
Length . . . . 220.1 inches
Weight . . . . 4100 lbs.
Width . . . . 77.9 inches
Standard Engine V8
Standard Brakes . . . . Front: drum type
Rear: drum type
Turning Diameter . . . . 48 feet
Gas mileage average
premium fuel . . . . 12.9 mpg.
Front leg room . . . . 41.9 inches
Front head room . . . . 38.9 inches
Rear leg room . . . . 37.6 inches
Rear head room . . . . 37.7 inches
Room for luggage . . . . 19.1 cubic feet

Car: POLARA
Year: 1974
Manufacturer: Dodge (Chrysler)

Wheelbase . . . . 122 inches
Length . . . . 222.7 inches
Weight . . . . 4300 lbs.
Width . . . . 79.3 inches
Standard Engine V8
Standard Brakes . . . . Front: disc type
Rear: drum type
Turning Diameter . . . . 43.8 feet
Gas mileage average
unleaded fuel . . . . 13.5 mpg.
Front leg room . . . . 42.4 inches
Front head room . . . . 38 inches
Rear leg room . . . . 38.2 inches
Rear head room . . . . 37 inches
Room for luggage . . . . 20.6 cubic feet

Car: POLARA
Year: 1969-1973
Manufacturer: Dodge (Chrysler)

Wheelbase . . . . 122 inches
Length . . . . 226.6 inches
Weight . . . . 4000 lbs.
Width . . . . 79.6 inches
Standard Engine V8
Standard Brakes . . . . Front: disc type
Rear: drum type

Turning Diameter . . . . .43 feet
Gas mileage average
   unleaded fuel . . . . 11.7 mpg.
Front leg room . . . . 41.7 inches
Front head room . . . . 38 inches
Rear leg room . . . . 39.1 inches
Rear head room . . . . 38.4 inches
Room for luggage . . . . 22.4 cubic feet

Car: POLARA
Year: 1967-1968
Manufacturer: Dodge (Chrysler)

Wheelbase . . . . 122 inches
Length . . . . .219 inches
Weight . . . . 3900 lbs.
Width . . . . .80 inches
Standard Engine V8
Standard Brakes . . . . Front: drum type
                               Rear: drum type
Turning Diameter . . . . .47 feet
Gas mileage average
regular fuel . . . . 13 mpg.
Front leg room . . . . 41.8 inches
Front head room . . . . 39.8 inches
Rear leg room . . . . 39 inches
Rear head room . . . . 38.5 inches
Room for luggage . . . . 16.2 cubic feet

Car: NEWPORT
Year: 1974
Manufacturer: Chrysler

Wheelbase . . . . 124 inches
Length . . . . .255 inches
Weight . . . . 4600 lbs.
Width . . . . .79.5 inches
Standard Engine V8
Standard Brakes . . . . Front: disc type
                               Rear: drum type
Turning Diameter . . . . 44.7 feet
Gas mileage average
   unleaded fuel . . . . .13.25 mpg.
Front leg room . . . . 42.2 inches
Front head room . . . . 38.7 inches
Rear leg room . . . . 39.9 inches
Rear head room . . . . 38.5 inches
Room for luggage . . . . 21.6 cubic feet

Car: NEWPORT
Year: 1969-1973
Manufacturer: Chrysler

Wheelbase . . . . 124 inches
Length . . . . .224.1 inches

Weight . . . . 4450 lbs.
Width . . . . 79.4 inches
Standard Engine V8
Standard Brakes . . . . Front: disc type
                               Rear: drum type
Turning Diameter . . . . 43.22 feet
Gas mileage average
   unleaded fuel . . . . 11 mpg.
Front leg room . . . . 41.8 inches
Front head room . . . . 38.7 inches
Rear leg room . . . . 41.5 inches
Rear head room . . . . 37.9 inches
Room for luggage . . . . 22.4 cubic feet

Car: NEWPORT
Year: 1967-1968
Manufacturer: Chrysler

Wheelbase . . . . 124 inches
Length . . . . .219.2 inches
Weight . . . . 4200 lbs.
Width . . . . 78.6 inches
Standard Engine V8
Standard Brakes . . . . Front: drum type
                               Rear: drum type
Turning Diameter . . . . .49 feet
Gas mileage average
premium . . . . 12.2 mpg.
Front leg room . . . . 41.8 inches
Front head room . . . . 39.8 inches
Rear leg room . . . . 39 inches
Rear head room . . . . 38.5 inches
Room for luggage . . . . 22 cubic feet

Car: BUICK
Year: 1969-1974
Manufacturer: Buick (G.M.)

Wheelbase . . . . 124 inches
Length . . . . .224.2 inches
Weight . . . . 4600 lbs.
Width . . . . .79.6 inches
Standard Engine
Standard Brakes . . . . Front: disc type
                               Rear: drum type
Turning Diameter . . . . .43.1 feet
Gas mileage average
regular fuel . . . . 12.5 mpg.
Front leg room . . . . 42.1 inches
Front head room . . . . 38.1 inches
Rear leg room . . . . 38.8 inches
Rear head room . . . . 37.4 inches
Room for luggage . . . . 20.4 cubic feet

Car: FURY
Year: 1974
Manufacturer: Plymouth (Chrysler)

Wheelbase . . . . 122 inches
Length . . . . 222.8 inches
Weight . . . . 4460 lbs.
Width . . . . 79.4 inches
Standard Engine V8
Standard Brakes . . . . Front: disc type
Rear: drum type
Turning Diameter . . . . 43.9 feet
Gas mileage average
  unleaded fuel . . . . 11.2 mpg.
Front leg room . . . . 42.2 inches
Front head room . . . . 38.0 inches
Rear leg room . . . . 38.2 inches
Rear head room . . . . 37.0 inches
Room for luggage . . . . 17.75 cubic feet

Car: FURY
Year: 1968-1973
Manufacturer: Plymouth (Chrysler)

Wheelbase . . . . 120 inches
Length . . . . 223.4 inches
Weight . . . . 4000 lbs.
Width . . . . 79.8 inches
Standard Engine V8
Standard Brakes . . . . Front: drum type
Rear: drum type
Turning Diameter . . . . 45.9 feet
Gas mileage average
  unleaded fuel . . . . 13.6 mpg.
Front leg room . . . . 41.8 inches
Front head room . . . . 38.8 inches
Rear leg room . . . . 38 inches
Rear head room . . . . 38.4 inches
Room for luggage . . . . 20.4 cubic feet

Car: FURY
Year: 1967-1968
Manufacturer: Plymouth (Chrysler)

Wheelbase . . . . 119 inches
Length . . . . 213 inches
Weight . . . . 3900 lbs.
Width . . . . 77.7 inches
Standard Engine . . . . 6 cylinders
Standard Brakes . . . . Front: drum type
Rear: drum type
Turning Diameter . . . . 46 feet
Gas mileage average
regular fuel . . . . 15 mpg.
Front leg room . . . . 41.8 inches
Front head room . . . . 39.5 inches

Rear leg room . . . . 37 inches
Rear head room . . . . 37.7 inches
Room for luggage . . . . 19.7 cubic feet

Car: FORD
Year: 1969-1974
Manufacturer: Frod

Wheelbase . . . . 121 inches
Length . . . . 219.5 inches
Weight . . . . 4631 lbs.
Width . . . . 79.5 inches
Standard Engine V8
Standard Brakes . . . . Front: disc type
Rear: drum type
Turning Diameter . . . . 41.9 feet
Gas mileage average
  unleaded fuel . . . . 9 mpg.
Front leg room . . . . 41.9 inches
Front head room . . . . 38.8 inches
Rear leg room . . . . 38.7 inches
Rear head room . . . . 37.6 inches
Room for luggage . . . . 171.1 cubic feet

Car: BUICK
Year: 1969
Manufacturer: Buick (G.M.)

Wheelbase . . . . 123.2 inches
Length . . . . 218.2 inches
Weight . . . . 4300 lbs.
Width . . . . 80 inches
Standard Engine V8
Standard Brakes . . . . Front: drum type
Rear: drum type
Turning Diameter . . . . 46 feet
Gas mileage average
regular fuel . . . . 13.1 mpg.
Front leg room . . . . 42.3 inches
Front head room . . . . 39.1 inches
Rear leg room . . . . 37.9 inches
Rear head room . . . . 37.7 inches
Room for luggage . . . . 17.3 cubic feet

Car: BUICK
Year: 1967-1968
Manufacturer: Buick (G.M.)

Wheelbase . . . . 123.2 inches
Length . . . . 218.2 inches
Weight . . . . 4300 lbs.
Width . . . . 80 inches
Standard Engine V8
Standard Brakes . . . . Front: drum type
Rear: drum type

Turning Diameter . . . . 46 feet
Gas mileage average
premium fuel . . . . 13.1 mpg.
Front leg room . . . . 42.3 inches
Front head room . . . . 39.1 inches
Rear leg room . . . . 37.9 inches
Rear head room . . . . 37.7 inches
Room for luggage . . . . 17.3 cubic feet

Car: FORD
Year: 1967-1968
Manufacturer: Ford

Wheelbase . . . . 119 inches
Length . . . . 213.3 inches
Weight . . . . 3700 lbs.
Width . . . . 78 inches
Standard Engine . . . . 6 cylinders
Standard Brakes . . . . Front: drum type
Rear: drum type
Turning Diameter . . . . 46 feet
Gas mileage average
regular fuel . . . . 16 mpg.
Front leg room . . . . 41.9 inches
Front head room . . . . 38.9 inches
Rear leg room . . . . 37.6 inches
Rear head room . . . . 37.9 inches
Room for luggage . . . . 19.1 cubic feet

Car: CHEVROLET
Year: 1971-1974
Manufacturer: Chevrolet (G.M.)

Wheelbase . . . . 121.5 inches
Length . . . . 222.6 inches
Weight . . . . 4666 lbs.
Width . . . . 79.5 inches
Standard Engine V8
Standard Brakes . . . . Front: disc type
Rear: drum type
Turning Diameter . . . . 41.7 feet
Gas mileage average
unleaded fuel . . . . 9.3 mpg.
Front leg room . . . . 42.5 inches
Front head room . . . . 38.9 inches
Rear leg room . . . . 38.8 inches
Rear head room . . . . 38 inches
Room for luggage . . . . 17.7 cubic feet

Car: CHEVROLET
Year: 1967-1970
Manufacturer: Chevrolet (G.M.)

Wheelbase . . . . 119 inches
Length . . . . 216 inches

Weight . . . . 4100 lbs.
Width . . . . 79.8 inches
Standard Engine . . . . 6 cylinders
Standard Brakes . . . . Front: disc type
Rear: drum type
Turning Diameter . . . . 46 feet
Gas mileage average
regular fuel . . . . 13.2 mpg.
Front leg room . . . . 42.3 inches
Front head room . . . . 38.3 inches
Rear leg room . . . . 35.1 inches
Rear head room . . . . 37.8 inches
Room for luggage . . . . 18.11 cubic feet

Car: MARATHON
Year: 1973-1974
Manufacturer: Checker

Wheelbase . . . . 120 inches
Length . . . . 204 inches
Weight . . . . 3700 lbs.
Width . . . . 76 inches
Standard Engine . . . . 6 cylinders (Chevrolet)
Standard Brakes . . . . Front: disc type
Rear: drum type
Turning Diameter . . . . 42.3 feet
Gas mileage average
unleaded fuel . . . . 13.9 mpg.
Front leg room . . . . 36 inches
Front head room . . . . 36 inches
Rear leg room . . . . 38 inches
Rear head room . . . . 35.75 inches
Room for luggage . . . . 12.2 cubic feet

Car: MARATHON
Year: 1967-1972
Manufacturer: Checker

Wheelbase . . . . 120 inches
Length . . . . 204 inches
Weight . . . . 3700 lbs.
Width . . . . 76 inches
Standard Engine . . . . 6 cylinders (Chevrolet)
Standard Brakes . . . . Front: drum type
Rear: drum type
Turning Diameter . . . . 42.3 feet
Gas mileage average
unleaded fuel . . . . 13.9 mpg.
Front leg room . . . . 36 inches
Front head room . . . . 36 inches
Rear leg room . . . . 38 inches
Rear head room . . . . 35.75 inches
Room for luggage . . . . 12.2 cubic feet

Car: AMBASSADOR
Year: 1969-1974
Manufacturer: American Motors

Wheelbase . . . . 122 inches
Length . . . . 219.4 inches
Weight . . . . 4118 lbs.
Width . . . . 77.2 inches
Standard Engine V8
Standard Brakes . . . . Front: disc type
                                          Rear: drum type
Turning Diameter . . . . 40.5 feet
Gas mileage average
   unleaded fuel . . . . 12.3 mpg.
Front leg room . . . . 41.8 inches
Front head room . . . . 39.6 inches
Rear leg room . . . . 38.6 inches
Rear head room . . . . 37.5 inches
Room for luggage . . . . 18.2 cubic feet

Car: AMBASSADOR
Year: 1967-1968
Manufacturer: American Motors

Wheelbase . . . . 118 inches
Length . . . . 202.5 inches
Weight . . . . 3500 lbs.
Width . . . . 78.36 inches
Standard Engine V8
Standard Brakes . . . . Front: drum type
                                          Rear: drum type
Turning Diameter . . . . 44 feet
Gas mileage average
   regular fuel . . . . 15 mpg.
Front leg room . . . . 41.6 inches
Front head room . . . . 38.7 inches
Rear leg room . . . . 36.5 inches
Rear head room . . . . 36.5 inches
Room for luggage . . . . 18.2 cubic feet

Car: VENTURA II
Year: 1971-1974
Manufacturer: Pontiac (G.M.)

Wheelbase . . . . 11 inches
Length . . . . 197.5 inches
Weight . . . . 3250 lbs.
Width . . . . 72.4 inches
Standard Engine . . . . 6 cylinders
Standard Brakes . . . . Front: drum type
                                          Rear: drum type
Turning Diameter . . . . 40.8 feet
Gas mileage average
   unleaded fuel . . . . 14.4 mpg.
Front leg room . . . . 39.3 inches
Front head room . . . . 42.6 inches

Rear leg room . . . . 35.3 inches
Rear head room . . . . 37.3 inches
Room for luggage . . . . 13.7 cubic feet

Car: VALIANT
Year: 1967-1974
Manufacturer: Plymouth (Chrysler)

Wheelbase . . . . 108 inches
Length . . . . 195.8 inches
Weight . . . . 3000 lbs.
Width . . . . 71.1 inches
Standard Engine . . . . 6 cylinders
Standard Brakes . . . . Front: drum type
                                          Rear: drum type
Turning Diameter . . . . 40 feet
Gas mileage average
   unleaded fuel . . . . 17.9 inches
Front leg room . . . . 41.6 inches
Front head room . . . . 38.4 inches
Rear leg room . . . . 34.6 inches
Rear head room . . . . 37.3 inches
Room for luggage . . . . 14 cubic feet

Car: OMEGA
Year: 1973-1974
Manufacturer: Oldsmobile

Wheelbase . . . . 110 inches
Length . . . . 197.5 inches
Weight . . . . 3280 lbs.
Width . . . . 72.4 inches
Standard Engine . . . . 6 cylinders
Standard Brakes . . . . Front: drum type
                                          Rear: drum type
Turning Diameter . . . . 41.2 feet
Gas mileage average
   unleaded fuel . . . . 14.8 mpg.
Front leg room . . . . 41.7 inches
Front head room . . . . 39.3 inches
Rear leg room . . . . 35.3 inches
Rear head room . . . . 37.3 inches
Room for luggage . . . . 13.8 cubic feet

Car: COMET
Year: 1971-1974
Manufacturer: Mercury—(Ford)

Wheelbase . . . . 109.9 inches
Length . . . . 192.3 inches
Weight . . . . 2850 lbs.
Width . . . . 70.5 inches
Standard Engine . . . . 6 cylinders
Standard Brakes . . . . Front: disc type
                                          Rear: drum type

Turning Diameter . . . . 38.7 feet
Gas mileage average
   unleaded fuel . . . . 18.2 mpg.
Front leg room . . . . 42.7 inches
Front head room . . . . 37.8 inches
Rear leg room . . . . 36 inches
Rear head room . . . . 36.5 inches
Room for luggage . . . . 10.1 cubic feet

Car: COMET
Year: 1967
Manufacturer: Mercury—(Ford)

Wheelbase . . . . 116 inches
Length . . . . 203.5 inches
Weight . . . . 3200 lbs.
Width . . . . 73.8 inches
Standard Engine . . . . 6 cylinders
Standard Brakes . . . . Front: drum type
                         Rear: drum type
Turning Diameter . . . . 43 feet
Gas mileage average
   regular fuel . . . . 16 mpg.
Front leg room . . . . 42.1 inches
Front head room . . . . 38.8 inches
Rear leg room . . . . 36 inches
Rear head room . . . . 37.6 inches
Room for luggage . . . . 17.1 cubic feet

Car: MAVERICK
Year: 1970-1974
Manufacturer: Ford

Wheelbase . . . . 103 inches
Length . . . . 183.3 inches
Weight . . . . 2850 lbs.
Width . . . . 70.5 inches
Standard Engine . . . . 6 cylinders
Standard Brakes . . . . Front: drum type
                         Rear: drum type
Turning Diameter . . . . 38.7 feet
Gas mileage average
   unleaded fuel . . . . 18.5 mpg.
Front leg room . . . . 40.7 inches
Front head room . . . . 37.8 inches
Rear leg room . . . . 36 inches
Rear head room . . . . 36.5 inches
Room for luggage . . . . 10.1 cubic feet

Car: FALCON
Year: 1967-1969
Manufacturer: Ford

Wheelbase . . . . 110 inches
Length . . . . 184.3 inches

Weight . . . . 3100 lbs.
Width . . . . 73.2 inches
Standard Engine . . . . 6 cylinders
Standard Brakes . . . . Front: drum type
                         Rear: drum type
Turning Diameter . . . . 41 feet
Gas mileage average
   regular fuel . . . . 19.7 mpg.
Front leg room . . . . 42.4 inches
Front head room . . . . 38.8 inches
Rear leg room . . . . 33.8 inches
Rear head room . . . . 37.7 inches
Room for luggage . . . . 12.2 cubic feet

Car: DART
Year: 1967-1974
Manufacturer: Dodge-(Chrysler)

Wheelbase . . . . 111 inches
Lenght . . . . 203.8 inches
Weight . . . . 3000 lbs.
Width . . . . 69.6 inches
Standard Engine . . . . 6 cylinders
Standard Brakes . . . . Front: drum type
                         Rear: drum type
Turning Diameter . . . . 39 feet
Gas mileage average
   unleaded fuel . . . . 17.5 mpg.
Front leg room . . . . 41.5 inches
Front head room . . . . 38.6 inches
Rear leg room . . . . 35.9 inches
Rear head room . . . . 37.3 inches
Room for luggage . . . . 14.3 cubic feet

Car: CHEVY II/NOVA
Year: 1968-1974
Manufacturer: Chevrolet (G.M.)

Wheelbase . . . . 111 inches
Length . . . . 194.3 inches
Weight . . . . 3200 lbs.
Width . . . . 72.4 inches
Standard Engine . . . . 6 cylinders
Standard Brakes . . . . Front: drum type
                         Rear: drum type
Turning Diameter . . . . 41.2 feet
Gas mileage average
   unleaded fuel . . . . 14.9 mpg.
Front leg room . . . . 41.7 inches
Front head room . . . . 39.3 inches
Rear leg room . . . . 35.3 inches
Rear head room . . . . 37.3 inches
Room for luggage . . . . 13.7 cubic feet

Car: CHEVY II
Year: 1967
Manufacturer: Chevrolet (G.M.)

Wheelbase	110 inches
Length	183 inches
Weight	2900 lbs.
Width	71.3 inches
Standard Engine	6 cylinders
Standard Brakes	Front: drum type
	Rear: drum type
Turning Diameter	39 feet
Gas mileage average regular fuel	17.8 mpg.
Front leg room	40.7 inches
Front head room	38.8 inches
Rear leg room	35.5 inches
Rear head room	37.3 inches
Room for luggage	13 cubic feet

Car: HORNET
Year: 1970-1974
Manufacturer: American Motors

Wheelbase	108 inches
Length	184.9 inches
Weight	2880 lbs.
Width	71 inches
Standard Engine	6 cylinders
Standard Brakes	Front: drum type
	Rear: drum type
Turning Diameter	36 feet
Gas mileage average unleaded fuel	18.2 mpg.
Front leg room	42.05 inches
Front head room	38.1 inches
Rear leg room	35.5 inches
Rear head room	37 inches
Room for luggage	11.2 cubic feet

Car: AMERICAN
Year: 1967-1969
Manufacturer: American Motors

Wheelbase	106 inches
Length	181 inches
Weight	3000 lbs.
Width	70.84 inches
Standard Engine	6 cylinders
Standard Brakes	Front: drum type
	Rear: drum type
Turning Diameter	40 feet
Gas mileage average regular fuel	18.9 mpg.
Front leg room	42 inches
Front head room	39 inches

Rear leg room	35 inches
Rear head room	36 inches
Room for luggage	12 cubic feet

Car: CORVAIR
year: 1967-1969
Manufacturer: Chevrolet—(G.M.)

Wheelbase	108 inches
Length	183.2 inches
Weight	2600 lbs.
Width	70 inches
Standard Engine	6 cylinders
Standard Brakes	Front: drum type
	Rear: drum type
Turning Diameter	40 feet
Gas mileage average regular fuel	18 mpg.
Front leg room	40.9 inches
Front head room	37.9 inches
Rear leg room	30.7 inches
Rear head room	36.5 inches
Room for luggage	7 cubic feet

Car: APOLLO
Year: 1973-1974
Manufacturer: Buick — (G.M.)

Wheelbase	111 inches
Length	200.2 inches
Weight	3300 lbs.
Width	72.4 inches
Standard Engine	6 cylinders
Standard Brakes	Front: drum type
	Rear: drum type
Turning Diameter	41.2 feet
Gas mileage average unleaded fuel	14.9 mpg.
Front leg room	41.7 inches
Front head room	39.3 inches
Rear leg room	35.3 inches
Rear head room	37.3 inches
Room for luggage	13.8 cubic feet

Car: SUPER BEETLE
Year: 1967-1974
Manufacturer: Volkswagon

Wheelbase	95.3 inches
Length	158.6 inches
Weight	1825 lbs.
Width	61 inches
Standard Engine	4 cylinders; opposed
Standard Brakes	Front: disc type
	Rear: drum type

Turning Diameter . . . . 36 feet
Gas mileage average
   unleaded fuel . . . . 29.8 mpg.
Front leg room . . . . 44.5 inches
Front head room . . . . 36.4 inches
Rear leg room . . . . 37.5 inches
Rear head room . . . . 32 inches
Room for luggage . . . . 10.2 cubic feet

Car: VW BEETLE
Year: 1967-1974
Manufacturer: Volkswagen

Wheelbase . . . . 94.5 inches
Length . . . . 158.6 inches
Weight . . . . 1825 lbs.
Width . . . . 61 inches
Standard Engine . . . . 4 cylinders; opposed
Standard Brakes . . . . Front: disc type
                           Rear: drum type
Turning Diameter . . . . 36 feet
Gas mileage average
   unleaded fuel . . . . 29.8 mpg.
Front leg room . . . . 44.5 inches
Front head room . . . . 36.4 inches
Rear leg room . . . . 37.5 inches
Rear head room . . . . 32 inches
Room for luggage . . . . 8.8 cubic feet

Car: TOYOTA CORONA
Year: 1967-1974
Manufacturer:

Wheelbase . . . . 95.7 inches
Length . . . . 168.2 inches
Weight . . . . 2190 lbs.
Width . . . . 61.8 inches
Standard Engine . . . . 4 cylinders; in-line
Standard Brakes . . . . Front: disc type
                           Rear: drum type
Turning Diameter . . . . 31.5 feet
Gas mileage average
   unleaded fuel . . . . 18.5 mpg.
Front leg room . . . . 41 inches
Front head room . . . . 35.5 inches
Rear leg room . . . . 38 inches
Rear head room . . . . 35.5 inches
Room for luggage . . . . 10.9 cubic feet

Car: PINTO (2 Door)
Year: 1971-1974
Manufacturer: Ford

Wheelbase . . . . 94 inches
Length . . . . 164.5 inches
Weight . . . . 2200 lbs.

Width . . . . 69.4 inches
Standard Engine . . . . 4 cylinders; in-line
Standard Brakes . . . . Front: disc type
                           Rear: drum type
Turning Diameter . . . . 31.5 feet
Gas mileage average
   unleaded fuel . . . . 22.4 mpg.
Front leg room . . . . 41 inches
Front head room . . . . 37.5 inches
Rear leg room . . . . 31.5 inches
Rear head room . . . . 36.3 inches
Room for luggage . . . . 5.9 cubic feet

Car: FIAT 124
Year: 1967-1974

Wheelbase . . . . 95.3 inches
Length . . . . 158.9 inches
Weight . . . . 2095 lbs.
Width . . . . 64 inches
Standard Engine . . . . 4 cylinders; in-line
Standard Brakes . . . . Front: disc type
                           Rear: disc type
Turning Diameter . . . . 35 feet
Gas mileage average
   unleaded fuel . . . . 27 mpg.
Front leg room . . . . 41.3 inches
Front head room . . . . 36 inches
Rear leg room . . . . 39 inches
Rear head room . . . . 34 inches
Room for luggage . . . . 14 cubic feet

Car: DATSUN 610
Year: 1974

Wheelbase . . . . 98.4 inches
Length . . . . 174 inches
Weight . . . . 2400 lbs.
Width . . . . 63 inches
Standard Engine . . . . 4 cylinders; in-line
Standard Brakes . . . . Front: disc type
                           Rear: drum type
Turning Diameter . . . . 32.2 feet
Gas mileage average
   unleaded fuel . . . . 22.8 mpg.
Front leg room
Front head room
Rear leg room
Rear head room
Room for luggage . . . . 12 cubic feet

Car: DATSUN 510
Year: 1968-1973

Wheelbase . . . . 95.3 inches

Length . . . . 162.2 inches
Weight . . . . 2115 lbs.
Width . . . . 61.4 inches
Standard Engine . . . . 4 cylinders; in-line
Standard Brakes . . . . Front: disc type
Rear: drum type
Turning Diameter . . . . 31.4 feet
Gas mileage average
unleaded fuel . . . . 26.9 mpg.
Front leg room . . . . 43 inches
Front head room . . . . 36 inches
Rear leg room . . . . 37 inches
Rear head room . . . . 33.5 inches
Room for luggage . . . . 12.5 cubic feet

Car: DATSUN 411
Year: 1967

Wheelbase . . . . 93.7 inches
Length . . . . 157.3 inches
Weight . . . . 1984 lbs.
Width . . . . 68.7 inches
Standard Engine . . . . 4 cylinders; in-line
Standard Brakes . . . . Front: disc type
Rear: drum type
Turning Diameter . . . . 31 feet
Gas mileage average
regular fuel . . . . 32.9 mpg.
Front leg room . . . . 42.9 inches
Front head room . . . . 36 inches
Rear leg room . . . . 36.3 inches
Rear head room . . . . 34 inches
Room for luggage . . . . 12 cubic feet

Car: VEGA
Year: 1971-1974
Manufacturer: Chevrolet — (G.M.)

Wheelbase . . . . 97 inches
Length . . . . 172.2 inches
Weight . . . . 2300 lbs.
Width . . . . 65 inches
Standard Engine . . 4 cylinders; aluminum in-line
Standard Brakes . . . . Front: disc type
Rear: drum type
Turning Diameter . . . . 33 feet
Gas mileage average
unleaded fuel . . . . 20.8 mpg.
Front leg room . . . . 41.1 inches
Front head room . . . . 38 inches
Rear leg room . . . . 29 inches
Rear head room . . . . 36.4 inches
Room for luggage . . . . 8 cubic feet

Car: GREMLIN
Year: 1970-1974
Manufacturer: American Motors

Wheelbase . . . . 96 inches
Length . . . . 165.5 inches
Weight . . . . 2800 lbs.
Width . . . . 70.6 inches
Standard Engine . . . . 6 cylinders
Standard Brakes . . . . Front: drum type
Rear: drum type
Turning Diameter . . . . 32.8 feet
Gas mileage average
unleaded fuel . . . . 19 mpg.
Front leg room . . . . 42.05 inches
Front head room . . . . 38 inches
Rear leg room . . . . 27.8 inches
Rear head room . . . . 36.4 inches
Room for luggage
(car has no trunk . . . . 6.4 cubic feet

Car: TOYOTA COROLLA
Year: 1969-1974
Manufacturer:

Wheelbase . . . . 91.9 inches
Length . . . . 161.4 inches
Weight . . . . 1935 lbs.
Width . . . . 59.3 inches
Standard Engine . . . . 4 cylinders; in-line
Standard Brakes . . . . Front: disc type
Rear: drum type
Turning Diameter . . . . 29.6 feet
Gas mileage average . . . . 28.9 mpg.
unleaded fuel
Front leg room . . . . 42 inches
Front head room . . . . 36 inches
Rear leg room . . . . 32 inches
Rear head room . . . . 33.5 inches
Room for luggage . . . . 11.2 cubic feet

Car: FIAT 128
Year: 1972-1974
Manufacturer:

Wheelbase . . . . 96.4 inches
Length . . . . 157.2 inches
Weight . . . . 1950 lbs.
Width . . . . 62.6 inches
Standard Engine . . . . 4 cylinders; in-line
Standard Brakes . . . . Front: disc type
Rear: drum type
Turning Diameter . . . . 33.8 feet
Gas mileage average . . . . 33.5 mpg.
unleaded fuel
Front leg room . . . . 44 inches

Front head room .... 35.7 inches
Rear leg room .... 39 inches
Rear head room .... 34 inches
Room for luggage .... 12.6 cubic feet

Car: GRAND PRIX
Year: 1971-1974
Manufacturer: Pontiac (G.M.)

Wheelbase .... 116 inches
Length .... 217.5 inches
Weight .... 4500 lbs.
Width .... 77.9 inches
Standard Engine V8
Standard Brakes .... Front: disc type
                     Rear: drum type
Turning Diameter.................... 39 feet
Gas mileage average
    unleaded fuel.................... 9.7 mpg.
Front leg room .... 42.1 inches
Front head room .... 37.4 inches
Rear leg room .... 32.8 inches
Rear head room .... 37.2 inches
Room for luggage .... 14.7 cubic feet

Car: GRAND PRIX
Year: 1969-1970
Manufacturer: Pontiac (G.M.)

Wheelbase .... 118 inches
Length .... 210.2 inches
Weight .... 4100 lbs.
Width .... 75.7 inches
Standard Engine V8
Standard Brakes .... Front: disc type
                     Rear: drum type
Turning Diameter.................... 42 feet
Gas mileage average
    premium fuel .... 10.6 mpg.
Front leg room .... 42.4 inches
Front head room .... 36.2 inches
Rear leg room .... 31.6 inches
Rear head room .... 36.2 inches
Room for luggage .... 14.3 cubic feet

Car: GRAND PRIX
Year: 1967-1968
Manufacturer: Pontiac (G.M.)

Wheelbase .... 121 inches
Length .... 216.3 inches
Weight .... 4200 lbs.

Width .... 79.8 inches
Standard Engine V8
Standard Brakes .... Front: drum type
                     Rear: drum type
Turning Diameter.................... 42.8 feet
Gas mileage average
    premium fuel..................... 9.9 mpg.
Front leg room .... 42.3 inches
Front head room .... 37.9 inches
Rear leg room .... 35.2 inches
Rear head room .... 37.2 inches
Room for luggage .... 18.9 cubic feet

Car: TORONADO
Year: 1971-1974
Manufacturer: Oldsmobile (G.M.)

Wheelbase .... 122 inches
Length .... 228 inches
Weight .... 4880 lbs.
Width .... 79.8 inches
Standard Engine V8
Standard Brakes .... Front: disc type
                     Rear: drum type
Turning Diameter.................... 47.7 feet
Gas mileage average
    unleaded fuel.................... 8.6 mpg.
Front leg room .... 42.4 inches
Front head room .... 38.1 inches
Rear leg room .... 35.8 inches
Rear head room .... 37.1 inches
Room for luggage .... 13.6 cubic feet

Car: TORONADO
Year: 1967-1970
Manufacturer: Oldsmobile (G.M.)

Wheelbase .... 119 inches
Length .... 214.3 inches
Weight .... 4600 lbs.
Width .... 78.8 inches
Standard Engine V8
Standard Brakes .... Front: disc type
                     Rear: drum type
Turning Diameter.................... 46 feet
Gas mileage average
    premium fuel .... 10.3 mpg.
Front leg room .... 41.3 inches
Front head room .... 37.7 inches
Rear leg room .... 35.5 inches
Rear head room .... 37.2 inches
Room for luggage .... 14.6 cubic feet

Car: MARK III
Year: 1972-1974
Manufacturer: Lincoln (Ford)

Wheelbase . . . . 120.4 inches
Length . . . . 228.4 inches
Weight . . . . 5250 lbs.
Width . . . . 79.8 inches
Standard Engine V8
Standard Brakes . . . . Front: disc type
Rear: drum type
Turning Diameter . . . . 43 feet
Gas mileage average
   unleaded fuel . . . . 8.6 mpg.
Front leg room . . . . 42 inches
Front head room . . . . 37.5 inches
Rear leg room . . . . 36.4 inches
Rear head room . . . . 36.8 inches
Room for luggage . . . . 14.8 cubic feet

Car: MARK III
Year: 1969-1971
Manufacturer: Lincoln (Ford)

Wheelbase . . . . 117.2 inches
Length . . . . 216.1 inches
Weight . . . . 5000 lbs.
Width . . . . 79.4 inches
Standard Engine V8
Standard Brakes . . . . Front: disc type
Rear: drum type
Turning Diameter . . . . 48.3 feet
Gas mileage average
   unleaded fuel . . . . 9.3 mpg.
Front leg room . . . . 41.5 inches
Front head room . . . . 37.1 inches
Rear leg room . . . . 34.7 inches
Rear head room . . . . 36.5 inches
Room for luggage . . . . 13.5 cubic feet